Bed & Champagne

World's Top Romantic Hideaways

OTHER WORKS BY BRADLEY S. O'LEARY

FICTION

Jade Cross (due in 1999 with Lee Seymour)

POLITICAL

Are You a Republican or a Democrat? (due in September 1998
    with Victor Kamber)
Presidential Follies (with Ralph Z. Hallow)
Are You a Conservative or a Liberal? (with Victor Kamber)
Top 200 Reasons <u>Not</u> to Vote for Bill Clinton

TRAVEL

Dining By Candlelight: World's Most Romantic Restaurants
    (1998)
Bed & Champagne: Top Romantic Hideaways (1997)
*Dining By Candlelight: America's 200 Most Romantic
    Restaurants* (1997)

VIDEO BOOKS

The Planet is Alive (the story of Pope John Paul II)
    (Co-produced with Robert Evans)
Ronald Reagan: Story of an American President

Bed & Champagne

World's Top Romantic Hideaways

Bradley S. O'Leary

Library of Congress Cataloging in Publication Data is available.

ISBN 1-887161-24-4

Published in the United States by
Boru Publishing, Inc.
11212 Ladera Drive
Austin, TX 78759

Distributed to the trade by
National Book Network, Inc.
4720 Boston Way
Lanham, MD 20706

Boru books are available in quantity for promotional or premium use. For information on discounts and terms, please write to Director of Special Sales, Boru Publishing, Inc., 11212 Ladera Drive, Austin, TX 78759.

Cover design by Whizbang! Studios
Interior design by Joyce C. Weston

Manufactured in the United States of America

99 98   5 4 3 2 1

To Wayne LaPierre in appreciation for his help and work in ensuring that this book reach an editor.

To Erin O'Leary for her research work and inspiration.

Contents

INTERNATIONAL

Foreword *by Laura McKenzie*

I take considerable pride in my efforts to learn everything about travel in the United States and abroad. I have written 38 award-winning travel videos, produced a travel radio show for the NBC Mutual Radio Network, hosted several travel and adventure television programs, and appeared on *Entertainment Tonight* and *Oprah* as a travel expert. During my global excursions, my husband, David, and I have sought out the most romantic restaurants, hotels, inns, and transportation. Whenever we prepare to travel, there is one person I turn to who also has, for decades, sought out the most romantic locations in the world. The expert I speak of is my good friend, Brad O'Leary.

Brad is not only well-travelled; more importantly, he is an incurable romantic and a restaurateur. He knows all of the necessary ingredients to turn dinner for two into a charming, cozy, delicious, and romantic memory. His laboratory happens to be Chasen's restaurant in Los Angeles, in which he is an owner along with Grady Sanders and a host of other investors. Together, they have resurrected one of the most romantic and storied restaurants in all of Los Angeles. Recently they moved this famous eatery from West Hollywood to a new lush location in Beverly Hills. The setting in Chasen's is a little reminiscent of Rick's Cafe in the movie *Casablanca*.

Brad knows a romantic spot the minute he sees it, and if something is lacking, he knows how to manufacture the mood. I recall the time Brad hired a violinist to play at our table so that the atmosphere at that particular restaurant could be enhanced and live up to our romantic expectations.

Brad lives life to the fullest. He's worked with some of the biggest names in Washington, DC and Hollywood. He's been a professional gambler, a political consultant, a newsletter publisher, an executive producer of movies and television shows, and he has his own nationally-syndicated radio show which airs on many NBC stations.

His travels have taken him to pre-Castro Cuba. He has roamed the hills of Afghanistan with the Mujahideen. He was recalled to active duty for the Berlin airlift. He was in Vietnam in 1963 and 1964 helping refugees, and for a time, helped to run orphanages in Saigon and Macao. He was in Russia two weeks after the coup failed.

During his many years in Washington, DC, Brad never let go of his California roots. His close cronies in Los Angeles include former Paramount chief and movie producer, Bob Evans, and actor, Paul Sorvino. In fact, the first time I met Brad was when he was involved in planning a weekend party for 300 special guests that included such luminaries as Tom Selleck, Joe Mantegna, Louise Mandrell, Erik Estrada, Stella Stevens, and Robert Conrad. The party was so impressive that Robert Stack rose to his feet and toasted Brad with, "Some people say that the old Hollywood is dead, but it lived again for this weekend." You see, Brad knows what it takes to "make the moment" and he's put a lot of his expertise into this second edition of *Bed & Champagne*.

Horse lovers and bettors alike might recognize Brad's name from the world of horseracing. Brad is part owner of several thoroughbred horses. Just last year one of his horses, Grady, won the Indian Nation Futurity Cup at Santa Fe Downs in New Mexico. This race offers the second richest payoff for owners of two-year old horses in the country.

Laura McKenzie

What is a Romantic Interlude?

WHAT IS ROMANCE?

Romance is a mood, and we create it—we make it happen. We can turn the most dismal experience into a romantic one if we work at it. Romance comes alive when you awaken the five senses.

Romance is thrilling the sense of sight by having a gift beautifully wrapped, by calling ahead and having flowers delivered to your room or your table at dinner. Romance is packing candles when you travel so you can enjoy the soft glow of candlelight when you turn out the lights. Or you can play with the lighting, dimming it to an intimate softness.

Romance is thrilling the sense of touch by stroking someone's hand or gently touching them to let them know you're there. Or it could be silk sheets on the bed, or standing on the balcony and feeling a breeze caress the two of you, or enjoying the touch of a hot shower or gentle massage. It could be a simple bottle of scented massage oil or bath oil. Or you might want to spread rose petals on the bed.

Romance is thrilling the sense of smell with fresh flowers, or biscuits freshly baked in the morning. The smell of the ocean, or the scent of incense you remembered to bring along for just the right aroma. But be careful with incense. One time in a London hotel room I set off the silent smoke alarm. Perhaps I had lit too many sticks of incense, and I had ignored the ringing telephone. Imagine my surprise when three firemen started beating on my door!

Romance is thrilling the sense of taste with each other's lips. Perhaps it's the wonderful meal you've just enjoyed together, or maybe you remembered to pack the chocolates or sweets your lover particularly likes, and you place one or two on her pillow at night. You may have called ahead to make sure that her favorite white wine was chilled so it has just the right taste when it rolls over her lips. Perhaps you ordered strawberries from room service, and when you share a kiss, you place the strawberries between your lips and savor the taste and the juices.

Romance is thrilling the sense of hearing. The sounds of the night, the crash of ocean waves, or gentle mountain breezes. Finding a perfect radio station the two of you can share. Or try buying a CD alarm clock and bring your favorite romantic CDs along with you. Your lover can also thrill to the sound of your voice telling her how beautiful she is, or expressing your most intimate thoughts. If you are too shy, try memorizing some of the poetry in this book to tell her the words she desires to hear.

Romance can happen anywhere, if you awaken the five senses of love.

A romantic interlude is a trip to someplace extraordinary, special, warm, and inviting. It is an escape from the mundane and into a paradise regained. A romantic spot should have something unique to offer. Whether it's the classy elegance of the Ritz-Carlton in Chicago or the wild natural scenery of the Post Ranch Inn at Big Sur, a romantic destination must offer you something you don't find in your everyday life.

What is it that makes a place romantic? Sometimes it's nature plus luxurious resort comforts in a beautiful beach or mountain setting. Or it could be the glamor and excitement of city life with all the civilized pleasures a grand hotel has to offer. If you live in the city, you probably want to escape to the wild. And if you live in a rural area, you might be drawn to the city lights.

Or you might want to choose a foreign destination. This revised edition of *Bed & Champagne* includes 100 new entries of accommodations outside the US. Taking a trip together overseas is sure to inspire romantic moments, and I've included some of the world's best places for you and your lover to stay. At the Hayman

Island Resort near Australia's Great Barrier Reef, you can enjoy excellent snorkeling or scuba, and later savor fresh seafood at La Fontaine as live music plays in the background. Or after a day of sampling the best sightseeing that Paris has to offer, relax together in your luxurious room at the grand Hotel Ritz. Or visit Chilean wineries outside Santiago, during your stay at Hacienda Los Lingues at the foot of the Andes Mountains. In this new edition, there are now many foreign destinations in the book for you to choose from.

Romance is a mood, and like most moods, it is fragile, even fickle. While it may not take much to get you into the mood, something as simple as a messy room or a surly waiter can ruin the moment. The little things are important. Attention to detail is what sets apart a pretty good hotel from an excellent one. Does the hotel offer concierge service? Is your bed turned down at night? Will room service let you order from the restaurant menus? Is your morning coffee hot or just tepid? These details add up to make the entire experience and will either enhance or detract from your visit.

Service is very important. And great service is both attentive and unobtrusive, respectful without being obsequious, warm without trying to be your next best friend. Excellent service is almost unnoticeable. You finish a course, and the plate is whisked away; your bed is made when you come back from breakfast. The concierge knows what you want, because he/she takes the time to ask. In some of the smaller inns and resorts, the owners take an active role in the day-to-day operations. This is one of the charms of staying in a smaller establishment, and while you might sacrifice some of the amenities of larger hotels, you get the feeling that you are staying in someone's own home. This kind of service cannot be taught in hotel school, nor can it be dictated by the guidelines of a corporate hierarchy. Unfortunately, for these very reasons, excellent personal service is often rare.

Luxury hotels are popping up in every city in the country. Many of them are operated by large hotel chains. There is nothing wrong with corporate hotel ownership; in fact, some fading old dowagers have been vastly improved once they have been taken over by a chain. However, you can't always judge how good a hotel is, and you certainly can't tell how romantic it is, just by the ownership. Service and amenities at chain hotels can vary widely from location to location, even within the same city. Nor should you try to go by the opposite criteria. Just because a hotel is privately owned and operated doesn't mean it's romantic or even any good.

You never can tell what staying at a hotel is like just by looking at the brochures or even reading most of the tour guides. For my various business ventures, I travel a lot. And I believe there's no reason not to mix business with pleasure. Why stay at an impersonal, nondescript hotel when you can choose a charming, romantic place instead? Over the years I have learned—slowly but surely—which are the most romantic places to stay.

That's why I wrote this book. While there are scores of travel and vacation guides already out on the market, there aren't any romantic ones. Sure, there are honeymoon planners and books on romantic destinations. But there isn't a comprehensive and detailed guide to hotels and resorts in the United States and around the world based on their romantic allure.

This book includes a wide variety of romantic interludes. There are first-class hideaways, private escapes that will both pamper you and allow you privacy. There are also several big city hotels, so if you're coming into town on either business or pleasure, your stay can be as romantic. I've added a few simpler inns, for people who find luxury distracting. And specialty vacations such as yacht charters, private railroad cars, and villa rentals are also listed.

While I have tried to list the most accurate and current information in this book, prices or offerings might have changed, so please call first to make sure that you can get what you want. Nothing can be more disappointing than having a particular plan in mind—say a sunset cocktail cruise or dancing to live music—only to discover upon arrival that it is no longer offered.

Romance is poetry itself, and I have included love

poems in the descriptions of these romantic hideaways. Sometimes the connection between the poem and the place is obvious, other times, the poem's meaning is more cryptic or personal. But then poetry, like love, should never have to explain itself, should it? I have found that people who frequent romantic hideaways tend to like love poetry, and I hope you will enjoy the selections I have included. Should you be so inclined, feel free to send me some romantic verse, either classics of great authors or your own creations, for inclusion in the next edition.

This is the second edition of *Bed & Champagne*. Subsequent editions will include changes to the lodgings themselves, new American and international entries, and comments based on reader response. Please take this book with you on your travels. And when you find a place that is either unique and undiscovered, or terribly overrated, let me know. Write to us at the address on the last page of this book. I'd also like to hear your answer to the age-old question—what is romance?

In the meantime, enjoy your romantic travels.

Brad O'Leary

Bed & Champagne

World's Top Romantic Hideaways

Alabama

MARRIOTT'S GRAND RESORT & GOLF CLUB
Point Clear

> It was a lover, and his lass,
> With a hey, and a ho, and a hey nonino,
> That o'er the green corn field did pass,
> In the spring time, the only pretty ring time,
> When birds do sing, hey ding a ding, ding.
> Sweet lovers love the spring.
>
> —untitled by William Shakespeare

The Grand Hotel is situated on the Gulf Coast, an area rich with history, scenic beauty, and steamy romance. First opened in 1847 as the Point Clear Hotel, the original hotel was accessible only by boat. Known as "The Queen of Southern Resorts," the hotel was a favorite among the southern gentility, who enjoyed parties, balls, and high-stakes poker games there. During the Civil War, the hotel served as an encampment and field hospital for Confederate soldiers. When the hotel opened for business after the war, a fire destroyed the kitchen and the main building. No guests were harmed, but all the records from the war were lost. Now the hotel maintains a Confederate Memorial Cemetery, where 150 unknown soldiers rest.

The property changed hands several times, with new owners making several improvements, but then the hotel was severely damaged by a hurricane. Soon thereafter, the hotel was bought by Marriott, which restored and improved the resort while retaining its history and charm. Now the hotel sits on 550 acres of manicured grounds, shaded by flowering magnolias and mossy oaks. Nearby are the lush foliage and charming homes of the Point Clear Historic District.

Three separate buildings offer guest accommodations

United States

1

overlooking the bay, marina, and surrounding gardens. All 306 rooms are newly renovated with careful attention to period detail. You can dance in the moonlight at Julep Point, or go for a walk along the waterfront. Pavilion Wharf offers exceptional fishing and crab trapping, and the chef will gladly prepare anything you catch. Point Clear Stables provide thoroughbred horses for riding along more than five miles of trails. Paddle boats, wave runners, and sailboats are all available for use on the Bay. Lakewood Golf course offers some of the best golf in the area. And the hotel's elegant 111-foot yacht, *Southern Comfort,* is the place for watching a spectacular sunset, or enjoying cocktail and dinner cruises under the southern moonlight.

The Grand Dining Room is formal yet relaxed, serving lavish breakfast and luncheon buffets, along with the legendary Sunday champagne jazz brunch. The Bayview Room offers great local seafood cooked to your taste and an exquisite view of Mobile Bay. The Clubroom at the golf course provides a country club atmosphere for more casual lunches. Afternoon tea is served in the rustic elegance of the main lobby every day.

The Grand Hotel combines southern hospitality with modern comforts, offering a vast array of amenities and activities in an environment of unparalleled historic charm.

Rates: Rooms $99–$219; Suites $169–$450
(based upon season)

MARRIOTT'S GRAND HOTEL RESORT & GOLF CLUB
1 Grand Boulevard
Point Clear, AL 36564-0639

Phone   334-928-9201
Toll free   800-544-9933
Fax   334-928-1149

Alaska

KACHEMAK BAY WILDERNESS LODGE
Homer

> In joy's excess, 'mid woodland shadows dark.
> The flowers join lips below; the leaves above;
> And every sound that meets the ear is Love.
>
> —"A Spring Morning" by John Clare

Some romantics, like Clare, find love in wild nature. If the two of you would like to revel in the splendid isolation of the Alaskan wild country, then Kachemak Bay is the place.

Accessible only by floatplane or ferry, this wilderness resort is situated on the spectacular Kenai Peninsula. A perfect spot for nature lovers who also want some luxury, the lodge is about a half an hour from Homer, but offers all the comforts (and more) of home while providing exciting activities in the wilds of Alaska. You can go hiking, canoeing, kayaking, and fishing. Get steamed in the sod-roofed sauna. Eat Dungeness crab that was pulled out of the bay that morning, along with homemade bread baked daily.

Kachemak is a family affair, managed with friendly hospitality and attention to detail. Mike and Diane McBride have been running the lodge for more than 20 years. Mike's a member of the Explorer's Club, a former bush pilot, a licensed skipper, and an expert on Alaska's wilderness. Diane knows all about the natural history of the area. In addition to being perfect hosts, both of them are helpful guides, always willing to answer your questions about the nature and history of this fascinating region.

Each of the four log cabins has a wood-burning stove, homemade quilts, and a porch. There's a stone fireplace in the main lodge and a private outdoor hot tub and sauna. And beyond that, nothing but spruce tree forests and pristine beaches. The wildlife is varied—with seals, sea birds, moose, bear, sea otters, whales, and bald eagles all nearby. And the region is home to the world's largest concentration of black bears. The McBrides offer photography workshops and guided nature tours. Or you can dig for clams and mussels on the beach. The fishing is some of the best in the world, offering trout, salmon, and halibut. The Kenai Peninsula is one of Alaska's most photographed places; when you arrive there, you might find that you recognize it from books or calendars.

Kachemak is listed in *America's Best 100* as "America's best wilderness lodge."

> Rates: $450 per day or $2,250 per week per person
>   (all meals and guide included)
>   (Season runs from May 1st—October 1st)

KACHEMAK BAY WILDERNESS LODGE
P.O. Box 956
Homer, Alaska 99603

Phone   907-235-8910
Fax   907-235-8911

Arizona

THE BOULDERS
Carefree

> Or would I were Narcissus, that sweet boy,
> And she her self the fountain crystal clear,
> Who ravish'd with the pride of his own joy,
> Drenched his limbs with gazing over near.
> So should I bring my soul to happy rest
> To end my life in that I loved best.
>
> —untitled by Sir Arthur Gorges

Imagine coming home to the enticing fragrance and romantic warmth of a wood-burning fireplace... enjoying a room service breakfast on your balcony overlooking the spectacular scenery of the High Sonoran Desert... or sunbathing by the pool and looking up at a mountain of boulders where a waterfall trickles down through the sun-drenched rock. That's what you get at The Boulders.

The Boulders is a desert hideaway, which blends so easily into its surroundings that it seems to be part of the natural landscape. The 160 guest quarters at The Boulders are adobe casitas, each one individually styled and shaped to fit into the terrain. Each has a patio, fireplace, wet bar, and refrigerator. The casitas are all clustered conveniently around the main lodge.

The Boulders is one of the best golf resorts in the country, its two eighteen-hole courses winning *Golf* magazine's Gold Medal Award. But there's more than just duffing. The Boulders also has eight tennis courts, a full service spa and health center offering personalized fitness programs, and two swimming pools. Or you can go for a trek on the hiking and jogging paths. Horseback riding, jeep tours, and hot air ballooning are also available.

But you can't just play all day. You've also got to eat. The Boulders has five restaurants. The Palo Verde serves regional cuisine enhanced by the spectacular beauty of the Sonoran terrain. Situated in the main lodge, the Latilla Room has its own waterfall. The formal room has a large picture window looking out onto a cascading waterfall and boulders. Sunday brunch features mesquite-grilled specialties served outdoors. You can also enjoy meals at the Cantina del Pedregal and the Bakery Cafe. The Boulders Club has a view of the golf course and the Sonoran foothills. Live entertainment is featured in the Discovery Lounge.

The Boulders was named favorite American resort by subscribers of *Hideaway Report* for eleven years in a row. They say that once you've stayed at The Boulders, it stays with you forever. If you like it enough, you can buy a house in the surrounding residential development.

Rates: $175–$525

THE BOULDERS
P.O. Box 2090
34631 North Tom Darlington Drive
Carefree, AZ 85377

Phone   602-488-9009
Toll free   800-553-1717
Fax   602-488-4118

SCOTTSDALE PRINCESS
Scottsdale

> Go, lovely rose—
> Tell her that wastes her time and me,
> That now she knows,
> When I resemble her to thee,
> How sweet and fair she seems to be.

> —"Song" by Edmund Waller

Those seeking romantic splendor beneath the warm Arizona sun need look no further than the posh Scottsdale Princess. The McDowell mountains add a dramatic backdrop to this resort's 450 exquisitely landscaped acres.

Spanish-colonial architecture rules at the Scottsdale Princess. Its 600 rooms are spread throughout the resort. Four hundred can be found in the red-tile-roof main building, while the remainder of the rooms are divided among 125 casitas and 75 villas. Regardless of which type of housing you choose, you will enjoy a private terrace and a room which is decorated in the muted tones of the Southwest but still contains all the luxurious appointments of a top-flight resort. This combination results in a mood of relaxed elegance that permeates the entire resort.

During the day, the Scottsdale Princess offers a wide variety of activities. If you're in the mood for relaxation, try the spa. Here you can enjoy any number of beauty treatments ranging from a Japanese shiatsu massage to a Finnish sauna. If you don't find the spa appealing, there are three pool areas where you can sun yourself or cool off with a swim. Sports enthusiasts will love the golf and tennis centers. The Scottsdale Princess boasts two TPC championship courses and plays host to the Phoenix Open. Meanwhile the tennis center and its seven courts have served the likes of Andre Agassi. Additionally, there is a fully equipped fitness center.

Boasting five restaurants, the Scottsdale Princess can satisfy the cravings of most gastronomes. Besides being the resort's premier restaurant, the Marquesa is also one of the best in the nation. Here you and your lover can enjoy fine Catalan cuisine in a regal setting. However, be sure to try the other restaurants, especially La Hacienda for authentic Mexican specialties.

The Scottsdale Princess is a recipient of AAA's Five Diamond Award, and it's no wonder why this resort consistently ranks as one of the world's top 100 destinations.

Rates: Doubles from $215

SCOTTSDALE PRINCESS
7575 East Princess Drive
Scottsdale, AZ 85255

Phone   602-585-4848
Fax   602-585-0091

California

BOB'S AT THE BEACH
Lake Tahoe

> What is love, 'tis not hereafter,
> Present mirth, hath present laughter:
> What's to come, is still unsure.
> In delay there lies no plenty
> Then come kiss me sweet and twenty:
> Youth's a stuff will not endure.
>
> —untitled by William Shakespeare

On the California side of Lake Tahoe, there is one very special place to stay, a vacation rental home that's as spectacular as the Sierras themselves.

Featured on *Lifestyles of the Rich and Famous,* this wet-and-wild 7,000-square-foot three-story beach house is located in an exclusive electronic-gated community of million dollar homes right on stunning Lake Tahoe. It's minutes away from skiing, casinos, and all the other attractions of this fantastic resort area. The house has four bedrooms, seven baths, five fireplaces, decks, a gourmet kitchen, wet bars, a Jacuzzi, a boat dock, and an indoor swimming pool. There's also a beautiful beach, an outdoor spiral staircase, and gorgeous glass architecture. A video is available for more details and a sense of how special this place really is.

Rates: House $750–$1,500 per day
(based upon season)

BOB'S AT THE BEACH
P.O. Box 8096
South Lake Tahoe, CA 96158

Phone   530-541-3731
Fax   530-541-3904

DOCKSIDE BOAT & BED
San Francisco and Oakland

> She tells her love while half asleep,
> In the dark hours,
> With half-words whispered low:
> As Earth stirs in her winter sleep
> And puts out grass and flowers
> Despite the snow,
> Despite the falling snow.
>
> —"She Tells Her Love While Half Asleep"
> by Robert Graves

Innkeepers Robert and Mollie Harris offer visitors to the San Francisco Bay area probably one of the most unique places to stay. Dockside Boat and Bed offers a fourteen-boat fleet to guests looking for something different but definitely romantic. If you have concerns about the quality of service you'll receive, fret not. In 1994, Dockside was certified as a bed and breakfast by the California Association of B&B Inns. In keeping with the B&B tradition, Dockside's service includes a continental breakfast brought right to your cabin door.

Each boat offers guests something different. Some yachts are sailing vessels, while others are motor-based. Whatever you choose, you're certain to be pleased. Master staterooms feature queen or full beds, color televisions, stereo cassettes, heating, refrigerator/freezers, microwaves, and full baths. A coffee maker with fresh ground coffee and teas are also on board.

A sampling of the fleet includes: *Carrie C*—a forty-one-foot Viking Sportfisher motoryacht that features a spacious, enclosed upper flybridge deck with views to Jack London Square and the Estuary. Some of the amenities you'll find aboard the *Carrie C* are a wet bar, sectional couch, and an entertainment system with a CD/cassette player and color TV/VCR. The master stateroom has a full bed with adjoining bath and the large aft deck is ideal for soaking up the rays. *Kweilin* is a fifty-four-foot Ketch-rigged CT. This sailboat features lots of deck space with cushioned seating for eight in the cockpit. The best part of your stay aboard *Kweilin* is its location at an end-tie with a great view of the Estuary and San Francisco. Inside are four staterooms and three baths. The interior is spacious yet intimate with lots of teak paneling.

Order a catered dinner aboard any of the yachts for that extra-romantic touch!

Your choice of activities is practically limitless. Some of the more popular include: hiking, sightseeing, bicycling, historic tours, theater, opera, concerts, shopping, cable cars, boating, sailing, speedboat and sail cruises, and harbor seal viewing.

Dockside has two locations in the Bay area: Pier 39 at Fisherman's Wharf in San Francisco and Jack London Square in Oakland. Snooze and cruise packages are available.

Rates: $95–$275 for two people,
$50 for each additional person

DOCKSIDE BOAT & BED

77 Jack London Square, Suite B
Oakland, CA 94607

Phone   510-444-5858
Fax   510-444-0420

Pier 39
San Francisco, CA 94133

Phone   415-392-5526
Toll free   800-436-2574

GINGERBREAD MANSION
Ferndale

> Come away, come, sweet love,
> The golden morning breaks,
> All the earth, all the air
> Of love and pleasure speaks,
> Teach thine arms then to embrace,
> And sweet rosy lips to kiss,
> And mix our souls in mutual bliss.

Eyes were made for beauty's grace,
Viewing, rueing love's long pain,
Procur'd by beauty's rude disdain.

Come away, come, sweet love,
The golden morning wastes,
While the sun from his sphere
His fiery arrows casts:
Making all the shadows fly,
Playing, staying in the grove,
Hunting thee hence with hunt's-up to the day.
O, now be gone! More light and light it grows.
ROMEO
More light and light-more dark and dark our woes.
   —"To His Love" by William Shakespeare

Just a few miles from Highway 101 lies the
Gingerbread Mansion, one of the most photographed
inns in California. Many tourists venture off 101 to view
the Gingerbread Mansion's gables, spindle roof, and icicle
eaves all painted in peach and yellow hues and to enjoy
the precisely landscaped and beautiful Victorian garden.

This one-time hospital has been lovingly restored by
proprietor Ken Torbert. Inspired by *Alice in Wonderland*,
Torbert sought to turn this Victorian and Eastlake gem
into a modern day version of Lewis Carroll's fantasy. To
do so, Torbert gave each room its own personality. Most
opulent of the inn's ten rooms is the Empire Suite. The
highlight of this room is the bed surrounded by Ionic
columns and the bathroom which features an oversized
tub in front of a marble fireplace. Guests of the Empire
Suite often take breakfast in their room; the suite
includes a living and dining area with a second fireplace.
Another interesting room is the Fountain Suite featuring
two side-by-side clawfoot tubs in front of a mirrored wall
and a corner fireplace.

In addition to the unique bedrooms, the Gingerbread
Mansion offers several other diversions. Four parlors are
set aside for reading or playing games. Additionally, the
inn has bicycles for guests to use to explore Ferndale or
the surrounding countryside. Yet perhaps the most

pleasant diversion of all is breakfast, which consists of fresh fruit, locally made cheeses, homemade granola, and a baked egg dish such as Eggs Florentine.

Rates: $140–$350

GINGERBREAD MANSION
400 Berding Street
Ferndale, CA 95536

Phone	707-786-4000
Toll free	800-952-4136
Fax	707-786-4381

HOTEL BEL-AIR
Los Angeles

> I loved thee, though I told thee not,
> Right earlily and long,
> Thou wert my joy in every spot,
> My theme in every song.
>
> And when I saw a stranger face
> Where beauty held the claim,
> I gave it like a secret grace
> The being of thy name.
>
> All the charms of face or voice
> Which I in others see
> Are but the recollected choice
> Of what I felt for thee.
>
> —"The Secret" by John Clare

Simply one of the best hotels in the country, the Hotel Bel-Air is famous for offering comfort, convenience, and privacy in a luxurious setting. Hidden away on eleven acres in the foothills of Bel-Air, the hotel is a secure and peaceful sanctuary among the glitz and bustle of Tinseltown. Lush gardens, flowers, streams, and lawns give the Hotel Bel-Air the feeling of a tropical oasis. You'll never think you're in America's second largest city. But you're only minutes away from the shopping at

Rodeo Drive, and close to Westwood and the LA beaches.

The Restaurant (that's what it's called) is excellent, popular both with the hotel's guests and the locals, featuring California cuisine with fresh ingredients and imaginative presentations. For dining alfresco, there's the terrace, draped with bougainvillea. This terrace is heated for year-round comfort and overlooks the hotel gardens and Swan Lake, home of the famous Bel-Air swans swimming among the gentle splash of a waterfall. But you don't have to leave your room to enjoy their fabulous cuisine. Room service provides a full menu, and the service is exquisite, yet discreet. Or you can lunch, Hollywood-style, by the heated pool.

Adjacent to The Restaurant is The Bar. It has a fireplace, wood paneling, and a baby grand piano. The Bar features nightly entertainment and is a favorite meeting place for guests and locals.

The Hotel Bel-Air provides luxurious comfort in unparalleled style. The hotel's ninety-two rooms are all designed individually with Mediterranean appointments. All are furnished with art and antiques, and many have wood-burning fireplaces, balconies, and patios. Hotel Bel-Air's casual but refined residential mood is enhanced by the private entrances and walled patios. Despite the privacy, all the rooms seem close to nature with beautiful views, skylights, or French doors.

The Hotel Bel-Air is a popular wedding and honeymoon site. Celebrities ranging from Joan Crawford to Farrah Fawcett have honeymooned here. But if you'd like to get married here, book well in advance.

Rates: Rooms $315–$435; Suites $495–$950

HOTEL BEL-AIR
701 Stone Canyon Road
Los Angeles, CA 90077

Phone	310-472-1211
Toll free	800-648-4097
Fax	310-476-5890

LA VALENCIA
La Jolla

> Love without hope, as when the young bird-catcher
> Swept off his tall hat to the Squire's own daughter,
> So let the imprisoned larks escape and fly
> Singing about her head, as she rode by.
>
> —"Love Without Hope" by Robert Graves

Built in 1926, La Valencia immediately became one of the top hotels on the West Coast and has never looked back. Today this coral-pink palace is better than ever.

Located in the prestigious town of La Jolla, just north of San Diego, La Valencia often offers guests some of the best weather in the United States. Beneath dazzling azure skies, you can play in the surf or lounge next to the heated heart-shaped pool set amidst palm trees and beautiful flower gardens.

The lobby of this seaside gem features European furnishings and Oriental screens and rugs. In contrast, the rooms are individually decorated in a Californian style with pastel hues.

For romantic dining, try the Sky Room. Perched upon the 10th floor, the restaurant's twelve tables are elegantly appointed with silver, crystal, Wedgewood china, and fresh flowers. If you prefer open-air dining, La Valencia's Ocean View Terrace serves breakfast, lunch, dinner, and the best oceanview dining in La Jolla.

Rates: $340–$675

LA VALENCIA
1132 Prospect Street
La Jolla, CA 92037

Phone	619-454-0771
Toll free	800-451-0772
Fax	619-456-3921

MEADOWOOD
Saint Helena

> She wore a new 'terra-cotta' dress,
> And we stayed, because of the pelting storm,
> Within the hansom's dry recess,
> Though the horse had stopped; yea, motionless
> We sat on, snug and warm.
>
> Then the downpour ceased, to my sharp sad pain
> And the glass that had screened our forms before
> Flew up, and out she sprang to her door:
> I should have kissed her if the rain
> Had lasted a minute more.
>
> —"A Thunderstorm In Town" by Thomas Hardy

There is no better way to experience the Napa Valley than a stay at the former private-club turned luxury-resort that is Meadowood. This exclusive hotel is set among oak and madrone trees on 250 acres of parkland.

The hotel features New England traditional architecture with wainscoting in the lobby and beamed cathedral ceilings in the rooms. Other room amenities include cushioned window seats, remote control skylights, heated tile floors, and a private balcony. Best of all, the rooms are offered in a variety of settings. You can opt for the lawnview terrace overlooking croquet lawns or one of the seventeen four-suite lodges scattered about the property. The lodges are located around the extensive list of attractions at Meadowood. For instance, you can stay at Poolside near one of the two swimming pools at the complex or you might pick the Fairway Lodge alongside the nine-hole executive golf course. Courtside situates you near one of Meadowood's seven tennis courts.

Couples looking for a special hideaway can request the Hideaway Lodge or the Treeline or Hillside terrace units that are tucked away deep in the woods. These units feature a king-sized bed, wet bar, and fireplace in the living room.

In addition to the pool, golf, and tennis, Meadowood offers three miles of hiking trails, cycling, and a state-of-the-art health spa that provides personal trainers, professional massages, and facial treatments. Nearby you can enjoy hot air ballooning, antique and boutique shopping, and wine tasting at over 100 wineries in the Valley.

Rates: Rooms $340–$550; Suites $540–$1,970

MEADOWOOD

900 Meadowood Lane
Saint Helena, CA 94574

Phone	707-963-3646
Toll free	800-458-8080
Fax	707-963-3532

POST RANCH INN
Big Sur

> But if thou wilt prove faithful then,
> And constant of thy word,
> I'll make thee glorious by my pen
> And famous by my sword;
> I'll serve thee in such noble ways
> Was never heard before;
> I'll crown and deck thee all with bays,
> And love thee more and more.
>
> —"I'll Never Love Thee More" by James Graham,
> Marquis of Montrose

A dramatic coastline of mountains and cliffs rising up from the ocean. The secluded beauty of unspoiled beaches and deep forest wilderness. Brilliant sunshine, the spray of salt water, spectacular sunsets, and quiet, starry nights. That's Big Sur, an unforgettable place and one of the most unique natural areas in the country.

The clock runs differently at Big Sur. You won't be hurried or harried. There will be no distractions or interruptions. You'll be able to enjoy each other in a peaceful "earthly" environment. Perhaps this is why Ed McMahon likes to come here for a romantic getaway.

The place to stay at Big Sur is Post Ranch Inn, a romantic country inn nestled in a mountain meadow with a spectacular ocean view. Post Ranch Inn enjoys some of the most dramatic meetings of land and sea in the world.

The entrance to the inn and its ninety-eight-acre grounds is located right off Highway One in Big Sur. After you arrive at the reception office, a van will take you up the winding road that leads to a secluded bluff where the thirty guest villas are located. Some of these are eccentrically designed, like the ones built on stilts, or covered in sod roofs. However they all blend harmoniously into the landscape, and inside they offer the most modern conveniences.

All the guest quarters have fireplaces, jacuzzis, wet bars, refrigerators, and private decks with spectacular views so you can absorb the surrounding beauty. The rooms have high ceilings and walls of stone and wood, with lots of windows to enjoy the view.

At the main lodge, a nonsmoking dining room offers a gorgeous view from a huge picture window. There is also a terrace bar, with a sweeping view of the ocean and mountains. The first-rate cuisine is complemented by an extensive wine list.

There is a lot to do in the Big Sur area. Hiking, swimming, and horseback riding are among the local activities. Or you can just kick back and do nothing at all.

Rates: Villas $365–$645

POST RANCH INN
P.O. Box 219
Big Sur, CA 93920

Phone   408-667-2200
Toll free   800-527-2200
Fax   408-667-2824

SEAL COVE INN
Moss Beach

> Light, so low in the vale,
> You flash and lighten afar,
> For this is the golden morning of love,

And you are his morning star.
Flash, I am coming, I come,
By meadow and stile and wood,
Oh, lighten into my eyes and heart,
Into my heart and my blood!

Heart, are you great enough
For a love that never tires?
O heart, are you great enough for love?
I have heard of thorns and briers.
Over the thorns and briers,
Over the meadows and stiles,
Over the world to the end of it,
Flash for a million miles.

—"Marriage Morning" by Alfred, Lord Tennyson

Country-inn researcher and author Karen Brown Herbert and her husband Rick decided to take their years of visits to inns and apply the things they liked best into a first-rate bed and breakfast of their own that leaves no detail unturned.

Follow the quiet road that leads you to this romantic Eden set among a meadow of beautiful wildflowers. The English-manor-style inn is ringed with fragrant cypress trees and is set back from the ocean bluffs. Guests are provided with a distant view of the ocean from private terraces.

Located only one half hour south of San Francisco, the Seal Cove Inn is certain to appeal to the well-heeled city crowd looking for a romantic escape in pampered style.

The rooms are decorated in warm fashion with country antiques, rich fabrics, and watercolors. You will also find that a wood-burning fireplace, heated towel racks, and a private terrace are features of each room. For that extra touch, Karen and Rick have fresh cut flowers throughout the inn and in your room you will find a mini-refrigerator stocked with complimentary wine, snacks, and soft drinks. For those amorous souls in search of a special stay, request the Fitzgerald or Cypress rooms which feature king-sized canopied beds and whirlpool bathtubs. Besides the guest rooms, the inn features a living room with fireplaces, a dining room, conference room, and a video library.

The beach is but a brief walk away and, if your timing is exquisite, watch for whales from the bluffs. Surfing and fishing are also options for guests.

A complimentary full breakfast is served each morning consisting of freshly squeezed orange juice, fruit, waffles, or French toast. Hors d'oeuvres and appetizers are served to guests at 5 pm.

Rates: Rooms $165-185; Suites $250

SEAL COVE INN
221 Cypress Avenue
Moss Beach, CA 94038

Phone   650-728-7325
Toll free   800-995-9987
Fax   650-728-4116

SECRET GARDEN INN & COTTAGES
Santa Barbara

Like the touch of rain she was
On a man's flesh and hair and eyes
When the joy of walking thus
Has taken him by surprise:

I do adore thee:
I know thee what thou art,
I serve thee with my heart,
And fall before thee.

—"Like The Touch Of Rain" by Anonymous

The Blue Quail Inn changed its name to Secret Garden Inn & Cottages a few years back and, given the inn's setting, the new name is very appropriate. Hidden away behind high hedges and romantic gardens with fragrant jasmine, Secret Garden Inn's complex of five bungalows offers an intimate and private locale for couples visiting the Santa Barbara area.

Each bungalow has a flavor all its own. The Wood Thrush cottage features large wicker arm chairs and there's luxurious French linens on the king-sized bed. Another avian-named offering is the Cardinal suite which is outfitted with a wicker bed, rich fabrics in stripes and paisleys, and botanical prints. The Kingfisher, Oriole, and Nightingale rooms and suites have been recently renovated, each with a unique luxurious touch that ranges from a hot tub to a private deck. The bathrooms include antique clawfooted bathtubs with modern shower attachments.

Pamper yourself with a massage in the privacy of your own deck and then spend some time with your loved one in front of a roaring fire.

Tennis, golf, hiking, bicycling, the beach, sailing, fishing, and whale watching are all within a few miles of the inn.

Rates: Rooms $110–$195

SECRET GARDEN INN & COTTAGES
1908 Bath Street
Santa Barbara, CA 93101

Phone	805-687-2300
Toll free	800-676-1622
Fax	805-687-4567

TWO BUNCH PALMS
Desert Hot Springs

> Now folds the lily all her sweetness up,
> and slips into the bosom of the lake:
> So fold thyself, my dearest, thou, and slip
> Into my bosom and be lost in me.
>
> —from *The Princess* by Alfred, Lord Tennyson

> "Most relaxing and romantic hotel/spa ever."
> —Powers Boothe

Relaxation and privacy are the main ingredients of a stay at this hideout turned hideaway. Once the secret desert oasis of American Indians, Two Bunch Palms was first developed by the infamous Al Capone. Here Capone built a casino, hot-spring fed pools, and a fortress complete with sentry turret. Today, however, couples retreat here not to hide from the law, but to escape the stresses of everyday life.

The first impression of Two Bunch Palms is one of privacy. Only expected guests are allowed to pass through the guarded gate. As a result, Two Bunch has become a favorite of many celebrities such as Mel Gibson, Goldie Hawn, and Robin Williams. Next you'll notice the overall serenity of Two Bunch. Rarely does anyone speak much above a whisper, and many of your fellow guests stroll around in bathing suits and bathrobes.

Besides being very private, Two Bunch is also very intimate. The majority of its guests are couples seeking a weekend getaway in one of the resort's forty-four guest rooms, each in a private bungalow or villa. The most sought-after dwelling is Capone's former fortress. Each guest room is individually decorated with a pleasantly eclectic mix of Victorian and Art Deco accents. Some accommodations even have enclosed patios for private sunning.

The activities at Two Bunch are centered around relaxation, not exertion. Two Bunch boasts one of the world's best spas and offers a smorgasbord of health and beauty treatments. The spa offers traditional shiatsu and Swedish massage in addition to several New Age techniques such as meditative acupressure and lymphatic massage. For beauty, try an herbal steam or a Roman Celtic Brush. Most of these can be performed à deux, so that you and your partner can relax together. Especially romantic is the Roman Tub Rejuvenator; an hour-long massage followed by a candlelit lavender Epsom salt bath.

Rates: $105 to $420

TWO BUNCH PALMS
67–425 Two Bunch Palms Trail
Desert Hot Springs, CA 92240

Phone   760-329-8791
Toll free   800-472-4334
Fax   760-329-1317

THE WHALE WATCH INN
Gualala

No simpering lips nor looks can breed
Such smiles as from your face proceed.
The sun must lend his golden beams,
Soft winds their breath, green trees their shade,
Sweet fields their flowers, clear springs their streams,
Ere such another smile be made.
But these concurring, we may say,
So smiles the Spring, and so smiles lovely May.

—"To The Lady May" by Aurelian Townsend

Located on a seaside bluff, the Whale Watch Inn stands as a world-class bed and breakfast. True, you can see whales during winter as they migrate between Alaska and the Sea of Cortez, but the real draw of the Whale Watch Inn is its intimacy and splendid service.

The inn's eighteen rooms are spread throughout five buildings. All have private decks and fireplaces and are individually decorated in styles ranging from Asian to Victorian. The unifying features of the rooms though are their high, skylighted ceilings and light color schemes. Additionally, many rooms boast an individual or two-person whirlpool bath. For those staying more than a couple of days, the Sea Bounty building houses four condo-like suites with fully equipped kitchens. No matter which room you stay in, you'll find such amenities as down comforters and soft bed linens.

The attentive yet unobtrusive service at the Whale Watch Inn compliments the intimacy of the rooms. Upon arrival, you are urged to relax in the lobby and enjoy a glass of wine. Best of all, breakfast is delivered to your doorstep each morning at a time preselected by you. Presented in cute wicker baskets, breakfast is a full meal with such treats as blueberry blintzes and quiche accompanied by muffins, croissants, fresh fruit, coffee, and juice.

After breakfast, you may want to linger in your room. Or you can walk down the long set of stairs—130 steps— to the beach and play in the tidal pools. Another pleasant option is to walk along the cliffside paths and marvel at the sea beneath you, the trees above you, or the love of the person next to you.

Rates: $170–$265

THE WHALE WATCH INN
35100 Highway 1
Gualala, CA 95445

Phone	707-884-3667
Toll free	800-942-5342
Fax	707-884-4815

Colorado

THE BROADMOOR
Colorado Springs

> The lark now leaves his wat'ry nest.
> And climbing, shakes his dewy wings;
> He takes this window for the east,
> And to implore your light, he sings,
> Awake, awake, the morn will never rise,
> Till she can dress her beauty at your eyes.
>
> The merchant bows unto the seaman's star,
> The ploughman from the sun his season takes;
> But still the lover wonders what they are,
> Who look for day before his mistress wakes.
> Awake, awake, break through your veils of lawn,
> Then draw your curtains, and begin the dawn.
>
> —"Song" by Sir John Davenant

Since its founding in 1918 by gold barons Spencer and Julie Penrose, the Broadmoor has stood for elegance. After traveling the world, the Penroses decided to bring the opulence and luxury of Europe and the Orient home with them and opened the Broadmoor as a retreat for their fellow millionaires. Since then, the Broadmoor has added two housing buildings and now spreads over 3,000 acres at the base of the Cheyenne Mountains.

The first thing one notices about the Broadmoor is its size. With 700 rooms, the Broadmoor is gigantic by luxury hotel standards. Thankfully, the Broadmoor's size does nothing to detract from its quality. Indeed, the level of service offered at the Broadmoor is rarely found elsewhere in the world. Somehow the bellmen manage to remember your name, the room service personnel—usually among the most hurried of any hotel's staff—always have smiles on their faces and do everything they can to make your stay memorable. It's refreshing to find service as gracious as the rooms are luxurious. This surely must be part of the reason why the Broadmoor has earned Mobil's Five Stars and AAA's Five Diamond Award every year since each was first handed out.

The vast array of amenities at the Broadmoor nearly eliminates the need to leave the resort. There are three championship golf courses used exclusively by guests. For a peaceful walk, follow the paths around Cheyenne Lake where you can also enjoy the resort's paddleboats. For fitness buffs, the Broadmoor's fitness center houses a complete gym, an aerobics room, an indoor pool, and an outdoor lap pool. Two other outdoor pools can be found elsewhere on the grounds. The resort also has a full-service spa where you can have your troubles caressed away. In addition, there's the Broadmoor's thirty+ shops to browse.

Deciding where to dine at the Broadmoor can be a daunting task. For formal dining, there's the Penrose Room. For slightly less formal dining, try the romantic Charles Court restaurant and sample unique "American Bounty" cuisine. After dinner, head to the Tavern where a four piece band plays dance music late into the evening.

Of special note, the Broadmoor offers carriage rides that can be especially romantic.

Rates: Rooms from $226

THE BROADMOOR
1 Lake Avenue
Colorado Springs, CO 80906

Phone   800-634-7711
Fax   719-577-5738

INN AT ZAPATA RANCH
Mosca

> Love alters not with his brief hours and weeks
> But bears it out even to the edge of doom:
> If this be error and upon me proved,
> I never writ, nor no man ever loved.
>
> —untitled by William Shakespeare

Nestled in a valley between the San Juan and Sangre de Cristo mountain ranges lies Mosca, Colorado. Mosca is home to Colorado's legendary Zapata Ranch on which you will find the Inn at Zapata Ranch and one of largest bison herds in the country.

With only fourteen rooms and one suite, the Inn at Zapata Ranch promises a stay that will be an intimate affair. From the outside, the guest houses look primitive with their rough-hewn log facades. Indeed with no televisions or phones, they are primitive to a degree, but not so much so that it's bothersome. Instead, the individually decorated rooms are charming enclaves filled with antiques, hand-crafted beds, claw-footed tubs, and pedestal sinks. Additionally there is absolutely nothing primitive about the cuisine served by the restaurant where you can enjoy inventive provincial cooking.

The resort offers golf and has a sauna, pool, and gym, and nearby you can hike, fish, or ride. Also, be sure to visit the Great Sand Dunes National Monument and stand in awe of the towering, continuously shifting dunes. Of course, if you do bring your clubs, the eighteen-hole course will challenge you with its tall prairie grass rough while endearing you with the natural beauty that abounds in this Colorado oasis.

Rates: $65–$99

INN AT ZAPATA RANCH
5303 Highway 150
Mosca, CO 81146

Phone	719-378-2357
Toll free	800-284-9213
Fax	719-378-2428

THE PEAKS AT TELLURIDE
Telluride

> So well I love thee, as without thee I
> Love nothing; if I might choose, I'd rather die
> Than be one day debarr'd thy company.
>
> —untitled by Michael Drayton

Until the mid-1980s, few people knew of Telluride, Colorado. Until then, this old gold town's mountain was frequented by hard-core skiers seeking steep slopes and deep powder. However, the secret of Telluride soon leaked out and those tired of Aspen's glitz began to frequent Telluride to enjoy skiing in this beautiful box canyon. To cater to these Aspen refugees, the Peaks at Telluride has evolved into one of the world's best mountain resorts.

Located mid-mountain at an altitude of 9,500 feet, the Peaks at Telluride commands breathtaking views of the surrounding San Juan Range and its 14,000 foot peaks. Before skiing, Telluride earned fame as the site of Butch Cassidy's first bank robbery, and the feeling of the Old West is carried on at the Peaks. The doorman, decked out in cowboy hat, leather riding gloves, flannel shirt, and range coat, greets you with a warm welcome. Inside you'll find a lobby enhanced by spectacular views from its large picture window, warmed by a charming stone fireplace, and filled with overstuffed chairs and sofas and dazzling rugs. In your room, you'll discover a down comforter, entertainment center, oversized marble bath, and a view that by itself justifies your stay.

The main attraction at the Peaks is the skiing. Located at mid-mountain, the Peaks offers the convenience of a ski-in/ski-out lounge. In the morning, a valet will fetch your skis—which were tuned the night before—and your boots, which are warmed for your comfort.

After a few days of skiing, many guests find themselves heading for the Peaks' full-service spa. Covering 42,000 square feet, the fitness center at the Peaks spans four floors and includes forty-four treatment rooms and an indoor seventy-five-foot lap pool. Among the many services offered are a Cybex weight center, aromatherapy massage, après ski facials, and eucalyptus-scented steam rooms.

If skiing or the spa don't catch your fancy, ask the concierge to arrange a snowmobile trip to an abandoned mining town. Or if you don't care for winter at all, return in the spring or summer and enjoy the Peaks' championship golf course and excellent tennis facilities.

Whichever season you visit, be sure to dine at the hotel's Legends of the Peaks restaurant which serves flavor-infused American and spa cuisine.

Rates: $150–$505

THE PEAKS AT TELLURIDE
136 Country Club Drive
Telluride, CO 81435

Phone	970-728-6800
Toll free	800-728-6567
Fax	970-728-6175

TRAPPER'S CABIN AT BEAVER CREEK RESORT
Avon

No one so much as you
Loves this my clay,
Or would lament as you
Its dying day.

You know me through and through
Though I have not told,
And though with what you know
You are not bold.

None ever was so fair
As I thought you:
Not a word can I bear
Spoken against you.

All that I ever did
For you seemed coarse
Compared with what I hid
Nor put in force.

—"No One So Much As You" by Anonymous

Here's a place where your heart can return to its old dwelling place or perhaps find a new one. Trapper's Cabin is a secluded log cabin 9,500 feet above sea level overlooking Beaver Creek. Combining impeccable service and mountain tranquillity, the 3,000-square-foot cabin gives you the best of both worlds. Enjoy elegant comfort in the most private setting imaginable.

When you arrive at Beaver Creak, your baggage is taken ahead of you, delivered by snowmobile (or Jeep, depending upon the season), and placed in your room before you even get up the mountain. At the site, there is a cabinkeeper who serves as host, bartender, and cleaner-upper to make sure that your needs are met and you are made as comfortable as possible.

Meanwhile a chef prepares your gourmet meal. You'll start out with appetizers with a Western flair, like grilled smoked wild meats and trout, or buffalo salami. Dinner might be such Rocky Mountain favorites as sautéed elk steaks in bourbon and wild mushroom sauce or salmon in dill butter. Dinner is served family-style with fine wine followed by coffee. The chef cleans up and then prepares a heap of midnight snacks before he and the cabinkeeper depart, leaving the two of you alone for the evening.

The cabin features three bedrooms, and is decorated in rustic charm, with lots of exposed beams. The dining room is hickory wood, and the living area is equipped with a player piano, a stone fireplace, a well-stocked library, and board games. A jacuzzi hot tub on the deck soothes muscles wearied by strenuous days of downhill and cross-country skiing.

Breakfast will be brought to you by the chef and cabinkeeper. Then you can plan the day's activities. In the winter, you can ski right from your doorstep (lift tickets are complimentary). In the summer, go horseback riding or hiking. Or you can do anything you like, including nothing at all.

The cabin is reserved for one couple or group at a time.

Rates: Cabin $400–$2,400 (based upon season)

TRAPPER'S CABIN
c/o Beaver Creek Resort
P.O. Box 36
Avon, CO 81620

Phone   970-845-5788
Fax   970-845-6204

Connecticut

STONEHENGE INN AND RESTAURANT
Ridgefield

> My true love hath my heart and I have his,
> By just exchange one for another given.
> I hold his dear, and mine he cannot miss:
> There never was a better bargain driven.
> My true love hath my heart and I have his.
>
> His heart in me, keeps him and me in one,
> My heart in him, his thoughts and senses guides:
> He loves my heart, for once it was his own:
> I cherish his, because in me it bides.
> My true love hath my heart and I have his.
>
>   —untitled by Sir Philip Sidney

New York City is just a short train-ride away, but you'd never know it once you've lost yourself in the bucolic surroundings of the Stonehenge Inn. Less than an hour from the excitement of the big city, you can enjoy the sylvan splendor of one of Connecticut's most exclusive suburbs.

The Stonehenge Inn is fabulously laid out, with a pond and rolling lawns giving way to a thicket of woods. It's conveniently located right off Route 7, yet far enough off the road that you won't hear the traffic. Instead you'll think you're visiting some stately manor house owned by someone with impeccable taste.

There are sixteen guest rooms on the ten-acre property. Make sure and get a room in the Guest House. The flagstone cocktail terrace is perfect for cooling off and winding down in the afternoon. The formal restaurant is one of the finest in an area full of great dining. In the morning, a breakfast basket and *The New York Times* are delivered to your room.

31

Ridgefield is a quaint town filled with antique shops and small specialty stores, in addition to all the necessary conveniences. You can walk the tree-lined streets of this lovely town or pop over the border into New York State and enjoy a picnic at Pound Ridge Reservation. Explore the coastal towns of Westport and Norwalk just a few miles south. Or stay close to the inn and enjoy the peaceful surroundings. The Stonehenge Inn and Restaurant is a classic, great weekend getaway from New York, or it could be the first stop on your travels north into New England.

Rates: Rooms $120; Suites $200

STONEHENGE INN AND RESTAURANT
Route 7
Ridgefield, CT 06877

Phone   203-438-6511
Fax   203-438-2478

District of Columbia

THE WATERGATE HOTEL
Washington, DC

> Loves flies with bow unstrung when Time appears,
> And trembles at the approach of heavy years.
> A few bright feathers leaves he in his flight,
> Quite, beyond recall, but not forgotten quite.
>
> —"Love and Age" by Walter Savage Landor

To people who've never stayed here, the Watergate Hotel means political scandal. But once you've spent a few nights at this hotel, Watergate only brings to mind memories of excellent food, exquisite service, and luxury accommodations in a convenient setting. The ambiance at the Watergate is a combination of classical elegance and contemporary sophistication. The modern architecture blends flawlessly with the period furnishings, creating a look that is both timeless and unique.

There are 232 rooms in the Watergate Hotel, 160 of which are suites. The accommodations are spacious and decorated as if they were residential apartments, instead of hotel rooms. The traditional decor is rounded out by gilt-framed botanical prints, and the beds are furnished with floral-print bedspreads and dust ruffles. Make sure to ask for a suite with a view of the Potomac.

The Aquarelle restaurant offers some of the finest cuisine in the nation's capital. The restaurant is open for breakfast, lunch, pre-theater and dinner, and for a wonderful Sunday brunch. Enjoy a cocktail at the Potomac Lounge, where light fare and afternoon tea are also served.

As you might expect at one of Washington's finest hotels, the service is impeccable, and the amenities offer that attention to detail demanded by the rich and powerful. There is twenty-four-hour room service and concierge service. Nightly turndown prepares your quarters for sleeping. And in the morning, you are offered a choice of seven daily newspapers. Facilities include an indoor lap pool and sundeck, jacuzzi, steam room, sauna, a state-of-the-art health club offering massage and spa treatments, a barber/beauty salon, the gift shop, and a jewelers. The Watergate shopping center offers a variety of clothing and specialty stores, as well as essentials such as a supermarket and post office.

Located between fashionable Georgetown and Foggy Bottom, and only a short cab ride from Midtown or the Capitol, the Watergate has an unbeatable location right on the Potomac River. The Watergate is a favorite with visiting celebrities, particularly those who are performing at the Kennedy Center. Recent celebrity guests have included James Earl Jones, Clint Eastwood, Patrick Swayze, Carol Channing, and Richard Chamberlain.

Rates: Rooms $175–$320; Suites $395–$1,885
(based upon season)

THE WATERGATE HOTEL
2650 Virginia Avenue, NW
Washington, DC 20037

Phone   202-965-2300
Toll free   800-424-2736
Fax   202-337-7915

Florida

BOCA RATON RESORT & CLUB
Boca Raton

> One day I wrote her name upon the strand,
> But came the waves and washed it away:
> Again I wrote it with a second hand,
> But came the tide, and made my pains his prey.
> Vain man, said she, that dost in vain assay
> A mortal thing so to immortalize,
> For I myself shall like to this decay,
> And eke my name be wiped out likewise.
> Not so, (quod I) let baser things devise
> To die in dust, but you shall live by fame:
> My verse your virtues rare shall eternize,
> And in the heavens write your glorious name:
> Where, whenas Death shall all the world subdue,
> Our love shall live, and later life renew.
>
> —untitled by Edmund Spenser

Between the intercoastal waterway and the Atlantic lies a 223-acre resort known as the Boca Raton Resort & Club. Since its opening in the 1920s, the Boca has impressed guests with its ability to continually improve itself. Perhaps this is why the Boca has become a regular fixture on Mobil's Five Star and AAA's Five Diamond lists.

A special feature of staying at the Boca is a wide choice of accommodations. Most charming is the Cloister building with its antiques, Mediterranean ambiance, and hidden gardens. In stark contrast to the Cloister is the Tower, a twenty-seven-story highrise filled with luxurious rooms and suites with magnificent views. For watersport enthusiasts, there's the Boca Beach Club and its ideal location. And lastly, for those seeking the ultimate in privacy, there are the Golf Villa Apartments with kitchens.

When you're not relaxing in your room, the Boca offers a wide variety of land- and sea-based activities. For tennis enthusiasts, the Boca has thirty courts and offers a full program of clinics and lessons. Meanwhile duffers rave about the resort's two eighteen-hole championship courses and the Dave Pelz Short Game School. If you're more nautically inclined, the Boca offers much more than the typical beach and pool scene. You can snorkel, or enjoy the resort's windsurfers and waverunners. The Boca even has a twenty-three-slip marina where you can charter fishing boats and try to catch your own dinner.

If you fail to catch your dinner, don't worry; the Boca has eight restaurants on site. You'll be able to choose from romantic elegance or burgers and beer.

Rates: $210–$515

BOCA RATON RESORT & CLUB

501 East Camino Real
Boca Raton, FL 33431

Phone	561-395-3000
Toll free	800-327-0101
Fax	561-447-3183

CHEECA LODGE
Islamorada

> So sweet the hour, so calm the time,
> I feel it more than half a crime,
> When Nature sleeps and stars are mute,
> To mar the silence ev'n with lute.
> At rest on ocean's brilliant dyes
> An image of Elysium lies:
> Seven Pleiades entranced in Heaven,
> Form in the deep another seven:
> Endymion nodding from above
> Sees in the sea a second love.
> Within the valleys dim and brown,
> And on the spectral mountain's crown,
> The wearied light is dying down,

And earth, and stars, and sea, and sky
Are redolent of sleep, as I
Am redolent of thee and thine
Enthralling love, my Adeline.
But list, O list,—so soft and low
Thy lover's voice tonight shall flow,
That, scarce awake, thy soul shall deem
My words the music of a dream.
Thus, while no single sound too rude
Upon thy slumber shall intrude,
Our thoughts, our souls—O God above!
In every deed shall mingle, love.

—"Serenade" by Edgar Allan Poe

In the Florida Keys, an hour south of Miami, lies Cheeca Lodge. Long known as an angler's paradise—George Bush is a frequent guest and even hosts an annual bonefish tournament here—Cheeca Lodge has undergone a multimillion dollar renovation and turned itself into one of the world's most romantic destinations.

Barefoot elegance is the trademark at Cheeca Lodge. Guest rooms are located in either the main building or in villas scattered throughout the resort's lushly landscaped twenty-seven acres. With ceiling fans and screened porches, the rooms at Cheeca Lodge encourage you to relax and leisurely enjoy the laid-back lifestyle of the Keys.

Cheeca's island location makes it a "has water sports." Besides world-class fishing, Cheeca boasts an excellent 1,000-foot-long, palm-lined, white-sand beach. From the Beach Hut, you can procure snorkeling gear or a catamaran for sailing. Divers can book a place on the resort's forty-two-foot catamaran for an excursion to the only living coral reef in the United States.

At night, Cheeca Lodge offers two restaurants from which to choose. One is the award-winning, fine dining Atlantic's Edge Restaurant. However, the other restaurant, the Ocean Terrace Grill, seems more appropriate for romance. As an open-air restaurant, the Ocean Terrace Grill serves casual fare indoors, outdoors, at poolside, or on the beach, and is the best place to enjoy a stunning Keys sunset.

Rates: $185–$1,000

CHEECA LODGE
Mile Marker 82
Islamorada, FL 33036

Phone   305-664-4651
Toll free   800-327-2888
Fax   305-664-2893

KONA KAI RESORT
Key Largo

> I ne'er was struck before that hour
> With love so sudden and so sweet,
> Her face it bloomed like a sweet flower
> And stole my heart away complete.
>
> —"First Love" by John Clare

The Florida Keys stretch south from Miami into the Gulf Stream. Wonderfully tropical, these islands offer a multitude of beautiful places to see and to stay. Kona Kai Resort is one of the more exceptional places to stay.

Located on Key Largo ninety minutes south of Miami, Kona Kai is a charming, lovingly restored resort built in the 1940s. Small in size, Kona Kai delivers big results. Its beautifully appointed nine guest rooms feature handsome furnishings, kitchens, and views of tropical gardens and Florida Bay.

Kona Kai's small size is not a negative. Instead, the resort is more of a hidden gem. Its heated bayfront pool and jacuzzi are exceptionally romantic, especially at sunset. In fact, due to its island location, Kona Kai allows you to enjoy not only dramatic sunsets but serene sunrises as well. Other amenities include hammocks, tikis, barbecues, and paddleboats. All in all, Kona Kai is the perfect place to retreat from the hustle and bustle of city life and enjoy a slice of tropical paradise.

Rates: $89–$299

KONA KAI RESORT
97802 South Overseas Highway
Key Largo, FL 33037

Phone   305-852-7200
Toll free   800-365-7829
Fax   305-852-4629

LITTLE PALM ISLAND
Little Torch Key

> I wish I could remember the first day,
> First hour, first moment of your meeting me;
> If bright or dim the season, it might be
> Summer or winter for aught I can say.
> So unrecorded did it slip away,
> So blind was I to see and to foresee,
> So dull to mark the budding of my tree
> That would not blossom yet for many a May.
>
> If only I could recollect it! Such
> A day of days! I let it come and go
> As traceless as a thaw of bygone snow.
> It seemed to mean so little, meant so much!
> If only now I could recall that touch,
> First touch of hand in hand!—Did one but know!
>
> —"The First Day" by Elizabeth Barrett Browning

This can be your home in the ever-freshened Keys. Little Palm Island is set on five acres of tropical hideaway that gives new meaning to the word seclusion. Located twenty-eight miles north of Key West, accessible only by water, Little Palm Island is a fifteen minute boat-ride away from Little Torch Key, but light years away from civilization. That doesn't mean it's not luxurious. In fact, all the comforts of home are here, without any of the nuisances or distractions.

Guest accommodations are in fourteen villas scattered across the island, all built on stilts to keep the flood-waters away. Inside the bamboo and thatched roof villas are twenty-eight luxury suites, with two more in a permanently moored houseboat. The suites all have large bedrooms, living rooms, mini-bars, whirlpool baths, private sundecks, and outdoor showers. Interiors are plush and tropical, furnished in rattan and wicker. The exteriors are screened and louvered, to keep the mosquitos and sunlight away while allowing the tropical breezes to pass through the rooms.

The fresh-water pool is fed by a waterfall, and heated by solar power; its loungers are fueled by tropical drinks and snacks from the poolside Palapa Bar. An intimate beach is ringed with white sand, uncommon in the Keys. There's a small-boat harbor for guests. And the docks are a great place to watch the spectacular sunset. The spa, which offers a vast array of treatments, will attend to your body. A dive shop will provide all you need for scuba or snorkeling. The well-stocked library has hammocks swinging outside, where you can curl up with a good book, or make bookends with someone special.

Of course even in paradise, you have to eat. And Chef Michel Reymond serves award-winning cuisine in the Cypress Dining Room or out on the deck. The tables are set with white linen, blue-rimmed plates, and hand-blown glassware. Fresh seafood is a specialty, often imaginatively prepared. Breakfast offerings include a fresh seafood delicacy and home-baked corn and banana bread. Lunch is popular with the local yachters, and salads and sandwiches are served along with more adventuresome fare like raw fish marinated in lime juice. Every Thursday is Gourmet Night which showcases Chef Michel's talents, and each Sunday brings a sumptuous Sunday brunch which is not only a feast for the palate but the eyes as well.

But the best part of Little Palm Island is still ahead, the gorgeous sunset and quiet, star-filled nights. This is what you've escaped civilization for—to sit out on the deck or lie in the hammock and enjoy each other's company in this blissful setting.

Rates: From $400–$725

LITTLE PALM ISLAND
28500 Overseas Highway
Little Torch Key, FL 33042

Phone	305-872-2524
Toll free	800-343-8567
Fax	305-872-4843

THE RITZ-CARLTON
Naples

> How do I love thee? Let me count the ways.
> I love thee to the depth and breadth and height
> My soul can reach, when feeling out of sight
> For the ends of Being and ideal Grace.
> I love thee to the level of every day's
> Most quiet need, by sun and candlelight.
> I love thee freely, as men strive for Right;
> I love thee purely, as they turn from Praise.
> I love thee with the passion put to use
> In my old griefs, and with my childhood's faith.
> I love thee with a love I seemed to lose
> With my lost saints,—I love thee with the breath,
> Smiles, tears, of all my life!—and, if God choose
> I shall but love thee better after death.
>
> —"Sonnet XLIII, From The Portuguese" by Elizabeth
>   Barrett Browning

This magnificent Mediterranean-style resort with old world glamor is one of the top-rated hotels in the United States. The Ritz-Carlton, Naples, was one of only twenty-five hotels in North America to win a Five-Star Award from the *1997 Mobil Travel Guide. Gourmet* magazine rated the Ritz-Carlton's beach the third best in the world and Conde Nast rated the Ritz-Carlton the third best resort in the mainland United States and fifth best in the world. You and your mate are bound to have a memorable experience at this resort.

Each of the 463 guest rooms and suites offers a view of the Gulf of Mexico. "Minimum view" rooms offer guests a clear view of the Gulf and overlook the tropical pool area. "Gulfview" rooms offer a view of the beach and the Gulf while the "Gulfront" rooms overlook the beach. There are twenty-six Gulfview one-bedroom suites and four Royal two-bedroom suites, and two Presidential suites. Inside the sizable guest rooms, you will find an armoire, a writing desk, club chairs, and either two double beds or one king-size. All rooms have a separate dressing area with vanity, two telephones, including one fax, computer hook-up capabilities, a stocked refreshment cabinet, terry robes, and luxury bath amenities. You'll also find a marbled bathroom complete with an oversized tub.

There is a seemingly endless list of things you can do at the Ritz-Carlton, Naples. You could spend a relaxing day on the property's three miles of pure white beach. You'll find Hobie sailboats, kayaks, cabanas, chaise lounges, and towels are all available at the beach. For those of you who prefer poolside to Gulfside, the Ritz-Carlton has an award-winningly designed swimming pool with an adjacent whirlpool. The pool bar is open year-round.

Fitness-minded guests can enjoy the state-of-the-art exercise center, a match at the hotel's tennis area, or an endless amount of golf provided by the region's forty-five courses. Guests of the Ritz-Carlton, Naples, receive special privileges at several of the local courses.

Cap off your activity-filled day with spa service that includes the expertise of a staff of licensed massage therapists.

While there are several fine restaurants in the Naples area, guests will discover many fine dining choices at the hotel. The Dining Room serves Florida cuisine with an Asian flair in a formal setting. Gumbo Limbo is the new open-air beach bar and restaurant that serves lunch, dinner, and cocktails. There is also the Grill which is a handsome, mahogany-paneled dining room serving grilled meats, chops, and fresh fish. You may also want to consider the Beach Pavilion, located directly on the Gulf of Mexico, for breakfast or lunch.

Rates: Rooms $165–$595; Suites $475–$3,345

THE RITZ-CARLTON
280 Vanderbilt Beach Road
Naples, FL 33941-2371

Phone	941-598-3300
Toll free	800-241-3333
Fax	941-598-6690

SANIBEL HARBOUR RESORT & SPA
Fort Myers

> Drink to me only with thine eyes,
> And I will pledge with mine;
> Or leave a kiss but in the cup
> And I'll not look for wine.
> The thirst that from the soul doth rise
> Doth ask a drink divine -
> But might I of Jove's nectar sup,
> I would not change for thine.
>
> —"To Celia" by Ben Johnson

This AAA Four Diamond resort consists of a lovely hotel surrounded by condominiums and numerous activity venues amid eighty acres of unspoiled natural beauty on a private peninsula situated across the water from Sanibel and Captiva Islands.

Each room at the resort is equipped with king- or queen-sized beds, a balcony, mini-bar, bathrobes, hair dryers, a full kitchen, and mini-washer/dryer. Guests can opt to stay in one of the hotel's 240 rooms that include forty-seven suites or they can stay in one of the resort's eighty luxury condominiums that range from two to three bedrooms.

The lush grounds, spa, tennis center with thirteen courts, marina, and four pools make for a veritable playground for active-minded guests. Sanibel Harbour Resort and Spa is bound to appeal to guests seeking a luxury resort with a more casual environment.

The world-class European spa leaves nothing to the imagination. Facials, wraps, massages, manicures, and coifs are just some of the many services offered. The state-of-the-art fitness center offers Cybex, Keiser, and Icarian equipment. The championship tennis facility with its thirteen courts is rated among the top-ten tennis resort facilities in Florida. In fact, the facility was home to the 1989 and 1992 Davis Cup matches. Visit Sanibel Resort's marina if water sports are on your agenda. You can rent everything from waverunners to boats and sailboats. Over fifty-four area golf courses can provide a limitless amount of challenging play during your stay.

Couples looking to add a romantic touch to their visit may want to try the Champagne Sunset Cruise that takes you through the waters of San Carlos Bay to the backdrop of tropical music. Sip complimentary champagne while you enjoy the spectacular sunset.

There are several dining options at the resort. Guests looking for something different should try a dinner cruise aboard the Sanibel Harbour Princess for a Sunday brunch or an evening dinner cruise.

> Rates: Rooms $130–$305; Suites $179–$329;
> Condominiums $179–$439;
> Condominium Penthouse $365–$600

SANIBEL HARBOUR RESORT & SPA
17260 Harbour Point Drive
Fort Myers, FL 33908

Phone	941-466-4000
Toll free	800-767-7777
Fax	941-466-2198

▬▬▬▬

THE TIDES
Miami

> She walks in beauty, like the night
> Of cloudless climes and starry skies;
> And all that's best of dark and bright
> Meet in her aspect and her eyes:
> Thus mellowed to that tender light
> Which heaven to gaudy day denies.
>
> One shade the more, one ray the less,
> Had half impaired the nameless grace
> Which waves in every raven tress,

Or softly lightens o'er her face;
Where thoughts serenely sweet express
How pure, how dear their dwelling place.

And on that cheek, and o'er that brow,
So soft, so calm, yet eloquent,
The smiles that win, the tints that glow,
But tell of days in goodness spent,
A mind at peace with all below,
A heart whose love is innocent!

    —"She Walks In Beauty" by Lord Byron

Built in 1936, The Tides is the tallest and most elegant Art Deco hotel on Ocean Drive in South Beach. Recently renovated, it is the flagship of Chris Blackwell's Island Outpost chain. The original 112 rooms have been converted into forty-five spacious 30s-style suites, each offering an incredible view of the ocean.

Luxury is evident whether you're staying in a deluxe room, the ninth floor suites, or the Terranova penthouse suite. All rooms are equipped with a TV/VCR, CD/cassette stereo, and a state-of-the-art telecommunications system with three two-line phones, a cordless phone, and data port connections. Other amenities include a fully stocked mini-bar that can be customized upon request, twenty-four-hour room service, and the essential telescope.

For couples vacationing with friends, try the interconnecting Goldeneye and Firefly suites that consume much of the ninth floor. Each suite has two full baths and a private terrace with yet more panoramic views of the ocean and coast. Couples looking for the ultimate stay might consider the palatial 3,200-square-foot Terranova Penthouse Suite.

Guests can enjoy the full exercise facilities with terrace on the ninth floor. Or take a dip in the private freshwater heated pool with bar and buffet on the mezzanine level where topless sunbathing is permitted.

A complimentary continental breakfast is available on each floor, and the Twelve Twenty Restaurant and Bar offers diners quality seafood. Twelve Twenty is expected to challenge other top South Beach establishments.

Rates: Suites $150–$2,000

THE TIDES
1220 Ocean Drive
Miami Beach, FL 33139

Phone	305-604-5000
Toll free	800-OUTPOST
Fax	305-604-5180

Georgia

THE CLOISTER
Sea Island

> Wine comes in at the mouth
> And love comes in at the eye;
> That's all we know for truth
> Before we grow old and die.
> I lift the glass to my mouth,
> I look at you, and I sigh.
>
> —"A Drinking Song" by William Butler Yeats

This classic vacation colony with beachfront solitude is set on an island along the Atlantic, and a causeway connects the smaller island to St. Simons Island. Experienced travelers consistently rate The Cloister as one of the best resorts in the country. The buildings are designed in Mediterranean style offering 265 rooms surrounded by stunning gardens and placed along a five mile beach.

The Cloister has some of the best golfing in the world. The two golf courses with a combined fifty-four holes are found on the historic Retreat Plantation along the majestic Avenue of Oaks. There are seventeen clay tennis courts as well as one automated court for private warm-ups and practice. Every morning there's a Seaside Morning Stretch or Morning Beach Walk. Other activities include horseback riding, a world-class spa, freshwater swimming pools, and shooting ranges. The beach club provides a variety of water sports. Sailing and fishing charters are offered at the resort's marina. Vintage motor and sailing yachts are available to be experienced by guests.

Throughout your stay, your own table is reserved for you, if you wish, and is adorned with fresh flowers. Friday nights feature a spectacular outdoor plantation

supper. And every night, except Sunday, The Cloister provides a variety of live music. You can dance to the orchestra before and after dinner. Big bands make The Cloister
one of America's top destinations for ballroom dancers.
The main dining room serves six-course dinners accompanied by live music. The Beach Club has indoor and
outdoor breakfast and lunch buffets, and seafood dinner
buffets.

Just because it's called The Cloister doesn't mean you
have to live like a monk. The staff is attentive to the
needs of romantic couples, and they specialize in
welcoming honeymooners and anniversary celebrations.
Honeymoon packages include amenities such as dancing,
champagne welcome, breakfast in bed, and a weekly honeymooner party.

Rates: Rooms $224–$614; Suites $470–$700
        (double occupancy, based upon season,
        all meals included)

THE CLOISTER
100 Hudson Place
Sea Island, GA 31561

Phone   912-638-3611
Toll free 800-732-4752
Fax   912-638-5159

JEKYLL ISLAND CLUB HOTEL
Jekyll Island

> Cloris, I cannot say your eyes
> Did my unwary heart surprise;
> Nor will I swear it was your face,
> Your shape, or any nameless grace:
> For you are so entirely fair,
> To love a part, injustice were;
> No drowning man can know which drop
> Of water his last breath did stop;
> So when the stars in heaven appear,
> And join to make the night look clear;

The light we no one's bounty call,
But the obliging gift of all.
He that does lips or hands adore,
Deserves them only, and no more;
But I love all, and every part,
And nothing less can ease my heart.
Cupid, that lover, weakly strikes,
Who can express what 'tis he likes.

—"To Cloris" by Sir Charles Sedley

Live on an island!

This resort has a history worth telling. The Jekyll Island Club was incorporated in 1886 by some of society's wealthiest elite including Astor, Gould, Rockefeller, Morgan, and Pulitzer as a place to form a winter hunting retreat. Over the years, condominiums were built by some of these wealthy men and others. However the island access was closed during World War II by the federal government, and after that period, the wealthy never returned. In the late '40s, the island was sold to the State of Georgia, and it was in 1978 that the 240-acre club was designated a National Historic Landmark. Seven years later, restoration began on the facilities.

Today you can enjoy the original grandeur of this exclusive retreat as Rockefeller and Morgan once did. Rooms at the Club are furnished with antique reproductions including two-poster mahogany beds, armoires, desks, tables and chairs, and sofas with rich fabrics. Many rooms feature fireplaces and/or jacuzzis and an array of bathroom amenities.

Club guests can choose from a variety of activities including a surfside Beach Club, sixty-three holes of golf, nine tennis courts (one indoor and five lighted), lawn games, a marina, and elegant shopping. There are also ten miles of beach, twenty miles of bicycling and jogging trails, and a health club. In addition, guests can enjoy other nearby golfing experiences, horseback riding, skeet and trap shooting, boating, and deep sea fishing at area facilities.

Couples looking for a magical getaway should try the Club's Romantic Fantasy which includes two nights deluxe accommodations with jacuzzi, continental champagne breakfast, long stem roses at turndown, gourmet chocolates upon arrival, picnic lunch (one day), complimentary tennis and bicycles (one day), and a commemorative photograph.

Rates: $85–$250

JEKYLL ISLAND CLUB HOTEL
371 Riverview Drive
Jekyll Island, GA 31527

Phone	912-635-2600
Toll free	800-535-9547
Fax	912-635-2818

Hawaii

FOUR SEASONS RESORT MAUI
Wailea

There is a garden in her face
Where roses and white lilies blow;
A heavenly paradise is that place,
Wherein all pleasant fruits do flow:
There cherries grow which none may buy
Till 'Cherry-ripe' themselves do cry.

Those cherries fairly do enclose
Of orient pearls a double row,
Which when her lovely laughter shows,
They look like rose-buds filled with snow;
Yet them nor peer nor prince can buy
Till 'Cherry-ripe' themselves do cry.

—"Cherry Ripe" by Thomas Campion

The Four Seasons at Wailea stands as a blissful retreat from the reality of everyday life. Rarely will one find another resort that pampers its guests like the Four Seasons. The hotel's elegant and enormous rooms serve as your own private sanctuary. And when you venture outside, the staff of the hotel will exceed your expectations. They even water down the beautiful sandy beach to prevent you from burning your bare feet.

Besides the beach, the cabana-lined pool is just one of the many opulent amenities at the Four Seasons. You'll have access to three of the best golf courses in Hawaii. Nearby horseback riding allows you to explore the lush foliage of the area's valleys. Yet perhaps the most enjoyable of all the amenities is the Seasons restaurant which combines fine dining with live music and dancing for a truly romantic experience.

Rates: Doubles from $295

FOUR SEASONS RESORT MAUI
3900 Wailea Alanui Drive
Wailea, HI 96753

Phone	808-874-8000
Toll free	800-334-6284
Fax	808-874-2244

GRAND WAILEA
Wailea

> Small is the worth
> Of beauty from the light retired:
> Bid her come forth,
> Suffer herself to be desired,
> And not blush so to be admired.
>
> —untitled by Edmund Waller

Grand Wailea lives up to its name; it is grand in every sense of the word. Indeed, a stay at this Maui gem is a case study in indulgence, a modern day Vanity Fair. Spread over forty-two acres on Maui's south shore, Grand Wailea is a resort designed to enhance the natural beauty of its setting. The result overwhelms the senses with feelings of elegance, luxury, and romance.

Water is incorporated throughout Grand Wailea. From its beach, you can spot an occasional humpback whale breaching in the distance. In addition, the hotel boasts a unique 2,000-foot multilevel riverpool, complete with waterfalls, rapids, and grottos, which provide the perfect place for a nighttime dip and kiss. During the day, you can relax next to the pool in your own cabana while waiters bring a cool drink.

Also at Grand Wailea is Spa Grande, rated by *Conde Nast Traveler* as America's top resort spa. Be sure to try the Terme Wailea hydrotherapy circuit. This consists of a series of whirlpools, cold plunges, steam room, sauna, and five different specialty baths: seaweed, aromatherapy, sea salts, mud, and tropical enzymes. After undergoing this treatment, not only do you feel relaxed but you actually notice your skin glowing. More intense therapies include a number of holistic Indian treatments straight from the subcontinent.

After your treatment or other activities of the day, you can dine at one of the resort's restaurants or retreat to your graciously appointed room. Outside your room, you'll enjoy the ocean view as you lounge on an over-stuffed chaise lounge. Or soak in your over-sized marble tub and enjoy the romance that is Grand Wailea.

Rates: Doubles from $380

GRAND WAILEA
3850 Wailea Alanui Drive
Wailea, HI 96753

Phone   808-875-1234
Toll free   800-888-6100
Fax   808-879-4077

HALEKULANI
Honolulu

> O mistress mine, where are you roaming?
> O! stay and hear; your true love's coming,
> That can sing both high and low.
> Trip no further, pretty sweeting;
> Journeys end in lovers meeting,
> Every wise man's son doth know.
>
> What is love? 'Tis not hereafter;
> Present mirth hath present laughter;
> What's to come is still unsure.
> In delay there lies no plenty;
> Then come kiss me, sweet and twenty;
> Youth's a stuff will not endure.
>
> —"Feste's Song From Twelfth Night" by William
> Shakespeare

Once part of an island paradise, Waikiki is now crowded and commercialized. Yet standing guard over part of Waikiki stands Halekulani, a tranquil oasis that ranks as one of the island's most romantic destinations.

The sleek luxurious building that forms the heart of Halekulani was built around the original historic 1931 building that began the Halekulani tradition of excellence. Not surprisingly, the resort offers the usual array of water sports, but what really sets this hotel apart is its attention to detail.

Excellent service is the cornerstone of the Halekulani experience. It all begins with the hotel's in-room check-in service that allows you to avoid annoying lines in the lobby. Once checked-in, you'll notice that your wood and marble room has a lanai, sitting area, bathrobes, and many other amenities that add to your stay. For extra romance, request a room overlooking nearby Diamond-head.

Halekulani's attention to detail carries over to the hotel's restaurants. Anchoring these restaurants is the elegant La Mer, one of the world's most romantic dining spots. Less formal is the beautiful Orchids restaurant, while House Without a Key offers oceanside dining. At all three, you will be treated to not only fine food but the attentive and knowledgeable service that makes Halekulani special.

Rates: $450–$1,000

HALEKULANI
2199 Kalia Road
Honolulu, HI 96815

Phone	808-923-2311
Toll free	800-367-2343
Fax	808-926-8004

HYATT REGENCY KAUAI RESORT & SPA
Koloa

> I cry your mercy—pity—love!—aye, love!
> Merciful love that tantalizes not,
> One-thoughted, never-wandering, guileless love,

Unmasked, and being seen—without a blot!
O! let me have thee whole,—all—all—be mine!
That shape, that fairness, that sweet minor zest
Of love, your kiss,—those hands, those eyes divine,
That warm, white, lucent, million-pleasured breast,
Yourself—your soul—in pity give me all,
Withhold no atom's atom or I die,
Forget, in the midst of idle misery,
Life's purposes, -- the palate of my mind
Losing its gust, and my ambition blind!

—untitled by John Keats

Kauai, the oldest of the Hawaiian islands, is known as the Garden Isle. This is the home of the Hyatt Regency Kauai Resort & Spa.

The Hyatt Regency Kauai overlooks Keoneloa Bay from atop cliffs. Built in 1990, the Hyatt's architecture evokes the classic Hawaiian style of the 1920s and '30s. Set on fifty acres, this Hyatt Regency features a man-made saltwater lagoon, cascading waterfall, and river pools.

After snorkeling or windsurfing in the Pacific, rinse the salt off at the outdoor lava rock showers. If you tire of the water, try the Robert Trent Jones II-designed eighteen-hole championship course.

For pure relaxation, visit the Anara Spa. Surrounding a lap pool, this spa is a world in itself. A unique specialty of Anara is the lomilomi massage; an experience that's so relaxing, you'll momentarily forget your mortal essence.

Rates: $275–$465

HYATT REGENCY KAUAI RESORT & SPA
1571 Poipu Road
Koloa, HI 96756

Phone	808-742-1234
Toll free	800-772-0122
Fax	808-742-1557

MAUNA LANI BAY HOTEL & BUNGALOWS
Kohala Coast

> To whom I owe the leaping delight
> That quickens my senses in our wakingtime
> And the rhythm that governs the repose of our
>   sleepingtime,
> The breathing in unison
>
> Of lovers whose bodies smell of each other
> Who think the same thoughts without need of speech
> And babble the same speech without need of meaning.
>
> No peevish winter wind shall chill
> No sullen tropic sun shall wither
> The roses in the rose-garden which is ours and ours
>   only
>
> But this dedication is for others to read:
> These are private words addressed to you in public.
>   —"A Dedication To My Wife" by T. S. Eliot

Located on the Kohala Coast of the Big Island of
Hawaii, the Mauna Lani Bay Hotel & Bungalows consists
of 345 rooms, five luxurious bungalows, and 3,200 acres
of paradise. The hotel's dramatic architecture
compliments the dramatic beauty surrounding it. From
the atrium lobby of waterfalls, ornamental fish ponds,
and towering palms, the hotel's six-story wings spread
out like a phoenix. Once inside the rooms, you'll discover
teak furniture, berber carpets, mini-bars, private lanais,
and elegant bathrooms.

In addition to its magnificent rooms, Mauna Lani Bay
offers world-class activities. Its three-mile stretch of beach
is one of the best places in the world to enjoy the sun and
surf. From here, you can take a catamaran or snorkel or
sail or experience some of the best diving in the world.
When you tire of the sea, the resort features two world-
class golf courses. The South Course, built on a young
lava flow, is the site of the Senior Skins Game. Besides
golf, the hotel's Racquet Club tennis center earns

accolades and is among one of the best tennis resorts in the United States.

After a long day of diving, golf, or tennis, your appetite will be ravenous. Thankfully, Mauna Lani's restaurants can satisfy even the most famished gastronome. The signature restaurant, Canoe House, serves innovative Pacific Rim cuisine. More relaxed than Canoe House, the Ocean Grill offers an oceanfront setting and light dining. Besides these two restaurants, Mauna Lani has another four to satisfy all your cravings.

Rates: $450–$895

MAUANA LANI BAY HOTEL & BUNGALOWS
68-1400 Mauna Lani Drive
Kohala Coast, HI 96743

Phone	808-885-6622
Toll free	800-367-2323
Fax	808-881-7000

Idaho

KNOB HILL INN
Ketchum

> I loved you; even now I may confess,
> Some embers of my love their fire retain;
> But do not let it cause you more distress,
> I do not want to sadden you again.
> Hopeless and tongue-tied, yet I loved you dearly
> With pangs the jealous and the timid know;
> So tenderly I loved you, so sincerely,
> I pray God grant another love you so.
>
> —untitled by Alexander Pushkin

This Tyrolean-style inn is the creation of native Austrian Josef Koenig, his wife Sandra, and their sons Greg and Andi. Couples will love this inn for a warmth and comfort that is customarily reserved for a private home. The interior of the main level, with its arches and cedar beams, creates a cozy and quiet air to the inn. Cedar is definitely in abundance at the Knob Hill Inn. The Koenig family influence is also everywhere. Josef Koenig made the eight-foot ceramic stove in the lobby, architect son Greg designed the rounded windows that line the inn's four stories, son Andi hand-carved the lobby's cedar bar, and Sandra oversees the kitchen staff that will make your breakfast to order.

The twenty double rooms with baths and the four suites all have views of the mountains. The rooms are decorated in a variety of motifs that range from country French to contemporary. The inn's two penthouse suites are favorites of celebrities, captains of industry, and sports figures. Four of the guests rooms and all four of the suites have fireplaces, and all rooms have cable television and mini-bars. Other inn amenities include exercise room, indoor lap pool, hot tub, sauna, ski equipment lockers, an in-house masseuse, fitness room, and transportation to the municipal airport. Downhill and cross-country skiing, a nature trail, four golf courses, and top-notch trout fishing are all nearby.

Guests can treat themselves to Felix, the Knob Hill Inn's restaurant. Felix is considered by many to be the area's finest restaurant.

Rates: Rooms $200–$300

KNOB HILL INN
960 North Main Street, Box 800
Ketchum, ID 83340

Phone   208-726-8010
Fax   208-726-2712

Illinois

THE RITZ-CARLTON
Chicago

> Come live with me and be my Love,
> And we will all the pleasures prove
> That hills and valleys, dales and fields,
> Or woods or steepy mountain yields.
>
> And we will sit upon the rocks,
> And see the shepherds feed their flocks
> By shallow rivers, to whose falls
> Melodious birds sing madrigals.
>
> And I will make thee beds of roses
> And a thousand fragrant posies;
> A cap of flowers, and a kirtle
> Embroidered all with leaves of myrtle.
>
> A gown made of the finest wool
> Which from our pretty lambs we pull;
> Fair-lined slippers for the cold,
> With buckles of the purest gold.
>
> —"The Passionate Shepherd To His Love" by
> Christopher Marlowe

The Windy City is a place that has much to offer in the way of excitement and nightlife. And for a real treat, choose to stay at the Ritz-Carlton during your visit. Located on the Magnificent Mile at Water Tower Place, the Ritz-Carlton offers guests a great location, timeless surroundings, exemplary guest facilities, and unparalleled service.

Thoughtful details in every guest room include luxurious marble bathrooms equipped with hair dryers and full-length cotton robes so you can travel light. Mini-bars and in-room safes provide convenience and safety. Twenty-four hour valet and room service are available to fulfill your every need. Of the 435 oversized guest rooms, ninety-one are suites. Among them, Four Seasons Executive Suites offer separate parlors. A baby grand piano, dining room, and study distinguish the two-level State Suite. And the Anniversary Suites are intimate accommodations with spectacular city views. Within these suites, the living areas and bedrooms are separated by French doors and the bathrooms feature oversized tubs and floor-to-ceiling windows overlooking Chicago.

Dining at the Ritz-Carlton offers a variety of enticing choices. French contemporary cuisine is served amidst a posh setting of crystal chandeliers and cozy banquettes in The Dining Room. This restaurant is regarded as one of Chicago's finest, and Chef Sarah Stegner and Pastry Chef En-Ming Hsu are among the Windy City's brightest culinary stars. The Cafe provides a casual setting for breakfast, lunch, dinner, and late-night dining. The Greenhouse serves a light luncheon buffet, traditional English afternoon tea, and evening cocktails in an atrium setting with a striking view of Chicago's lakefront. Evening piano music sets a graceful tone for a romantic night in the heart of the city. The Trianon also provides an intimate atmosphere for cocktails.

The Ritz-Carlton specializes in catering to pet owners, offering a full range of pet-friendly accommodations and services like gourmet pet room service menu and on-premise kennel and dog walking service. Now you don't have to leave Fido or Kitty behind during your romantic getaway.

The Ritz-Carlton offers a variety of weekend packages such as The Special Occasion which includes welcome cocktails at The Bar or Greenhouse; accommodations in the quiet luxury of an elegant guest room, where you'll enjoy complimentary French champagne accompanied by chocolate-dipped strawberries; full American breakfast for two; and use of the Carlton Club and Spa. What you do with the rest of your time is up to you.

Rates: Rooms $355-425; Suites $475–$3,500

THE RITZ-CARLTON

160 East Pearson Street
Chicago, IL 60611

Phone	312-266-1000
Toll free	800-661-6906
Fax	312-266-1194

SIERRA HOTEL RAILWAY

Chicago

> The grey sea and the long black land;
> And the yellow half-moon large and low;
> And the startled little waves that leap
> In fiery ringlets from their sleep,
> As I gain the cove with pushing prow,
> And quench its speed i' the slushy sand.
>
> Then a mile of warm sea-scented beach;
> Three fields to cross till a farm appears;
> A tap at the pane, the quick sharp scratch
> And blue spurt of a lighted match,
> And a voice less loud, through its joys and fears,
> Than the two hearts beating each to each!
>
> —"Meeting At Night" by Robert Browning

If you wish to share the engineer's joys (but don't want any of his responsibilities), you can rent your own rail car. The Sierra Hotel features private deluxe rail cruising. With private bedrooms and three lounge areas, you can move around your luxurious train car as it travels through scenic locales. A special dome level has a glass-ceiling viewing area so you can take in the sights. This is where the meals prepared on board are served. Relax in the spacious main lounge or in the cocktail area located on the lower level, underneath the dome.

Rates: Vary with itineraries. Please call.

SIERRA HOTEL RAILWAY

77 West Wacker Drive, 17th Floor
Chicago, IL 60601

Toll free	800-449-7796
Fax	805-481-0985

Indiana

THE CANTERBURY HOTEL
Indianapolis

'Twas a new feeling—something more
Than we had dared to own before,
Which then we hid not;
We saw it in each other's eye,
And wished, in every half-breathed sigh,
To speak, but did not.

She felt my lips' impassioned touch -
'Twas the first time I dared so much,
And yet she chid not;
But whispered o'er my burning brow,
'Oh, do you doubt I love you now?'
Sweet soul! I did not.

Warmly I felt her bosom thrill,
I pressed it closer, closer still,
Though gently bid not;
Till—oh! the world hath seldom heard
Of lovers, who so nearly erred,
And yet, who did not.

—"Did Not" by Thomas Moore

Travel back to the romantic past at the Canterbury Hotel. This National Historic Landmark was built in 1928 and has retained much of its Jazz Age splendor without sacrificing modern comforts. The rooms are luxurious, decorated with Chippendale furniture and four-poster beds decked in Irish linen. The bathrooms are constructed of fine marble with elegant fittings. A mahogany-paneled sitting room off the lobby has a carved wooden fireplace and exquisite library and is the perfect place to relax and converse. The lobby itself is a work of art, furnished with antiques and offering a stately yet comfortable ambiance.

Arriving in Indianapolis, you can have the Canterbury's Mercedes limousine pick you up at the airport and take you to the hotel. The atmosphere is "veddy" British with afternoon tea served in the atrium. The focus at the Canterbury is on personal service.

The Restaurant at Canterbury features American and Continental fare. Candlelight dining, wood paneling, and a hunting theme decor add to the romantic atmosphere along with the superb cuisine. After dinner at the Restaurant at Canterbury, you can take a horse-drawn carriage through downtown Indianapolis, or enjoy a quiet cocktail in the hotel's lounge.

The location can't be beat. The Canterbury is close to the train station, convention center, Monument Circle, and Hoosier Dome. A Canterbury Honeymoon package includes champagne and strawberries on arrival and continental breakfast the next morning.

Rates: $125–$1,200

THE CANTERBURY HOTEL
123 South Illinois Street
Indianapolis, IN 46225

Phone	317-634-3000
Toll free	800-538-8186
Fax	317-685-2519

▬▬▬▬

Kentucky

THE SEELBACH HOTEL
Louisville

> I gently touched her hand: she gave
> A look that did my soul enslave;
> I pressed her rebel lips in vain:
> They rose up to be pressed again.
> Thus happy, I no farther meant,
> Than to be pleased and innocent.
>
> —Anonymous

The Seelbach Hotel had already been famous for twenty years before Fitzgerald immortalized it in his novel, *The Great Gatsby.* The hotel was built in 1905 by brothers Louis and Otto Seelbach, who wanted to bring a grand hotel to this Ohio River city. The brothers brought marble from Italy and Switzerland for the entrance and decorated the lobby with murals depicting Kentucky's pioneer days. The lobby is nothing less than spectacular, with a flowing grand stairway, rich with the original brass, marble, and mahogany the Seelbachs were justly proud of.

The hotel has 323 rooms decorated in 18th century style, complete with armoires, four-poster beds, marble baths, and various pieces of mahogany furniture, including traditional writing tables. Concierge-class accommodations offer a special level of personal service and luxury, including a private lounge with beverages and complimentary hors d'oeuvres.

The renowned Oakroom Restaurant offers refined service and an eclectic menu created by some of the finest chefs in the region. The exquisite American cuisine features both seasonal and classic entrees. A luxurious setting of burnished oak and detailed hand-carvings, the Oakroom is stately yet intimate. The tables are comfortably set apart for intimate dining and private conversation. For romantic entertainment, enjoy piano jazz in the Old Seelbach Bar, which *Esquire* rated as one of the best bars in the South.

The hotel is a few short blocks from Louisville's riverfront and the world's largest floating fountain, the Falls Fountain, where computerized jets propel water into a 375-foot-high fleur-de-lis pattern, the symbol of Louisville. Anchored nearby is the Belle of Louisville, the oldest operating riverboat in the United States. A number of presidents have stayed at the Seelbach: William Howard Taft, Woodrow Wilson, Franklin Roosevelt, Harry Truman, John Kennedy, and Lyndon Johnson.

If you'd like to visit the Seelbach during Kentucky Derby week, make your reservations way, way in advance. Sorry, but reservations are no longer taken for Daisy Buchanan's wedding....

Rates: Rooms $132–$180; Suites $210–$510

THE SEELBACH HOTEL
500 Fourth Avenue
Louisville, KY 40202

Phone	502-585-3200
Toll free	800-333-3399
Fax	502-585-9239

Louisiana

THE DELTA QUEEN
New Orleans

> At dawn she lay with her profile at that angle
> Which, when she sleeps, seems the carved face of an
>   angel.
> Her hair a harp, the hand of a breeze follows
> And plays, against the white cloud of the pillows.
> Then, in a flush of rose, she woke, and her eyes that
>   opened
> Swam in blue through her rose flesh that dawned.
> From her dew of lips, the drop of one word
> Fell like the first of fountains: murmured
> 'Darling', upon my ears the song of the first bird.
>
> —"Daybreak" by Stephen Spender

Looking for a romantic cruise with flair? Then try the Delta Steamboat Company. Since 1890, the Delta Steamboat Company has served as the keeper of the steamboat legacy, offering memorable cruises on America's only three steam-powered overnight paddlewheelers: *The Delta Queen, The Mississippi Queen,* and *The African Queen.*

The Delta Queen was built in 1926 and is a National Historic Landmark. Her Victorian features harken back to the era of Mark Twain. She showcases rare and exotic hardwoods, brass fittings, and a grand staircase. All the accommodations aboard *The Delta Queen* are outside staterooms, and many have private verandas that offer a view of the antebellum landscape of plantation homes. The limited number of staterooms also adds an intimate touch to your cruise and makes you feel like an honored guest.

Theme cruises such as Big Band, World War II, and Civil War are offered annually. The steamboats travel the entire length of the Mississippi, Ohio, Tennessee, Cumberland, Arkansas, and Atchafayala Rivers with thrity-two ports of embarkment.

Rates: Three nights, $163 per person (double
    occupancy) and up; 3-14 nights, $490–$1,840
    (includes four meals a day and entertainment)

THE DELTA QUEEN
Robin Street Wharf
1380 Port of New Orleans Place
New Orleans, LA 70130-1890

Toll free   800-543-1949
Fax   504-585-0690

MADEWOOD PLANTATION
Napoleonville

> Stay, O sweet, and do not rise,
> The light that shines comes from thine eyes;
> The day breaks not, it is my heart,
> Because that you and I must part.
> Stay, or else my joys will die,
> And perish in their infancy.
>
> —"Aubade" by Anonymous

This magnificent Greek Revival mansion, designed by noted Irish architect Henry Howard, is located halfway between New Orleans and Baton Rouge amid a lush country setting overlooking Bayou Lafourche.

The live oaks and magnolias that surround this mansion and the six massive ionic columns that support the portico all add to the stunning visual appearance of Madewood Plantation. This National Historic Landmark was built in 1846 for Colonel Thomas Pugh. The mansion eventually fell into disrepair before being renovated after the Marshall family purchased the property in 1964.

The interior is every bit as stunning as the exterior. The main hallway is lined with tall fluted Corinthian columns. Hardwood floors, Oriental rugs, crystal chandeliers, fresh flowers, and 18th- and 19th-century antiques lend an elegant air to this stately mansion.

There are five bedrooms in the mansion. All are tastefully decorated with watercolor hues on the drapes and walls. The bedrooms are furnished with canopied beds and feather pillows, and each has a private bath (however the back two rooms upstairs must access their baths through the hallway).

Three additional suites are available in the Charlet House which was once home to a riverboat captain before it was moved eight miles to the Madewood Plantation. Couples looking for an extra-special touch may want to try the honeymoon suite complete with fireplace and a large screened porch.

Guests will no doubt enjoy the candlelit dinner, usually presided over by a member of the Marshall family. This meal will serve to round out this thoroughly Southern and delightful visit.

Madewood Plantation has been featured in numerous publications and was named in 1994 as one of "The Year's Top Twelve Inns" by *Country Inn* magazine.

Guests take note that the rooms in the main mansion must be vacated between 10 a.m. and 5 p.m. for tours and noon to 3 p.m. in the Charlet House.

Rates: Rooms $175

MADEWOOD PLANTATION
4250 Route 308
Napoleonville, LA 70390

Phone	504-369-7151
Toll free	800-375-7151
Fax	504-369-9848

WINDSOR COURT HOTEL
New Orleans

Good God, what a night that was,
The bed was so soft, and how we clung,
Burning together, lying this way and that,
Our uncontrollable passions
Flowing through our mouths.

> If I could only die that way,
> I'd say goodbye to the business of living.
>
> —untitled by Petronius Arbiter

Southern hospitality melds with European style at New Orleans' premier hotel. That the well-heeled are drawn to this fine, elegant, and luxurious establishment should come as no surprise. Exquisite describes everything from the fine art that adorns the walls to the service.

Most of the rooms at the Windsor Court Hotel are very large suites. There are only fifty-eight rooms in the hotel compared with 264 suites. As you might expect, the rooms are outfitted with canopy and four-poster beds, stocked wet bars, marble vanities, dressing areas, and oversized mirrors.

Afternoon tea is served in the lobby at Le Salon's. Try out the Polo Club Lounge for light meals and cocktails. Don't miss out on the fine dining experience at the Windsor Court's Grill Room, which won recognition in *Dining by Candlelight.* Many residents consider the Grill Room to be the city's best restaurant.

Guests will find plenty of recreational amenities for a hotel located just a short walk from the French Quarter. Among the amenities is a health club, an outdoor pool, steam room, hot tub, and masseuse. Tennis and racquetball are available nearby.

Rates: Rooms from $325–$460 (depending upon time of year); Suites $410–$650

WINDSOR COURT HOTEL
300 Gravier Street
New Orleans, LA 70130

Phone	504-523-6000
Toll free	800-262-2662
Fax	504-596-4513

Maine

CAPTAIN LORD MANSION
Kennebunkport

> Critics: in your sight
> no woman can win:
> keep you out, and she's too tight;
> she's too loose if you get in.
>
> —From "A Satirical Romance" by Sor Juana
>   Ines de la Cruz

Built during the War of 1812, this stately, three-story, yellow Federal-style home is the former residence of a sea captain. The mansion is located in Kennebunkport's Historic District and is on the National Register of Historic Places.

The lavish interior is exquisitely appointed with priceless antiques in the public salons. Each of the mansion's sixteen guest rooms is named after a ship that Captain Lord built and is meticulously decorated with period antiques and oil paintings. Most of these rooms have fireplaces, and each chamber has its own unique character. For instance, you can curl up on the clawfoot sofa in front of the fireplace in the Lincoln Room or you can relax on the English four-poster queen-sized bed. More deluxe accommodations are available in the Merchant Captain's Suite which has a huge bathroom that incorporates a double whirlpool tub and an over-sized shower for two. For elegance, try the Brig Merchant Room on the ground floor. This room is decorated with a fishnet canopy bed and dark mahogany period furniture.

Enjoy a full family-style breakfast in the kitchen before venturing out into Kennebunkport to explore the town's architecture or the shops of Dock Square.

Rates: $149–$250

CAPTAIN LORD MANSION
Pleasant & Green Streets
Box 800
Kennebunkport, ME 04046

Phone   207-967-3141
Toll free   800-522-3141
Fax   207-967-3172

FISHERMAN ISLAND
Fisherman Island

> In every dream thy lovely features rise;
> I see them in the sunshine of the day;
> Thy form is flitting still before my eyes
> Where'er at eve I tread my lonely way;
> In every moaning wind I hear thee say
> Sweet words of consolation, while thy sighs
> Seem borne along on every blast that flies;
> I live, I talk with thee where'er I stray:
>
> And yet thou never more shalt come to me
> On earth, for thou art in a world of bliss,
> And fairer still—if fairer thou canst be -
>
> Than when thou bloomed'st for a while in this.
> Few be my days of loneliness and pain
> Until I meet in love with thee again.

—"Sonnet" by William Barnes

If you're looking for a romantic getaway with a maximum of privacy, then look no further than Fisherman Island. When you stay at Fisherman Island, you have an *entire* island to yourself because you rent all of its sixty-eight acres. This very private, fully staffed retreat is just fifteen minutes by lobster boat from Boothbay Harbor, Maine, and provides you with your own little playground.

Lodging on the island is provided in an impressive 6,000-square-foot Tudor-style stone house that sleeps a maximum of fifteen people. The house was built in 1928 as a retreat for a Unitarian minister. The property was eventually sold and the house completely renovated in 1994.

All the bedrooms in the house have compelling ocean views, and a sauna and steambath complement the five stylish bathrooms which adjoin the double bedrooms. Romantic spots can be found in front of the fireplace in the Great Room or on the west-facing porch where you can watch the sunset.

The property features a rock-rimmed saltwater pool and plenty of sandy beach. Birdwatching, hiking, swimming, snorkeling, water-skiing, picnicking, and berry picking are just some of the many activities to while away your time.

Seal watching, whale watching, diving, lobster excursions, and shopping at Boothbay Harbour, Freeport, Wiscasset, and Damariscotta are all but a short boatride away.

Jim and Judy Kinson manage Fisherman Island. Their bountiful meals include home-baked breads, island-grown vegetables, and Maine seafood.

Rates: May 1–June 14 and September 3–
       November 30,$8,000 per week;
       June 15-September 2, $12,000 per week

FISHERMAN ISLAND (RESERVATIONS)
P.O. Box 195
Boothbay Harbor, ME 04538

Phone   207-441-0837 or 207-757-8368
Fax   207-557-4832

Maryland

THE INN AT PERRY CABIN
St. Michaels

> Twilight—and you
> Quiet—the stars;
> Snare of the shine of your teeth,
> Your provocative laughter,
> The gloom of your hair;
> Lure of you, eye and lip,
> Yearning, yearning,
> Languor, surrender;
> Your mouth
> And madness, madness
> Tremulous, breathless, flaming,
> The space of a sigh;
> Then awaking—remembrance,
> Pain, regret—your sobbing;
> And again quiet—the stars,
> Twilight—and you.
>
> —"El Beso" by Angelina Grimke

If you like the Laura Ashley look, you'll love the Inn at Perry Cabin. Owned by Sir Bernard Ashley, chairman of Laura Ashley, the inn is decorated with the latest of this exquisite designer line. But it's more than just a fabric pattern, the inn has the elegant and historic charm of an English country house, maintained by an accommodating old friend.

Situated on the peaceful, civilized, and serenely beautiful eastern shore of Maryland, this 1820 Greek Revival mansion was originally built by a navy veteran of the War of 1812. This first owner named the house after his commanding officer, Commodore Oliver Perry, famous for saying, "We have met the British, and they are ours." There is a morning room, a well-stocked library, a conservatory, and a snooker room, all furnished with heirloom pieces and antiques from Sir Bernard's personal collection, making it look like an English manor house. The library has a secret passageway, a hinged bookshelf that leads into the Morning Room.

The Inn at Perry Cabin has forty-one guest rooms, all exquisitely decorated with lush fabrics and canopy beds. The rooms are luxurious and comfortable. Fresh flowers decorate your room, a fireplace is there to keep you cozy. These and other exquisite appointments vie with the views of Chesapeake Bay.

The inn is set on twenty-five acres overlooking the Miles River, which feeds into the Bay. Terraces look out onto the meticulously maintained gardens and grounds. The cathedral ceilinged nonsmoking-only restaurant is overseen by Chef Mark Salter. Venetian chandeliers and banks of mullioned windows give this room a romantic aura. And let's not forget the fireplace and candlelight. The restaurant offers an exciting menu featuring local seafood specialties, and provides one of the finest dining experiences in the region. And in keeping with English country-house fashion, afternoon tea is served with scones and clotted cream.

The lawn rolls down to the water, dock, and estuary where the inn keeps its boats. You can go fishing or sailing, and cruises are also available to tour the Chesapeake Bay. There is golf nearby too. And you can always buzz into St. Michaels to shop for arts, crafts, and antiques. How about a romantic carriage ride through the village? Or a candlelight dinner on the dock? If you want to get the big picture, charter a helicopter ride over the bay. And there's a sunset cruise where you can enjoy cocktails as the sun goes down on another perfect day.

Rates: Rooms $195–$375; Suites $525–$695

THE INN AT PERRY CABIN
308 Watkins Lane
St. Michaels, MD 21663

Phone	410-745-2200
Toll free	800-722-2949
Fax	410-745-3348

Massachusetts

BLANTYRE
Lenox

> To-day there have been lovely things
> I never saw before;
> Sunlight through a jar of marmalade;
> A blue gate;
> A rainbow
> In soapsuds on dishwater;
> Candlelight on butter;
> The crinkled smile of a little girl
> Who had new shoes with tassels;
> A chickadee on a thorn-apple;
> Empurpled mud under a willow,
> Where white geese slept;
> White ruffled curtains sifting moonlight
> On the scrubbed kitchen floor;
> The under side of a white-oak leaf,
> Ruts in the road at sunset;
> An egg yolk in a blue bowl.
>
> —"Vision" by May Thielgaard Watts

Lenox has long been popular with the cosmopolitan set. During the Gilded Age it, along with Newport, was the place to be seen.

Though the Gilded Age has long since passed, Yankee cosmopolites still come here every summer to escape the city heat and enjoy the cooler climate of the leafy mountains. Over the years, the Berkshires have become a summer resort area with an enviable array of cultural (as well as natural) offerings. And the Blantyre, a Tudor mansion situated on eighty-five acres of meticulously maintained grounds, epitomizes the region's blend of tradition, elegance, and natural beauty.

Blantyre is a 1902 replica of a Scottish castle. The main

house contains eight guest quarters, while the recently renovated Carriage House and several cottages round out the compound to give Blantyre twenty-three rooms in total. In the main house, the Great Hall has wood paneling, fresh flowers, and antique furnishings.

In keeping with the region's harmonious blend of rural sophistication, Blantyre offers a wide range of activities, but doesn't make you feel as if you must be doing something. On the grounds, there are a swimming pool, four tennis courts, and two croquet lawns. Croquet was a favorite game among the 19th-century socialites who first put the Berkshires on the map.

The atmosphere is aristocratic yet comfortable. Rather than having to claim its prestige with fancy trappings, Blantyre expresses itself with understated elegance. Return guests and travel writers who appreciate this classy ambiance have made Blantyre one of the most renowned estate inns in the country. Fine French food is on the menu in the formal dining room, where the service is excellent. Breakfast is offered in the sun-filled conservatory. And you can also relax in the music salon.

Of course there is life beyond the compound. You can visit Edith Wharton's "cottage," where there are often live readings and other performances. Go to Tanglewood for a concert out on the lawn or in the newly built performance barn. There's nothing like camping out under the stars on a blanket, sharing the moment with the person you'd most like to be with, and listening to the gorgeous music waft from the concert stage and into the green mountains beyond. The Boston Symphony plays here in the summer, and the stage is host to a wide variety of classical and popular performers. And don't forget the Boston Pops, who are also regulars. And there's summer theater, ballet, and a host of other attractions. The Norman Rockwell Museum is nearby.

Rates: Rooms and Cottages $265–$485; Suites
$300–$675; Closed from November to April

BLANTYRE
16 Blantyre Road
Lenox, MA 01240

Phone   413-637-3556
Fax   413-637-4282

BOSTON HARBOR HOTEL
Boston

> Those who love the most,
> Do not talk of their love,
> Francesca, Guinevere,
> Deirdre, Iseult, Heloise,
> In the fragrant gardens of heaven
> Are silent, or speak if at all
> Of fragile inconsequent things.
>
> And a woman I used to know
> Who loved one man from her youth,
> Against the strength of the fates
> Fighting in somber pride
> Never spoke of this thing,
> But hearing his name by chance,
> A light would pass over her face.
>
> —"Those Who Love" by Sara Teasdale

If you're the type who likes to add a dash of history to a romantic getaway then you'll love the Boston Harbor Hotel. Located at Rowes Wharf, site of the Boston Tea Party, the sixteen-story complex includes the hotel, office space, retail shops, private residences, and a thirty-slip marina should you arrive by sea. At Rowes Wharf you'll find the Boston Tea Party Museum and *Beaver II,* a replica of the ship that served as center stage for the Tea Party. Also nearby are the State House, Faneuil Hall, the New England Aquarium, the Old North Church, and Paul Revere's house.

After a long day of sightseeing you'll be ready to return to the hotel. Before dressing for dinner take a moment to inspect the hotel's magnificent marble lobby adorned with arches, intricate woodwork, fresh flowers, and original artwork. The artwork is of special importance since it includes several maps and charts from colonial America, among them a map drawn by Captain John Smith in 1614 that actually guided the Pilgrims to Plymouth.

The hotel's 230 guest rooms occupy the top eight floors of the structure. All offer magnificent views of either the harbor and its maritime activities or of Boston's dazzling skyline. Inside your spacious rooms you'll find the ordinary hotel accompaniments: TV, phone, and clock. You'll also find a few amenities that set the Harbor Hotel apart such as, slippers, thick terry robes, umbrellas, and Chippendale desks. Not surprisingly, the Harbor Hotel offers excellent service as well. Highlights include nightly turndown, complimentary shoeshine, and twenty-four hour room service.

Downstairs you'll find the Rowe's Wharf Restaurant, the hotel's premier eatery. Run by renowned chef Daniel Bruce, this wood paneled gem has won numerous awards including *Boston Magazine*'s Best New England Cuisine award. Guests should stop for breakfast as well and try the Boston version of corned beef hash; beets, beef, and potatoes.

Rates: $215–$1,600

BOSTON HARBOR HOTEL
70 Rowes Wharf
Boston, MA 02110

Phone	617-439-7000
Toll free	800-752-7077
Fax	617-330-9450

THE WAUWINET
Nantucket

> Who has not seen their lover
> Walking at ease,
> Walking like any other
> A pavement under trees,
> Not singular, apart,
> But footed, featured, dressed,
> Approaching like the rest

In the same dapple of the summer caught;
Who has not suddenly thought
With swift surprise:
There walks in cool disguise,
There comes, my heart.

—"The Avenue" by Frances Cornford

During the hot, humid days of summer, the cities of
the Northeast become places of misery to be escaped
from at every chance. Those seeking a romantic escape
try their luck at winning one of the few rooms at the
Wauwinet on Nantucket. If you're lucky enough to get a
room, getting to the Wauwinet will take some effort. First
you'll have to take the ferry from Hyannis to Nantucket
Town. From there, you'll take a jitney to Nantucket's
most remote peninsula, the home of Wauwinet.

Once there, you'll experience the classic romance of
Nantucket. Inside the cedar-shingled hotel, twenty-nine
rooms are individually decorated in a style that reflects
the charm of old New England. For a more private
encounter, the Wauwinet offers five cottages.

Just a minute's walk through the dunes brings you to
the Atlantic and miles of beach. In contrast to the pound-
ing surf of the Atlantic, swimmers may enjoy the
calmness of the bayside beach more. Additionally, the
Wauwinet has eighteen-speed mountain bikes for you to
use in exploring the island in search of the perfect picnic
spot.

At night, you'll enjoy Wauwinet's restaurant,
Topper's. One of the best on the island, Topper's serves
fine New American cuisine with an emphasis on fresh
seafood dishes.

Rates: $290–$450

THE WAUWINET
Wauwinet Road
Box 2580
Nantucket, MA 02584

Phone   508-228-0145
Toll free   800-426-8718
Fax   508-228-6712

Michigan

GRAND HOTEL
Mackinac Island

> Did I boast of liberty?
> 'Twas an insolency vain
> I do only look on thee,
> And I captive am again.
>
> —From "Urania" by Lady Mary Wroth

A stately presence on secluded Mackinac Island, the Grand Hotel is a great place for a Midwestern getaway. The Indians called this island Michilimackinac, or the Great Turtle, because that's what it looks like from the mainland. And like turtles, visitors to Mackinac Island like to hide away and escape into privacy.

Originally built in 1887, the Grand retains its historic charm. Situated on a high bluff overlooking the straits of Mackinac, the hotel commands a breathtaking view. No cars are allowed on Mackinac Island. After you step off the ferry, a horse-drawn carriage will arrive to take you to the hotel. Once you're there, footmen in white gloves will greet you, and take you inside to the Victorian decorated lobby.

Or you might want to linger on the "world's largest porch," a comfortable Victorian affair replete with wicker furniture, a picturesque spot for relaxing conversation and people-watching. Or you could take a turn on the expansive and meticulously gardened grounds. Eventually, you'll want to see your room, one of the hotel's 330 individually decorated guest accommodations. Among the most unique lodgings is the Wicker Suite, furnished with a brass bed and white wicker furniture.

Dining at the Grand is an experience to savor. The food is exquisite, and the atmosphere is unbeatable. At the main dining room, local, fresh-caught seafood is a

81

specialty, and many dishes are garnished with Michigan cherries. Jackets and ties are required at dinner, which is a five-course affair. After dinner, relax over coffee in the Parlor or enjoy cocktails at the Geranium or Audubon wine bars. The Jockey Club at the Grand Stand offers lighter fare, and the pool grill provides snacks and beverages. Afternoon tea is served in the Parlor, accompanied by a string quartet.

Live music and ballroom dancing are specialties here at the Grand. Dinner is accompanied by an orchestra, and there is a small dance floor in the dining room. After dinner, the dancing continues in the Terrace Room, where the Grand Hotel Dance Band plays in the manner of the great bands of the 1930s and '40s.

When you're not cutting a rug, there are other activities to enjoy. The hotel has a huge swimming pool and acres of grounds to walk through. There's a private golf course for duffers. Tennis courts and nature trails offer a pleasant workout. You can rent bicycles or saddle horses to get around the island. Take a scenic tour of this beautiful and historic island in a vis-à-vis, an antique carriage drawn by horses in dress harness.

Rates: Rooms $320–$520; Suites $590

GRAND HOTEL
P. O. Box 286
Mackinac Island, MI 49757

Phone	906-847-3331
Toll free	800-334-7263
Fax	906-847-3259

Minnesota

THAYER INN
Annandale

> How can I write about you
> When you are all the world?
> When I know
> That all that is good or just in me is only
> An echo of you:
> When all that I think is what you have breathed on my
> heart: And all I say,
> Although I am praised for it,
> Is your book read aloud.
>
> —"My True Love Hath My Heart" by Naomi
> Mitchison

If you glanced at a map of Minnesota, Annandale might not seem to be the place to visit for a romantic repast. But then again, most maps don't mention the Thayer Inn. Built at the turn of the century, the inn was later gracefully restored, and it was added to the National Register of Historic Places in 1978. Its charming architecture is highlighted by its triple-tiered porch exterior.

Inside, Thayer features eleven rooms, a dining room, and the Depot Lounge. The rooms are all individually decorated with period antiques. Many feature beds hand-made by local artisans. Others offer such comforts as fireplaces and whirlpool baths which are sure to take the chill out of even the coldest Minnesota night. Downstairs you'll find the dining room and the Depot Lounge. The dining room serves fresh American cuisine with an emphasis on simple preparation and classical presentation. At the Depot Lounge, you'll find everything from fine cognacs and scotches to the latest microbrews, all of which you can enjoy over a game like checkers or cribbage.

To make your stay even more special, the Thayer Inn

offers a wide variety of romantic packages. They range from the classic Romantic Hideaway, to the decadent Fantastic Fantasy. Features of the packages include roses, champagne, robes, sauna, hot tub, breakfast delivered to your door, and most importantly, a late check-out.

Rates: $80–$135

THAYER INN
60 West Elm Street
Box 246
Annandale, MN 55302

Phone	320-274-8222
Toll free	800-944-6595
Fax	320-274-8222

Mississippi

THE CEDARS PLANTATION
Church Hill

> Now lies the Earth all Danae to the stars,
> And all thy heart lies open unto me.
>
> Now slides the silent meteor on, and leaves
> A shining furrow, as thy thoughts in me.
>
> Now folds the lily all her sweetness up,
> And slips into the bosom of the lake;
> So fold thyself, my dearest, thou, and slip
> Into my bosom and be lost in me.
>
> —"Now Sleeps The Crimson Petal" by Lord
> Alfred Tennyson

This three-story Greek Revival plantation home is located ninety miles southwest of Jackson. The large double-tiered galleries and Doric columns are visually stunning, as are the beautiful gardens and ponds which surround the home. As you step from your automobile, you immediately notice the aromatic azaleas and magnolias and the moss-draped trees.

Inside you will find four guest rooms with private baths. The rooms feature queen canopy beds, period furniture, and personal refrigerators. Those looking for something a little more grand should reserve the spacious suite. Couples will no doubt find the fireplace and jacuzzi a romantic touch.

Public areas include the library and the enclosed porch. The library offers music, books, magazines, television, and a fireplace. The enclosed porch is great for relaxed conversation, a book, or cards.

Couples should also take a pleasant walk around the grounds and enjoy a view of the lake. Along your walk, you could stop and spend some time relaxing in the gazebo, or perhaps visit the pond to feed the ducks.

Don't miss the full breakfast which is served on antique china, silver, and crystal.

Historic Natchez is a short drive away where you will find antique shops, antebellum home tours, and riverboat gambling.

Rates: Rooms $135-155

THE CEDARS PLANTATION
Route 553
Church Hill, MS 39120

Phone   601-445-2203
Fax   601-445-2372

Missouri

BIG CEDAR LODGE
Ridgedale

> She dwelt among the untrodden ways
> Beside the springs of Dove,
> A Maid whom there were none to praise
> And very few to love:
>
> A violet by a mossy stone
> Half hidden from the eye!
> - Fair as a star, when only one
> Is shining in the sky.
>
> She lived unknown, and few could know
> When Lucy ceased to be;
> But she is in her grave, and, oh,
> The difference to me!
>
> —"She Dwelt Among The Untrodden Ways" by
> William Wordsworth

In the ancient Ozarks lies Branson, Missouri, the newest Mecca of country music. Developed in an ad-hoc fashion, Branson offers world-class entertainment but little in the way of world-class romantic accommodations. Fortunately, just several miles south on the shores of Table Rock Lake lies Big Cedar Lodge.

Constructed of limestone and cedar, Big Cedar Lodge cuts an imposing figure. Designed to feel like an upscale hunting lodge, Big Cedar succeeds. The decor of the main lodge features mounted grizzlies, antler chandeliers, a delightful timbered restaurant, and a beautiful mahogany bar. The rooms continue this theme and include many luxuries. Be sure to request a room with a fireplace and jacuzzi bath; the suites in Valley View Lodge are especially posh. For more privacy, Big Cedar has eighty cabins spread along the lake and surrounding hillsides.

While nearby Branson offers a multitude of attractions, Big Cedar Lodge's activities are impressive in their own right. Table Rock Lake boasts some of the best bass fishing in the world and Big Cedar offers guided fishing trips. If fishing doesn't appeal to you, there's horseback riding, tennis, the par-3 Jack Nicklaus designed golf course, or the spa and fitness center.

Rates: $230–$379

BIG CEDAR LODGE
612 Devil's Pool Road
Ridgedale, MO 65739

Phone	417-335-2777
Fax	417-335-2340

Montana

BAD ROCK COUNTRY BED & BREAKFAST
Columbia Falls

> Believe me, if all those endearing young charms,
> Which I gaze on so fondly to-day,
> Were to change by to-morrow, and fleet in my arms,
> Like fairy-gifts fading away,
> Thou wouldst still be adored, as this moment thou art,
> Let thy loveliness fade as it will,
> And around the dear ruin each wish of my heart
> Would entwine itself verdantly still.
>
> —"Believe Me, If All Those Endearing Young
> Charms" by Thomas Moore

Located in the Flat Head Valley and set on thirty acres of rolling Montana paradise, the Bad Rock Country Bed and Breakfast is the perfect romantic stop for guests exploring northwest Montana. Innkeepers Jon and Sue Alper have created an elegant inn in the style of early Montana country living that earned the inn a "Top Twelve Inns" award in 1995 from *Country Inns* magazine. Spectacular views of the Swan Mountain range of the Rockies can be seen from a number of perspectives.

Bad Rock Country Bed and Breakfast offers lodging in either the main house or in the two newly constructed log buildings. The master bedroom in the main house features a queen bed, a full bath with a tub/shower, and a balcony which looks out to the west for a magnificent view of the sunsets. There are two other bedrooms on the upper level of the main house with a bath located across the hall. The bedroom on the lower level offers a queen bed, bath with steam shower, and garden and sunset views.

You'll also find a stocked refrigerator with soft drinks

and fruit juices in the television room of the main house. The great room has a bay window which looks out onto the Swan Mountains, and the dining room is decorated with 1890s furniture.

Each log building contains two stunning guest rooms with private entrances, private baths, and gas log fireplaces. The interiors of these guest rooms feature beautiful handmade lodgepole pine furniture.

Outdoor activities are limitless in this part of Montana. Guests are only twenty minutes from fishing, rafting, and hiking, from the towns of Whitefish and Kalispell, and from Glacier National Park. Before you leave for the day, consider making a reservation for time in the relaxing hot tub upon your return.

Rates: Rooms $110–$129;
       Log building rooms $136–$155

BAD ROCK COUNTRY BED & BREAKFAST
480 Bad Rock Drive
Columbia Falls, MT 59912

Phone	406-892-2829
Toll free	800-422-3666
Fax	406-892-2930

TRIPLE CREEK
Darby

> The night has a thousand eyes,
> And the day but one;
> Yet the light of the bright world dies
> With the dying sun.
>
> The mind has a thousand eyes,
> And the heart but one;
> Yet the light of a whole life dies
> When love is done.
>
>   —"The Night Has A Thousand Eyes" by Francis
>   William Bourdillon

This romantic mountain hideaway in the Big Sky State combines rugged beauty and plush elegance. Adjacent to millions of acres of scenic Rocky Mountain wilderness near the Idaho border, you can't get much more secluded than Triple Creek. But seclusion doesn't mean you have to skimp on creature comforts. There's one staff member for every guest, so you are assured personalized and efficient service. And this resort has all the amenities you could wish for. Plus it's couples only, so you're ensured the quiet and privacy you seek during a romantic escape.

Triple Creek is located at the foot of Trapper Peak just outside Darby, a small town a little more than an hour south of Missoula. The ranch features eighteen cabins, and three of these accommodate two couples. These cabins all have spectacular views of the creek and nearby mountains. Each cabin has a fireplace, fully stocked refrigerator, and wet bar. The large cabin suites feature separate living rooms, huge baths, and private hot tubs (a perfect place to tickle the rib of love) on the scenic decks.

The main lodge has a cozy bar with a wood-burning fireplace and an excellent dining room, which serves complimentary wine with its gourmet cuisine. The dining room's executive chef, Martha McGinnis, has been featured in *Southern Living, The Hideaway Reports,* and *Bon Appetit.* After dinner, you can groove to live music in the bar or sip a post-meal drink in the hot tub.

Sporting activities are wide and varied. You can swim in the outdoor pool or play tennis. Flyfish in the stream that runs through the resort, or watch the herd of buffalo that's kept by the Triple Creek Ranch. Nearby is the Bitterroot River, made famous by the book and movie, *A River Runs Through It.* Further along is the equally famous Salmon River, great for rafting trips down the dramatic rapids. Horseback riding is also conveniently available. Or you can explore the many hiking trails. In the winter, enjoy cross-country skiing, snowmobiling, and sleigh rides. Downhill ski areas are only a half hour away.

Like most of the region, Triple Creek is laid-back and

unpretentious, a perfect romantic getaway for those who want to enjoy the wild country in comfort and pleasure.

Rates: Cabins $475–$995

TRIPLE CREEK

5551 West Fork Road
Darby, MT 59829

Phone	406-821-4600
Toll free	800-654-2943
Fax	406-821-4666

Nevada

HARD ROCK HOTEL AND CASINO
Las Vegas

> She was a phantom of delight
> When first she gleamed upon my sight;
> A lovely apparition, sent
> To be a moment's ornament;
> Her eyes as stars of twilight fair;
> Like twilight's, too, her dusky hair;
> But all things else about her drawn
> From May-time and the cheerful dawn;
> A dancing shape, an image gay,
> To haunt, to startle, and waylay.
>
> > —"She Was A Phantom Of Delight" by William
> > Wordsworth

If you're going to Vegas and don't like rock 'n' roll, then don't stay at the Hard Rock. If you do like that type of music, then escape from the excess of the strip to the intimacy of the Hard Rock Hotel and Casino.

This plush eleven-story resort has only 340 rooms, few by Vegas standards. Yet despite its relatively small size, the resort cost nearly $100 million to build. As a result, you are rewarded with large comfortable rooms done in soothing desert tones. You'll even discover that your windows open (a rarity in Vegas where casinos pump extra oxygen into the rooms to help keep their guests awake and at the gaming tables) to let in the fresh desert air. Be sure to get a room overlooking the gorgeous pool area complete with a wave pool, white sand beach, and volleyball.

Music and the casino are the main attractions at the Hard Rock. Besides the music-influenced decor, like saxophone-shaped chandeliers, the Hard Rock houses The Joint. The Joint is a 1,200-seat theater featuring the top acts in rock. Recent performers have included Santana, George Thorogood, the Indigo Girls, and the Rolling Stones. Where else will you get to see Mick and Keith perform up close? Rock music is also played in the background in the 30,000-square-foot casino. Even the chips have rock motifs based on such bands as the Red Hot Chili Peppers and Jimi Hendrix.

Mortoni's offers fine Italian cuisine. You'll enjoy their regally appointed dining room, but in warm weather, they also serve dinner in perhaps Vegas's most romantic setting—near the pool's beach area.

Rates: $75–$250

HARD ROCK HOTEL & CASINO
4455 Paradise Road
Las Vegas, NV 89109

Phone	702-693-5000
Toll free	800-473-7625

New Hampshire

THE MANOR ON GOLDEN POND
Holderness

> My heart is like a singing bird
> Whose nest is in a watered shoot;
> My heart is like an apple-tree
> Whose boughs are bent with thick-set fruit;
> My heart is like a rainbow shell
> That paddles in a halcyon sea;
> My heart is gladder than all these,
> Because my love is come to me.
>
> —"A Birthday" by Christina Rossetti

You won't find Golden Pond on any map, but the site where Katherine Hepburn and Henry Fonda filmed the movie, *On Golden Pond,* was actually Squam Lake. The number of private homes makes it next to impossible to enjoy Squam Lake unless you stay at the Manor on Golden Pond. Located on fifty acres of wooded land with meandering stone walls, split rail fences, and foliage, the Manor on Golden Pond is just forty-five minutes north of Concord.

This rambling stucco and timber house built in 1907 features eight individually decorated guest rooms with private baths. Couples looking for a maximum of amenities should ask for the Buckingham Room which features a king-sized canopy bed and marble fireplace. All the bedrooms in the main house are decorated in Early American style with braided curtains and rugs. Other rooming options include a six-room carriage house and four two-bedroom cottages on the grounds. Although the rooms in the carriage house are less ornate, they are furnished with English antiques.

Guests will find many different ways to relax at the inn. A sixty-foot screened porch provides a relaxing setting. A sitting room with large picture window provides a view of the grounds. Other amenities include a television room, a swimming pool, and tennis courts.

Squam Lake provides guests with immediate access for sunning, swimming, fishing, or boating. Hiking and walking trails provide you with an opportunity to explore the area. You may also opt for a walk down to the town beach or the Science Center of New Hampshire. Downhill and cross-country skiing are also nearby options in the winter months.

> Rates: Main inn $190–$325; Carriage house
> $85–$110; Cottages $950–$1,725 per week

THE MANOR ON GOLDEN POND
Route 3 & Shepard Hill Road
Holderness, NH 03245

Phone	603-968-3348
Toll free	800-545-2141
Fax	603-968-2116

▬▬▬▬

NESTLENOOK FARM ON THE RIVER
Jackson

> Wild nights! Wild nights!
> Were I with thee,
> Wild nights should be
> Our luxury!
>
> Futile the winds
> To a heart in port -
> Done with the compass,
> Done with the chart.
>
> Rowing in Eden!
> Ah! the sea!
> Might I but moor
> Tonight in thee!
>
> —"Wild Nights" by Emily Dickinson

This elegant Victorian estate is situated on sixty-five acres of land on the banks of the scenic Ellis River. The inn features seven exquisitely decorated guest rooms and each contains a two-person jacuzzi that's perfect after a day of skiing, hiking, or tennis. Guests can snuggle up to the fireplace in the parlor, laze by the outdoor pool, or enjoy the game room, depending upon the weather and their mood.

But regardless of the season, Nestlenook Farm has something to offer for everyone. You can take an Austrian sleigh ride, and go snowshoeing, snowmobiling, or ice-skating during the winter months. Hiking, flyfishing, row boating, tennis, bicycling, swimming, golfing, and shopping are all enjoyed during the summer months.

Rates: Rooms from $125 for two
(including full breakfast)

NESTLENOOK FARM ON THE RIVER
Dinsmore Road, P. O. Box Q
Jackson, NH 03846

Phone   603-383-9443
Fax   603-383-4515

New Mexico

GALISTEO INN
Galisteo

> The hour of the waning of love has beset us,
> And weary and worn are our sad souls now;
> Let us part, ere the season of passion forget us,
> With a kiss and a tear on thy drooping brow.
>
> —"The Falling Of The Leaves" by William Butler
>   Yeats

This 240-year-old Adobe hacienda is surrounded by giant cottonwoods and was once the estate of the region's original settlers. The inn's setting of eight acres features a duck pond and a creek and plenty of fresh, clean air in the historic village of Galisteo.

The inn has twelve guest rooms that are individually decorated in a Southwestern motif. Some of the rooms have sitting areas, fireplaces, and eight of them have private baths. The rooms also offer varying views of the pasture, lawn, back courtyard, and pool.

Guests looking for extra-special accommodations should request Cottonwood Cottage which features skylights, a fireplace, and high ceilings that are perfect for a romantic retreat.

Other amenities at the Galisteo Inn include a library, a dining room that's perfect for intimate meals, and a cozy living room. The meals offered at the inn are mouthwatering and should not be missed.

Rates: Rooms $95–$170

GALISTEO INN
9 La Vega, off Highway 41
Galisteo, NM 87540

Phone   505-466-4000
Fax   505-466-4008

INN OF THE ANASAZI
Santa Fe

> The young heroes, the generous young men,
> Wasting themselves like pennies at a wedding,
> Will, when the sleep of exhaustion eludes them,
> Think of her face.

> —"Young Girl" by Menzies McKillop

They call New Mexico the Land of Enchantment, and it's easy to see why. There's something almost mystical about the desert mountains, the spectacular sunsets, the Native American heritage, and the Southwestern culture. Here is a place where time seems to stand still, and every day the ancient earth is renewed once again.

Of course, Santa Fe is the most exciting and romantic city in New Mexico. And the Inn of the Anasazi is the place to stay here. Located right in the heart of Santa Fe, near the galleries and shops of the historic main plaza, the inn is a luxurious, yet intimate resort, converted into a Pueblo-style hotel from its original incarnation as a municipal building.

The inn is named after the Anasazi Indians, who were the earliest inhabitants of this region, so entrenched that the Navajos called them "the ancient ones." They built dwellings in cliffsides, such as Mesa Verde and Chaco Canyon, and established highly developed farming communities. Their legacy is continued at the inn, which recaptures the patterned masonry techniques and colorful murals favored by the Anasazi. The common rooms have smooth-plastered walls and ceilings with rough-hewn wood vigas and latillas, and traditional support beams. The wrought-iron lighting fixtures and snake-patterned sconces provide a romantic glow downstairs. The upstairs is lit with rope-patterned floor lamps and more traditional ironwork fixtures. Kava fireplaces warm the library and boardroom. The wine cellar has painted, hand-carved wooden doors.

The inn features fifty-one guest rooms and eight deluxe rooms. All the rooms are furnished with four-poster beds, entertainment centers, and gas-burning fireplaces. The deluxe rooms have fax machine capability and stereos, for those who don't want to completely cut themselves off from civilization. Hand-crafted rugs and Anasazi-styled bedding give the rooms a distinctive Southwestern feeling. The bathrooms are decorated in handmade Mexican tile.

The famous Anasazi Restaurant combines Native American, New Mexican, and cowboy cuisine into a fascinating and tantalizing dining experience. After dinner, relax by the fireside in the living room or browse the legends of the Southwest in the cultural library.

Convenient to every attraction in Santa Fe, the inn is a perfect jumping off point for tours of the Southwest. You can visit the ancient Indian ruins and sites of the Anasazi and the Pueblo. Fishing, hiking, rafting, and skiing tours can be arranged by the inn's staff.

The Inn of the Anasazi is consistently ranked the best lodging in Santa Fe by a wide range of travel experts.

Rates: Rooms $199–$279; Deluxe rooms $345–$399
(based upon season)

INN OF THE ANASAZI
113 Washington Avenue
Santa Fe, NM 87501

Phone	505-988-3030
Toll free	800-688-8100
Fax	505-988-3277

New York

THE CASTLE AT TARRYTOWN
Tarrytown

> In a field by a river my love and I did stand,
> And on my leaning shoulder she laid her snow-white
> hand.
> She bid me take life easy, as the grass grows on the
> weirs;
> But I was young and foolish, and now am full of tears.
>
> —"Down By The Salley Gardens" by W.B. Yeats

Built in 1900 by wealthy New York journalist General Howard Carroll, the Castle at Tarrytown is based on Scottish and Welsh castles Carroll had seen while traveling abroad. Here guests have a chance to experience the fantasy of staying in a luxurious castle.

Although the exterior looks like a Gothic castle, the interior is elegant and decorated in dark woods that are accented with tapestries, plants, prints, and exquisite antiques. The main house has seven guest rooms and the new wing offers an additional twenty-four rich and comfortable rooms. Try the Linsmore Suite for something extra special. This room is in a turreted tower that is the highest point in Westchester County. The suite features a fireplace and a cut velvet sofa that faces the hearth and a panoramic view of the lush forest that runs down to the Hudson River.

For adventure, take a stroll around the property's ten acres which include an English garden and a rock-carved swimming pool.

Guests have several dining options at the Castle including the Equus Restaurant which has become a popular stop for the locals. The Oak Room offers a more baronial setting while the Tapestry Room's intimate ambiance should appeal to couples. The Garden Room offers expansive views of the river and New York City, and The Terrace is a popular choice for dinner and cocktails in the warmer months.

Rates: Rooms from $495

THE CASTLE AT TARRYTOWN
400 Benedict Avenue
Tarrytown, NY 10591

Phone   914-631-1980
Fax   914-631-4612

▬▬▬▬▬▬

THE INN AT IRVING PLACE
New York City

> When she rises in the morning
> I linger to watch her;
> She spreads the bath-cloth underneath the window
> And the sunbeams catch her
> Glistening white on the shoulders,
> While down her sides the mellow
> Golden shadow glows as
> She stoops to the sponge, and her swung breasts
> Sway like full-blown yellow
> Gloire de Dijon roses.
>
> —"Gloire de Dijon" by D.H. Lawrence

"Intimate," "private," and "low-key" are adjectives typically reserved for countryside retreats, not hotels in New York City. Yet they all apply to the Inn at Irving Place, a twelve-room retreat in the genteel neighborhood of Gramercy Park.

The Inn at Irving Place is luxurious in every respect. The two conjoined federalist townhouses that form the inn took three years to renovate. The results include gorgeous wood floors, handsome mantlepieces, and beautiful window sills. This backdrop is complemented by exquisite furniture.

Each room at the inn is unique. Some have separate studies, while others boast bathrooms bigger than some New York City apartments. While a guest at this comfortable inn, you'll be attended by an unobtrusive yet attentive staff who will make your stay a memorable one.

Rates: $275–$375

THE INN AT IRVING PLACE
56 Irving Place
New York, NY 10003

Phone	212-533-4600
Toll free	800-685-1447
Fax	212-533-4611

MOHONK MOUNTAIN HOUSE
New Paltz

> With the earth and the sky and the water, remade, like
> a casket of gold
> For my dreams of your image that blossoms a rose in
> the deeps of my heart.
>
> —"The Lover Tells Of The Rose In His Heart" by
> W.B. Yeats

A stay at the Mohonk Mountain House reflects the romance of a bygone era. Located in the Shawangunk Mountains of New York, Mohonk is a mere ninety miles from New York City, yet sits amid the 6,300 acres of the Mohonk Preserve.

Housed in a Victorian castle, Mohonk Mountain House rises from the shores of Lake Mohonk like a modern day Camelot. An all-inclusive retreat, Mohonk's 261 guest rooms offer serene sanctuary. For the most romantic experience, be sure to reserve a room with a fireplace, for there may not be a more beautiful setting on the East Coast for fireside snuggling. Fireplaces are also found among the many nooks of the main floor and are the perfect place to curl up with a good book.

Outdoor activities are an essential part of the Mohonk Mountain House experience. The hotel's 2,200-acre National Historic Landmark property and the surrounding reserve offer a multitude of activities that you and your love can enjoy together. During the summer, you can dip into the cool waters of Lake Mohonk, or simply enjoy—on foot or on horseback—the miles of trails that wind through the towering forest. During the winter, these trails become fabulous avenues for cross-country skiing. However, during the cold weather, the most romantic activity takes place on the lake. Here, men grab chair-skates and push their seated lover across the ice in a scene reminiscent of a Rockwell painting.

Rates: $110–$474

MOHONK MOUNTAIN HOUSE
Lake Mohonk
New Paltz, NY 12561

Phone	914-255-1000
Toll free	800-772-6646
Fax	914-256-2161

THE POINT
Saranac Lake

> And the flame of the blue star of twilight, hung low on
> the rim of the sky,
> Has awakened in our hearts, my beloved, a sadness that
> may not die.
>
> —"The White Birds" by W.B. Yeats

If you enjoy high-class service in rustic solitude, this is the place for you. Deep in the Adirondack Forest, this former Rockefeller family compound is located on the secluded peninsula of Upper Saranac Lake. It is one of the few lodges continuing the tradition of the great camps of the Adirondacks.

Much about the Point evidences its opulent history. The huge timbers used to construct the living room roof were brought in from Canada. Gigantic boulders form the large fireplaces in the Great Hall. The property includes two acres of lake frontage and seven acres of wooded land. The guest quarters are eleven rooms in several different buildings, lodges, cabins, and boathouses scattered around the property for privacy. Each room has a lake view, custom-made bed, bath with chrome and brass fixtures, and a fireplace. The accommodations are furnished in the Adirondack style with lots of exposed wood and a rustic simplicity.

"We try to make our guests feel that they have come to a house party in the woods," says owner Christie Garrett. This feeling is reinforced by service with attention to details. Your day at the Point begins with a soft knock on the door and morning coffee, served in a thermos so you can take your time enjoying it. Later, a slightly bolder knock announces the arrival of breakfast. You can have the meal in bed, at your breakfast table overlooking the lake, or before the fire on a chilly morning.

Outdoor activities abound. You can go canoeing, rowing, sailing, or water-skiing on the lake. Swimming is also popular, in the crystal clear fresh water. Take a hike on the Point's nature trails, or if you're looking for bigger mountains to climb, venture out into the vast Adirondacks. For those who have other sporting tastes, golf and tennis are available at the nearby country club. The Point is a great place to stay for a winter ski vacation, with many downhill mountains and excellent cross-country trails within easy reach.

Lunch is served on the terrace outdoors or packed into baskets for picnics at the lakeside or on one of the many islands dotting the lake. The dining room, supervised by Chef Albert Roux, of Gavroche in London, is only open to paying guests. Jacket and tie are required for dinner, where the guests sit together at a great table, just like a formal dinner party. Candlelight and fresh flowers decorate the table, and classical music plays in the background. Wednesday and Saturday dinner are black tie optional affairs. After dinner, enjoy an apéritif in the Great Hall or take one of the Point's regular sunset cocktail cruises on the lake.

Children under eighteen are not allowed, which lets the adults enjoy a little peace and privacy.

Rates: $850–$1,350 (all meals, open bar and recreation included)

THE POINT
HCR #1, Box 65
Saranac Lake, NY 12983

Phone	518-891-5674
Toll free	800-255-3530
Fax	518-891-1152

▬▬▬▬

THE REGENCY
New York City

> 'And when we die
> All's over that is ours; and life burns on
> Through other lovers, others lips,' said I,
> 'Heart of my heart, our heaven is now won!'
> —"The Hill" by Rupert Brooke

The Regency is the embodiment of its prestigious neighborhood of Park Avenue: powerful, glamorous, luxurious, and refined. And at this location, the Regency is convenient to the theater district, museums, world-class shopping, and Central Park. Indeed, the Regency is in the heart of it all. Perhaps that is why celebrities like Steve Guttenberg find it so enticing.

The Regency's 362 rooms and ninety-three suites pamper you. Understated luxury best describes the decor of these spacious rooms highlighted by the bathroom complete with terry robes, telephone, and TV. Downstairs you'll find the Regency's recently renovated 2,000-square-foot fitness center and the hotel's restaurant. It was in this restaurant that the power breakfast originated twenty-two years ago. At night, enjoy live music and drinks at the Regency Lounge. If none of this impresses you, the Regency's service will. Many consider it the best in New York.

Rates: $285–$900

THE REGENCY
540 Park Avenue
New York, NY 10021

Phone	212-759-4100
Toll free	800-233-2356
Fax	212-826-5674

North Carolina

THE FEARRINGTON HOUSE
Pittsboro

> O never give the heart outright,
> For they, for all smooth lips can say,
> Have given their hearts up to the play.
> And who could play it well enough
> If deaf and dumb and blind with love?
> He that made this knows all the cost,
> For he gave all his heart and lost.
>
> —"Never Give All the Heart" by W.B. Yeats

On the outskirts of Pittsboro lies Fearrington Village, a residential community transformed from a 200-year-old dairy farm. Its creators R.B. and Jenny Fitch studied restaurants and inns throughout Europe before they began their project, and the result is a community that seems more at place in the English countryside than Dixie. At the heart of this bucolic community lies the Fearrington House and its restaurant.

The inn's rooms and suites encircle a central courtyard highlighted by its charming garden and center fountain. The rooms are individually decorated with English pine, antiques, and floral print fabrics. They overlook the pasture where Belted Galloway cows and sheep now graze. Luxury bathrooms complete with towel warmers are another standard at Fearrington House.

The Fearrington family's farmhouse, built in 1927, serves as the restaurant. With much of its initial charm preserved, the restaurant is a collection of small intimate dining rooms and two glass-enclosed porches. Antiques and original art fill the candle-lit rooms and create the perfect atmosphere for a romantic meal.

At both the inn and the restaurant, you'll come to appreciate Fearrington House's service. Never obtrusive, but always attentive, the staff ensures that your stay here will be pleasant. It is because of them that Fearrington House is a member of Relais & Châteaux and a AAA Five Diamond property.

Rates: $165–$275

THE FEARRINGTON HOUSE
2000 Fearrington Village Center
Pittsboro, NC 27312

Phone   919-542-4000
Fax   919-542-4202

THE SWAG COUNTRY INN
Waynesville

> And as we stray further from love
> We multiply the words,
> Words and sentences long and orderly.
> Had we remained together
> We could have become a silence.
>
> —"Quick and Bitter" by Yehuda Amichai

Perched high upon a private, 5,000-foot mountain in the Smokies, the Swag arguably has the best views of any entry in this book. From this charming rustic retreat, you and your lover can gaze fifty miles into the distance and marvel at the unspoiled beauty of the Smoky Mountains.

Rustic romance best describes the Swag. The main building is dominated by its massive stone fireplace. Rustic timber planking, hand-hewn log walls, exposed beams, and Appalachian art all add to the ambiance of the cathedral lounge. This theme continues to the guest rooms. All rooms feature hand-made quilts, coffee grinders and makers, and your own refrigerator (an attractive amenity in this dry, BYOB county). For the ultimate in romance, pay a little extra and get one of the rooms with a balcony, fireplace, jacuzzi, and steam shower.

Located on the border of the Great Smoky Mountains National Park, the Swag is a nature lover's paradise. It even has its own private entrance to the 500,000-acre park and its network of scenic trails. Inside the park, you and your lover can do everything from visiting an old frontier village to chasing salamanders in the mountain streams. Back at the Swag, you can relax in the spring-fed swimming hole or a nearby hammock. After a delicious dinner (rates include three meals a day), proceed to the porch, pull a couple of rocking chairs together, and enjoy the serenity of a Smoky Mountain night.

Rates: $125–$325

THE SWAG COUNTRY INN
2300 Swag Road
Waynesville, NC 28786

Phone	828-926-0430
Fax	828-926-2036

Ohio

THE CINCINNATIAN HOTEL
Cincinnati

> Your kisses close my eyes and yet you stare
> As though God struck a child with nameless fears;
> Perhaps the water glitters and discloses
> Time's chalice and its limpid useless tears.
>
> —"Goodbye" by Alan Lewis

In a city not usually associated with romance, the Cincinnatian Hotel is making a reputation for itself. The hotel originally opened in 1882, but a $23 million facelift has left it anything but old fashioned. Now it's a European-style hotel with modern details mixing comfortably with the original architecture.

The atrium lobby is stunning evidence that the renovation was a success. The hotel's original walnut-and-marble grand staircase has been preserved and rises into the contemporary furnishings of the atrium. You might like the looks of the atrium enough to request a room with a flower-decked balcony that faces out onto it.

There are two restaurants at the Cincinnatian Hotel. The Palace features progressive American cuisine and is one of Cincinnati's finest restaurants. This restaurant is setting standards for impeccable classic service, with dishes presented under silver domes, and there's an impressive wine selection. And the Cricket Lounge, at the base of the atrium lobby, serves lighter fare and has a piano bar. Afternoon tea is served on the weekdays at the Cricket Lounge, and the pastries are superb. In fact, the ritual is getting so popular that local businesspeople now talk of "power teas" at the Cincinnatian Hotel.

Celebrities are beginning to make the Cincinnatian the hotel of choice in the Queen City. The Rolling Stones have stayed here, as have Tom Cruise and Bob Hope. The hotel is located right in the center of downtown Cincinnati, just off Fountain Square, the city's traditional business, shopping, and entertainment center.

The hotel offers weekend packages for romantic couples. The Celebration Package includes queen-bed accommodations, valet parking, the delivery of a bottle of Chandon champagne and a half dozen chocolate-covered strawberries to your room the evening of your arrival, a bath amenity, and a $25 voucher towards break-fast in the Palace Restaurant or from room service.

Rates: Rooms $210–$285; Suites $350–$1,500
(based upon season)

THE CINCINNATIAN HOTEL
601 Vine Street
Cincinnati, OH 45202

Phone   513-381-3000
Toll free   800-942-9000
Fax   513-651-0256

Oregon

COLUMBIA GORGE HOTEL
Hood River

> And it seems, wherever I look,
> Phantoms of irreclaimable happiness taunt me.
> Then I see her, petalled in new-blown hours,
> Beside me—'All you love most there
> Has blossomed again,' she murmurs, 'all that
>   you missed there
> Has grown to be yours.'
>
> —"The Album" by Cecil Day Lewis

Situated on the green banks of the Columbia River Gorge in Hood River, Oregon, this is a great place to experience the natural splendor of the Pacific Northwest. Just an hour east of Portland, the Gorge is a setting of exquisite dramatic beauty. The hotel first opened in 1921 and quickly developed an international reputation for elegant hospitality amidst rugged beauty. Presidents Roosevelt and Coolidge were visitors, as were Myrna Loy and Jane Powell. It's rumored that Rudolph Valentino and Clara Bow used the Columbia Gorge Hotel as a romantic hideaway.

The hotel sits not far from the base of Mt. Hood and the 206-foot Wah-Gwin-Gwin Falls are nearby. Recently renovated, the hotel's forty-two rooms and its elegant public areas have been designed to allow the gorgeous surrounding scenery to dramatically infuse the interior.

One of the most amazing meals you'll ever see is "The World Famous Farm Breakfast" where you can "gorge" yourself. Here's all of what you get: seasonal fruits, apple fritters with sugar and spice, old fashioned oatmeal with brown sugar and sweet cream, three farm fresh eggs, bacon, a smoked pork chop, apple and maple flavored sausage, hash browns, baking powder biscuits and honey, a stack of buttermilk pancakes with hot maple syrup, and coffee. Of course you can also enjoy a breakfast drink from their outstanding selection of champagne and other cocktails.

If you're ever hungry again, there's a fantastic dinner menu, including items such as fresh Columbia River salmon in lemon-butter Chardonnay sauce and grilled medallions of venison. And save room for the Apple Tart, Columbia Gorge style: Hood River apples, thinly sliced and blended with a rich butter caramel sauce, are baked under a covering of puff pastry. This delicious treat is served hot with French vanilla ice cream.

Travel writers have called the hotel, "one of the most romantic places on Earth," and it's easy to see why. The spectacular views and lush gardens, fantastic food and rural seclusion make this a romantic's dream spot. The Columbia Gorge Hotel is a great place to have a wedding, featuring five different reception rooms and a varied banquet and hors d'oeuvres menu. And the hotel has its own in-house florist to take care of flower arrangements.

Rates: Rooms $150–$270; Suites $295–$365

COLUMBIA GORGE HOTEL

4000 Westcliff Drive
Hood River, OR 97031

Phone	541-386-5566
Toll free	800-345-1921
Fax	541-387-5414

SALISHAN LODGE
Gleneden Beach

> I am two fools, I know,
> For loving, and for saying so
> In whining poetry;
> But where's that wise man, that would not be I,
> If she would not deny?
>
> —"The Triple Fool" by John Donne

Salishan Lodge has long enjoyed the reputation of being Oregon's premier resort and it's easy to see why. Spectacularly set among 700 forested acres adjacent to the Pacific Ocean, Salishan Lodge is conveniently located only about ninety miles southwest of Portland.

All 198 rooms and three suites are cozy and include fireplaces and balconies that are certain to lend to a romantic atmosphere. Other room amenities include a mini-bar, VCR and large-screen TV, a coffeemaker, and robes.

There's an exhaustive list of activities thanks to the resort's vast resources. Golfers can hit a few rounds at the eighteen-hole championship golf course or practice on the putting green. Tennis buffs can enjoy a friendly match regardless of the weather thanks to three indoor courts. Guests can also partake in a more strenuous work-out at the fitness center, swim laps at the pool, and walk or jog on the resort's many trails. Afterwards guests can relax in the sauna or the whirlpool.

The Lodge's Dining Room is ideal if you're looking to sample superb innovative Pacific Northwest cuisine complimented by an excellent selection of wines. Guests in search of more casual dining may want to try the Cedar Tree which offers Sunday brunch or the Sun Room.

Rates: Rooms $112–$575

SALISHAN LODGE
7760 Highway 101N
Gleneden Beach, OR 97388

Phone	541-764-2371
Toll free	800-452-2300
Fax	541-764-3681

Pennsylvania

FOUR SEASONS HOTEL
Philadelphia

> Hither with crystal vials, lovers come,
> > And take my tears, which are love's wine,
> And try your mistress' tears at home,
> For all our false, that taste not just like mine;
> > Alas, hearts do not in eyes shine,
> Now can you more judge woman's thoughts by tears,
> > Than by her shadow, what she wears.
> O perverse sex, where none is true but she,
> > Who's therefore true, because her truth kills me.
>
> —"Twickenham Garden" by John Donne

Often overwhelmed by its sister cities along the Atlantic coast, Philadelphia is an unappreciated gem. The cultural attractions are world-class, with an excellent art museum and one of the best orchestras in the world. Center City has a dynamic nightlife, and the residential neighborhoods of Society Hill and Rittenhouse Square offer an elegant respite from urban stress. You can visit the many historic sights, including the Liberty Bell, or enjoy the latest novelties in cuisine or entertainment. As W.C. Fields once said, "On the whole, I'd rather be in Philadelphia."

And the best place to stay in Philadelphia is the Four Seasons Hotel. There are 365 rooms in this massive hotel, including ninety-six executive suites. The suites provide a sleeping area that is separated from the sitting area by French doors. There are only six parlor suites. The room decor blends contemporary fabrics with Federal-style furniture. The Presidential Suite has a large marble bath with a whirlpool.

Candles and fresh flowers decorate the tables in the Fountain Restaurant. Live music plays during tea and on weekend evenings, and ranges from classical to jazz. After dinner, go for a romantic walk to the Swann Fountain in nearby Logan Square. Viennese dessert buffet is served on Friday and Saturday nights from 9 p.m. until 1 a.m. in the morning. In addition to enjoying delectable pastries and sinful desserts, you can dance to the trio playing in the Swann Lounge.

The Four Seasons offers a Suite Romance package. The king-sized bed is turned down and dressed with a soft white sheet and comforter. A single long-stemmed rose lies upon the lace boudoir pillow. Champagne is served and a room-service breakfast is on order for the morning after.

Rates: Rooms $320–$480; Suites $875–$2,350

FOUR SEASONS HOTEL
One Logan Square
Philadelphia, PA 19103

Phone   215-963-1500
Toll free   800-332-3442
Fax   215-963-9506

GLENDORN
Bradford

Now thou hast loved me one whole day,
Tomorrow when thou leav'st, what will thou say?
Will thou then antedate some new made vow?
Or say that now
We are not just those persons, which we were?

—"Woman's Constancy" by John Donne

Glendorn offers couples the opportunity for an exclusive escape on a vast amount of private land. The estate, which is tucked away on almost 1,300 acres of fenced-in land in northwestern Pennsylvania, provides guests with the ultimate playground for fun and romance. The privacy of this retreat is virtually guaranteed by the Allegheny National Forest which surrounds Glendorn on three sides.

Built in 1929 for the locally prominent Dorn family who used the resort as a "summer camp," Glendorn opened its doors to the public in 1995. Rooms and suites are offered in the magnificent redwood lodge which serves as the centerpiece for the property. Additional guest quarters are available in rustic and elegant cottages that mostly offer one to four bedrooms. All guest accommodations have private baths, telephones, and robes. Fresh fruit, cookies, and candies are placed in the rooms each day. You can have a continental breakfast delivered to your room, suite, or cabin each morning, or you can opt for the full country breakfast at the Big House or terrace depending upon the weather. You can also arrange for a lovely romantic picnic.

The 1,300 acres of private land provide a limitless variety of activities including hiking, bicycling, cross-country skiing, fishing in the lake or streams, canoeing, tennis, trap and skeet, billiards, bridge card games, swimming in the sixty-foot heated outdoor pool, or a workout at the gym. There's even golf nearby. Wind down your fun-filled day relaxing by a two-story fireplace.

Rates: Rooms $295–$895 (includes meals
and recreation)

GLENDORN
1032 West Corydon Street
Bradford, PA 16701

Phone   814-362-6511
Toll free   800-843-8568
Fax   814-368-9923

South Carolina

CHARLESTON PLACE
Charleston

> Come live with me, and be my love,
> And we will some new pleasures prove
> Of golden sands, and crystal brooks,
> With silken lines, and silver hooks.

> —"The Bait" by John Donne

Charleston is a spectacular city, rich with history and timeless beauty. Horse-drawn carriages make their way down cobblestone streets that lead to some of America's most beautifully preserved antebellum homes along with antique shops, museums, and piazzas. Every spring the town comes alive with celebrations, most notably the Spoleto Festival, a world-class performing arts marathon that attracts performers and fans from all over the globe to this exquisite gem of a city. Whether you're here for Spoleto or at any other time of year, the place to stay is Charleston Place.

Modern day Rhetts and Scarletts, guests of Charleston Place, are swept into tradition in the reception area of the hotel, and embraced by a grand, curving double staircase lit by an enormous crystal chandelier. Upstairs, the 440 rooms and forty suites provide guests with elegant period-style furnishings, ceiling fans, and opulent bathrooms with Botticino marble and glass fixtures. Premier accommodations crown the two top floors where the Club offers a higher level of luxury service. Here you will enjoy a private elevator, concierge service, special check-in and check-out privileges, and complimentary food and cocktails.

Relaxation and recreation begin at the Fitness Center where a retractable glass roof allows year-round sunning and swimming in the heated indoor pool. A fully equipped exercise room, steam room, and sauna are also available. Or you can soak in the huge jacuzzi while overlooking the view of downtown Charleston.

Southern Living calls afternoons in the Lobby Lounge "the best known of tea times in the city." Evenings in the Lounge are nearly as famous, when hors d'oeuvres, cocktails, and desserts are served to the accompaniment of live piano music. Chef Bob Waggoner, recipient of the coveted Mobil Four Star Award, offers a unique Low Country cuisine at Charleston Grill. Here you can dine in a relaxed atmosphere and ambiance, entertained by a wonderful jazz trio and vocalist. The Palmetto Cafe is another popular dining room which features breakfast and brunch buffets during the weekends.

Charleston Place spares no effort in entertaining its guests with fine southern hospitality and has earned a reputation as one of the finest hotels in the Carolinas.

Rates: Rooms $325–$375; Suites $425–$2,500

CHARLESTON PLACE
130 Market Street
Charleston, SC 29401

Phone   803-722-4900
Toll free   800-611-5545
Fax   803-722-0728

PALMETTO DUNES RESORT
Hilton Head

> Yet, love and hate me too,
> So, these extremes shall neither's office do;
> Love me, that I may die the gentler way;
> Hate me, because thy love is too great for me;
>
> —"The Prohibition" by John Donne

Located on Hilton Head Island just off the South Carolina coast, Palmetto Dunes Resort is a vast conglomeration of rental villas, homes, and two hotels in a semitropical setting.

Couples looking for a romantic getaway may want to

consider contacting one of the property rental companies that handle villa and home rentals for Palmetto Dunes. What makes Maximum Resort Rentals especially attractive are their honeymoon and romance packages they can tailor to your desires. The typical honeymoon/romance package includes comfortable accommodations, a romantic dinner at a fine southern restaurant, a bottle of champagne (or wine), and bicycle rentals for two. For an additional charge, Maximum Resort Rentals will arrange horseback riding for two, sunset or daytime catamaran cruises for two, kayaking on a two-hour nature tour, or trolley rides in nearby Savannah, Georgia.

Typical rental villas have a full kitchen, living room, dining area, and a deck or patio. Many also have a whirlpool tub or fireplace. Ask for an oceanfront villa and you will be rewarded with scenic ocean views and a fabulous sunrise.

Palmetto Dunes offers a playground of activities. The resort features five golf courses that won praise from *Golf* magazine for providing some of the best golfing in America. The twenty-five-court tennis center has won accolades as one of the best tennis resorts in America by *Tennis* and *Racquet* magazines. You'll also find three miles of beach for basking or walking, thirty swimming pools, and several peaceful lagoons and scenic creeks. Your boating and water sports needs are met at the Shelter Cove Harbour Marina.

Whatever your needs, Maximum Resort Rentals can help you design a fun-filled and romantic retreat.

Rates: Villas, $490–$2,140 per week (depending
    upon season)

PALMETTO DUNES RESORT
22 New Orleans Road, Suite 2
Hilton Head Island, SC 29928

Phone   803-842-6069
Toll free   800-231-6622
Fax   803-842-6906

Tennessee

ADAMS EDGEWORTH INN
Monteagle

> O my first love! Even so you lie
> Near the base of my precipitous, ever lonelier and
>   colder life
> With your fair hair still rippling out
> As I remember it between my fingers
> When you let me unloosen first
> (Over thirty chaotic years ago!)
> That golden tumult forever!
>
> —"Of My First Love" by Hugh MacDiarmid

If you're the type who finds historical places romantic, then Adams Edgeworth Inn is for you. Adams sits amid Monteagle Assembly, a ninety-six-acre Victorian village listed on the National Register of Historic Places. Originally built in 1896 as a boardinghouse, the inn was renovated and reopened in 1977. Today the inn is run by David and Wendy Adams who have taken great care in preserving the inn's authenticity.

With only thirteen rooms and one suite, the Adams Edgeworth Inn sets the stage for an intimate stay. The luxurious rooms feature twelve-foot ceilings and are decorated in Victorian cottage style with lots of warm colored chintzes. Be sure to get a room with a four-poster bed (the others have twin brass beds) and a fireplace. Downstairs you'll find the dining room where breakfast and dinner are served. Wendy, a graduate of the Culinary Institute of America, creates delightful meals that are presented on antique china. The long wrap-around porch is the perfect place to retire to after dinner, especially on a rainy night when the drops of rain dance on the tin roof playing a soothing symphony.

If at all possible, visit during the summer. It's during

the summer months that Monteagle Assembly comes alive and hosts an eight-week program of events that range from classical music concerts to literary seminars. If you miss this event, the inn has a 2,000-volume library and an excellent art collection. A short drive away is South Cumberland State Park where you can hike, play in waterfalls, or even explore some of the region's caves.

Rates: $75–$175

ADAMS EDGEWORTH INN
Monteagle Assembly
Box 340
Monteagle, TN 37356

Phone   931-924-4000
Fax   931-924-3236

MUSIC ROAD HOTEL
Pigeon Forge

Shall I compare thee to a summer's day?
Thou art more lovely and more temperate:
Rough winds do shake the darling buds of May,
And summer's lease hath all too short a date:

But thy eternal summer shall not fade,
Nor lose possession of that fair thou ow'st,
Nor shall death brag thou wander'st in his shade,
When in eternal lines to time thou gow'st,
So long as men can breathe, or eyes can see,
So long lives this, and this gives life to thee.

—"Shall I Compare Thee To A Summer's Day?" by
    William Shakespeare

When Pigeon Forge first became a tourist spot, it was characterized as one long strip of go-cart tracks and mini-golf with the *Hee-Haw* studio serving as the main cultural attraction. As the South developed over the last twenty years, so did Pigeon Forge. So much so that the Music Road Hotel is now a favorite with romantics like country singer Louise Mandrell.

She describes the Music Road Hotel as "magical." "The lobby has a huge stone fireplace and antique furniture throughout. It's as though you've stepped into someone's magnificent home. The rooms are elegant with antique sleighbeds and jacuzzis as well as a refrigerator in every room. My husband and I love eating breakfast out on the balcony which faces the beautiful Smokies and overlooks a small stream."

Rates: $69–$129

MUSIC ROAD HOTEL
303 Henderson Chapel Road
Pigeon Forge, TN 37863

Phone   800-429-7700
Fax   423-429-3626

RICHMONT INN
Townsend

> A down the pale-green glacier river floats
> A dark boat through the gloom—and whither?
> The thunder roars. But still we have each other!
> The naked lightnings in the heavens dither
> And disappear—what have we but each other?
> The boat has gone.
>
> —"On The Balcony" by D.H. Lawrence

Brenda Vaccaro and Guy Hector call the Richmont, "The most romantic inn in Tennessee." I think they may be right.

Designed in the architectural style of a historic Appalachian cantilever barn, the Richmont Inn is a romantic sanctuary nestled in the woods of Tennessee's Smoky Mountains. The decor of the main living room is an eclectic mix of beamed ceilings, broad-plank floors, English and American antiques, and French paintings.

Eclecticism continues in the individually decorated rooms named after people prominent in Appalachia's history. Most romantic is the Nanye-hi Room, named after the Cherokee Chieftainess. Its spacious layout includes a cathedral ceiling, a large wood-burning fireplace, jacuzzi tub for two, private balcony, king bed, and skylight views of the valley and mountains. If this room is unavailable, try for the Robert Mize Room with its folk art decor, double jacuzzi, and fireplace.

Start your day by enjoying the inn's grand breakfast. Then you can fill your day by exploring the Great Smoky Mountains National Park. When you return in the evening, you'll find one of the inn's award-winning desserts waiting for you before you settle in for another night of romance.

Rates: $95–$150

RICHMONT INN
220 Winterberry Lane
Townsend, TN 37882

Phone   423-448-6751
Fax   423-448-6480

Texas

CIBOLO CREEK RANCH
Marfa

> Forth, Love, and find this made,
>> Wherever she be hidden:
> Speak, Love, be not afraid,
>> But plead as thou art bidden;
> And say, that he who taught thee
>> His yearning want and pain,
> Too dearly, dearly bought thee
>> To part with thee in vain.
>
> —"Amaturus" by William Johnson Cory

This restored working Longhorn ranch is situated on 25,000 acres in Big Bend country. The ranch was built around remains of pre-Civil War adobe forts and provides guests with eleven elegant adobe-insulated guest rooms. Most of the rooms have luxury touches such as fireplaces and down comforters. Each room is decorated in a motif that reflects the period for which it was named, such as Cowboy, Colonial South, and Texas.

Request the Master Suite if you're looking to make a Texas-sized impression. The suite comes complete with a private dining room, jacuzzi, huge bathroom, and walk-in closet, and it opens out onto a glass-walled veranda that looks upon a private fishing lake and a nearby swimming pool.

Recreational activities include horseback riding, fishing, and swimming. Wind down your day with a giant gourmet spread enjoyed with a soothing margarita. You can even sit around the campfire at night gazing up at the big starry sky.

Rates: Rooms $250; Master Suite $390

CIBOLO CREEK RANCH
Highway 67
Shafter, TX 79850

Phone   915-229-3737
Fax   915-229-3653

FOUR SEASONS HOTEL
Austin

> A book of Verses underneath the Bough,
> A Jug of Wine, a Loaf of Bread—and Thou
>   Beside me singing in the Wilderness—
> Oh, Wilderness were Paradise now!
>
> Yet Ah, that Spring should vanish with the Rose!
> That Youth's sweet-scented manuscript should close!
>   The nightingale that in the branches sang,
> Ah whence, and wither flown again, who knows!
>
> Ah Love! Could you and I with Him conspire
> To grasp this sorry Scheme of Things Entire,
>   Would not we shatter it to bits—and then
> Re-mold it nearer to Heart's Desire!
>
>   —"The Rubaiyat" by Omar Khayyám

Located in the heart of downtown Austin, just a short ride away from the state capitol building, the University of Texas, and the L.B.J. Library, the Four Seasons is a great place to stay, whether you're in Austin for a romantic weekend, or you're there on a business trip.

The Four Seasons is consistently ranked as the best hotel in Austin. The atmosphere is distinctly Texan, with the service and amenities that you've come to expect from Four Seasons' hotels. But this hotel is more laid-back than others in the chain. The lobby is warm and comfortable, with a large fireplace and lots of luxurious furniture to relax in. Have a drink in the Lobby Lounge, and watch the people go by. There are 291 rooms in the hotel, all of them offering amenities like twenty-four-hour room service, terry-cloth bathrobes, and complimentary newspapers. But the best accommodations are the executive suites.

The hotel is nestled on the banks of Town Lake, with its park land surroundings, and hiking and biking trails. Enjoy a swim in the heated outdoor pool overlooking the lake. The fully equipped health club includes saunas, whirlpool, and other facilities.

The Four Seasons offers some of Austin's finest restaurants. The Cafe features a lakeside terrace, where imaginative American and southwestern cuisine are served. The terrace is a great perch for bat-watching, a favorite Austin pastime. And it's also a popular place among locals for Sunday brunch.

At night, check out the exciting night scene on Austin's famous 6th Street. Live music from country to jazz to "grunge rock" is played (often without cover charges) in the street's countless bars and nightclubs.

Rates: Rooms $195–$240; Suites $245–$425

FOUR SEASONS HOTEL
98 San Jacinto Boulevard
Austin, TX 78701

Phone   512-478-4500
Toll free   800-332-3442
Fax   512-478-3117

LA COLOMBE D'OR
Houston

> No—yet still steadfast, still unchangeable,
>   Pillow'd upon my fair love's ripening breast,
> To feel forever its soft fall and swell,
>   Awake forever in a sweet unrest,
> Still, still to hear her tender-taken breath,
> And so live ever—or else swoon to death.
>
> —"Bright Star" by John Keats

Nothing compares to La Colombe D'Or. This unique and spectacular prairie-school-style residence was first built in 1923. Then Steve Zimmerman turned it into a

European-style boutique hotel. Zimmerman calls his pleasure palace "the smallest luxury hotel in the world." And in this case, small is good, especially when you want peace, quiet, privacy, and personalized service.

The hotel has only six guest rooms, and a staff of thrity-six, so you can imagine the level of attention you'll enjoy here. Some of the suites are residences all to themselves. The Degas Suite, for example, has an intimate dining room decorated with a French crystal chandelier and Queen Anne chairs.

Chef Tan Binh Doan is an artist, supervising a restaurant that produces authentic French cuisine served with impeccable style. Fresh seafood is brought in daily by local fishermen from the Gulf, and many of the herbs used in the menu dishes are grown in the La Colombe D'Or herb garden. Start with a cocktail in the wood-paneled library or the Bacchus Bar. The restaurant does not turn over tables, so when you reserve a table, it's yours for the whole evening. Instead of being rushed through the several courses of a fine French meal, you'll be allowed to relax and savor both the food and the atmosphere of the elegant dining room. Rich desserts are a specialty here.

La Colombe D'Or is located in the artsy Montrose district of Houston. It's close to most of the city's attractions, particularly the Museum of Fine Arts, the Contemporary Arts Museum, Rice University, and the unavoidable Astrodome. But once you walk into this beautifully appointed little jewel of a hotel, you might never want to leave your room.

Rates: Rooms $195–$275; Penthouse Suite $575

LA COLOMBE D'OR
3410 Montrose Boulevard
Houston, TX 77006

Phone   713-524-7999
Fax   713-524-8923

THE MANSION ON TURTLE CREEK
Dallas

> How say you? Let us, O my dove,
> Let us be unashamed of soul,
> As earth lies bare to heaven above!
> How is it under our control
> To love or not to love?
>
> —"Two In The Campagna" by Robert Browning

Caroline Rose Hunt has created several of the best hotels in America, among them the Hotel Bel-Air in Los Angeles. And the Mansion on Turtle Creek is one of her crowning achievements. Consistently ranked as one of the top hotels in the world by a wide range of travel authorities, the Mansion is an exquisite place. It is particularly appealing to romantics because of the fine attention to detail, exceptional restaurants, and superlative service.

There are 126 rooms in this Mansion, and fifteen of them are suites which happen to be simply stunning. Individually decorated with original art, the suites have living rooms, wet bars, and separate powder rooms. Some even feature two bedrooms and a full kitchen. Suites on the ninth floor have roof gardens with a view of the Dallas skyline. Baths feature marble shower stalls and vanities, custom brass fixtures, and large dressing areas. Room service offers a full menu, so you never have to leave your room.

Set on a low rise above meandering lawns, the Mansion is situated near the neighborhood of Highland Park. It has the feeling of a private residence, which isn't surprising, because that's what it initially was. And the pace at the Mansion is like you are the guest at a country home. There's plenty to do nearby, but no one will force you to do anything. Instead you are encouraged to take it easy, to simply enjoy the surroundings and amenities. At the Mansion, you are pampered with prompt, personal attention. But when you wish to be left alone, you are. This is a place to just "be": sleeping until noon if you feel like it, waking up only for breakfast in bed followed by lounging by the pool.

Then there's dinner to look forward to. The restaurant at the Mansion is one of the finest in the country. Chef Dean Fearing is recognized as the founding father of haute southwestern cuisine, combining the regional flavors of Native American, Spanish, Mexican, Southern, and American-cowboy cookery to produce a unique and unparalleled menu. Specialties include lobster taco, tortilla soup, salad with smoked salmon, and roasted quail.

According to a reader's poll in *D Magazine,* a local Dallas periodical, the Mansion is the best restaurant in Dallas. It was also judged the most romantic: "From the quick takeover of your car by beaming attendants to the ritual welcome at the maitre de station, right on through exquisite service of fine fare and wines in a setting of no-stone-unturned splendor, dinner *à deux* here is an evening to remember." The same survey said the Mansion served the best desserts. Chef Fearing is so confi-dent that no one can make crème brûlée as well as he can that he even made his secret recipe public.

After dinner, relax in the lounge and get a hand-written weather report for the next day. But you don't need to decide right then whether you want to sleep in.

Rates: Rooms $290–$425; Suites $525–$1,775

THE MANSION ON TURTLE CREEK
2821 Turtle Creek Boulevard
Dallas, TX 75219

Phone	214-559-2100
Toll free	800-527-5432
Fax	214-528-4187

Utah

STEIN ERIKSEN LODGE
Park City

> See! The mountains kiss high heaven,
>   And the waves clasp one another;
> No sister flower would be forgiven
>   If it disdained its brother;
> And the sunlight clasps the earth,
>   And the moonbeams kiss the sea: -
> What are all these kissings worth,
>   If thou kiss not me?
>
> —"Love's Philosophy" by Percy Bysshe Shelley

Utah ski resorts don't get the attention that their glitzy cousins in Colorado receive, and for many that's part of their charm. Sure, there's not as lively a night scene in predominantly Mormon Utah, but that doesn't mean you can't make your own excitement.

The Stein Eriksen Lodge is one of the premier ski lodges in Utah. Forty-five minutes from Salt Lake City, the lodge is nestled in the alpine splendor of the Deer Valley Resort at Park City. The Lodge is on the mountainside, and most of the rooms have a view of the mountain (make sure to ask for one of these rooms). About half the rooms have fireplaces. The suites also have spacious decks. The rooms are decorated in Scandinavian color and theme. Bathrooms are equipped with oversized whirlpools. And the lobby has a huge stone fireplace, creating a warm and cozy atmosphere. Candlelight and fresh flowers are a regular feature in the Glitretind Gourmet room, where the menu is superb. The restaurant has an excellent wine selection.

Other amenities include a heated, year-round outdoor swimming pool, and a health spa with exercise room, sauna, hot tub, and massage rooms. There's also a ski locker room, and ski rental and repair shop for your equipment needs. You can buy a lift ticket right at the Lodge and ski out to Deer Valley's Sterling lift. And the outdoor walkways are heated so you don't get chilled coming in or going out.

Celebrities eager to enjoy mountain solitude have taken advantage of the Stein Eriksen's impeccable hospitality. Folks like Dustin Hoffman, Ann-Margret, Sidney Poitier, Bruce Springsteen, and Gerald Ford have stayed here, and although it's made its reputation as a ski resort, don't dismiss Stein Eriksen when planning a summer vacation. The summer days in the mountains are warm and dry, with virtually no humidity. Nights are cool enough for a sweater, and provide a sky full of stars. Summer events in the area include rodeos, concerts, and sports competitions.

> Rates: Rooms $175–$650; Suites $225–$2,500
> (based upon season)

STEIN ERIKSEN LODGE

P.O. Box 3177
Park City, Utah 84060

Phone	435-649-3700
Toll free	800-453-1302
Fax	435-649-5825

SUNDANCE RESORT

Provo

> For a breeze of morning moves,
>   And the planet of love is on high,
> Beginning to faint in the light that she loves
>   On a bed of daffodil sky,
> To faint in the light of the sun she loves,
>   To faint in his light, and to die.
>
> All night have the roses heard
>   The flute, violin, bassoon;
> All night has the casement jessamine stirred

> To the dancers dancing in tune;
> Till a silence fell with the walking bird,
> And a hush with the setting moon.

—"Song From Maud" by Alfred, Lord Tennyson

Sundance was created in 1969 by actor Robert Redford who envisioned a resort where the arts, environment, and recreation would flourish in harmony. The resort has become a major success and earned kudos as "Resort Sanctuary of the Year" by *Harper's Hideaway Report.*

Sundance is located on the slopes of 12,000-foot Mount Timpanogos about an hour drive from Salt Lake City. At the resort are ninety rustically elegant cottages that have won the attention of *Architectural Digest.* All the cottages are within a short walking distance to Sundance Village. Each cottage contains three guest quarters apiece with varying levels of amenities and decorated with Navajo rugs and Native American crafts. The standard room provides you with a queen bed, private bath, and separate vanity area. The junior suite features a kitchenette, fireplace, private patio, queen bed, and private bath. The master suite has a full kitchen, dining table, fireplace, private patio, queen bed, and bath. All guest quarters have a private entrance and come with a full American breakfast for two served daily in the Foundry Grill.

The resort has two restaurants which offer authentic regional cooking. The signature restaurant, the Tree Room, offers candlelight dining with food prepared from the kitchen of award-winning Chef Jean Louis Montecot. The restaurant is graced with Native American art and Western memorabalia from Robert Redford's personal collection.

There's something to do for everyone who visits Sundance. You can enjoy the fresh air and gorgeous scenery as you hike to Stewart Falls or try your hand at flyfishing or horseback riding.

Winter activities abound here. Sundance Resort closes its slopes to the first 1,200 skiers to ensure a quality skiing experience. Downhill skiers have their choice of forty-one trails spread over 450 acres. Cross-country skiing is also available as is skating, snowshoeing, and sledding.

Rates: Standard Room $150–$195;
Junior Suite $195-325; Master Suite $275–$425

SUNDANCE RESORT

North Fork Provo Canyon
RR 3, Box A-1
Provo, UT 84604

Phone	801-225-4107
Toll free	800-892-1600
Fax	801-226-1937

Vermont

1811 HOUSE
Manchester

> Wi' lightsome heart I pu'd a rose
> Upon its thorny tree;
> But my fause luver staw my rose,
> And left the thorn wi' me.
>
> —"The Banks o'Doon" by Robert Burns

Parts of this rambling bed and breakfast date to 1750, its history recognizable in the low ceiling of the foyer. This inn has been in operation since 1811, and several rooms were added through the years. The only interruption of service occurred when it was the home of Abraham Lincoln's granddaughter.

Relaxed Federal decor gives 1811 House a charming and authentic feeling. Stenciled floral borders ring the ceiling, while dozens of horse paintings line the walls. Waterford crystal and the ornately carved chairs of the dining room give this colonial inn a touch of British charm. The pub also has a decidedly British ambiance. Dark, intimate, and decorated with exposed rafters, the pub stocks more than fifty fine single malt scotches.

The B&B's fourteen rooms and one suite are all elegantly appointed. While some of the bathrooms are a bit dated, like the inn itself, each room features gracious English and early American antiques. More modern, but just as charming, are the three cottages that dot the seven-and-a-half acre property. Surrounded by English gardens, terraces, and a pond, the cottages are ideal for romance.

Rates: $160–$200

1811 HOUSE
Route 7A
Manchester, VT 05254

Phone   802-362-1811
Toll free 800-432-1811
Fax   802-362-2443

INN AT SHELBURNE FARMS
Shelburne Farms

> If things on earth may be to heaven resembled,
> It must be love, pure, constant, undissembled.
> But if to sin by chance the charmer press,
> Forgive, O Lord, forgive our trespasses.
>
> —"And Forgive Us Our Trespasses" by Aphra Behn

This fascinating sixty-room brick-over-wood Queen Anne mansion sits amidst 1,400 acres of working farmland on a crowning bluff overlooking Lake Champlain. This National Historic Site features grounds that were designed by noted landscape architect Frederick Law Olmsted of Central Park fame and this perhaps explains why it was named the "Most Fascinating Country Inn" in 1992 by *Harper's Hideaway Report.*

The Inn at Shelburne Farms has two dozen authentically appointed guest rooms, most of which have private baths. The Rose Room, W. Seward Webb Room, Overlook Room, and Brown Room are particularly recommended for your stay. They are decorated with fine antiques, private baths, and offer a view of the lake from their second floor perch. Third floor rooms are less expensive and decorated in a more basic style. They have shared bathrooms but offer garden views.

There are crackling fires to be enjoyed at times in the public areas. These actually become a necessity in winter since this home has no heating (so pack accordingly). There are plenty of lounging areas that are lined with ancestral family portraits. Take in a brisk morning or evening on porches filled with wicker chairs.

The many activities available to the guests include fishing, swimming, boating, tennis, and hiking.

Rates: Rooms $85–$250 (depending upon size
         of room and view)

INN AT SHELBURNE FARMS
1611 Harbor Road
Shelburne Farms, VT 05482

Phone   802-985-8498
Fax   802-985-1233

THE INN ON COVERED BRIDGE GREEN
Arlington

> Love's weather is so fair,
>   Like perfumed air.
> Each word such pleasure brings
>   Like soft-touched strings;
> Love's passion moves the heart
>   On either part;
> Such harmony together,
>   So pleased in either.
>
>   —"Fulfillment" by William Cavendish

Anyone who's ever seen Norman Rockwell's "Saying Grace" or "The Four Freedoms" is bound to have wondered if such an America ever existed. Not only did such a place exist, you can now stay there in Rockwell's old house.

On the shores of the Battenkill River, just over a covered bridge, lies the Inn on Covered Bridge Green. Just a stone's throw away lies the picture-perfect town of Arlington. It's a place where the white steepled church is still used for harvest dinners, and life moves a lot slower than in the cities of the Northeast. From his old farmhouse, now 206 years old, Rockwell observed this charming little hamlet and created images that have warmed the souls of many Americans. The B&B still contains many of Rockwell's possessions, and its intimate rooms are filled with many period antiques. Out back is Rockwell's studio, now a two-bedroom, two-bath cottage perfect for a romantic weekend.

Nearby you can enjoy skiing at Bromley or Stratton. During the spring, summer, and fall, the Battenkill River offers some of the best trout fishing in the nation.

Rates: $110–$180

THE INN ON COVERED BRIDGE GREEN
R.D. 1
Box 3550
Arlington, VT 05250

Phone   802-375-9489
Fax   802-375-1208

TWIN FARMS
Barnard

> I cried for madder music and for stronger wine,
> But when the feast is finished and the lamps expire,
> Then falls thy shadow, Cynara, the night is thine;
> And I am desolate and sick of an old passion,
>   Yea hungry for the lips of my desire:
> I have been faithful to thee, Cynara, in my fashion.
>
> —"Non Sum Qualis Eram Bonae Sub Regno
>   Cynarae" by Ernest Dowson

In the past, Twin Farms served as the retreat of Nobel Prize winner Sinclair Lewis. Today, Twin Farms serves as an exclusive refuge for those seeking a little bit of fantasy amid the Vermont wilderness.

Located near Woodstock, Twin Farms spreads out over 235 acres. Lewis's house still stands and is the heart of Twin Farms. An all-inclusive retreat, the highlight here is the rooms. The main house has several, the star being the Washington Suite, but the cottages are by far the best lodging available. From the outside, the eight individually designed cottages seem bland. They're painted in the muted greys, greens, and blues of New England, and their only apparent luxury is a screened porch. Yet once you cross the threshold, you enter a world of opulent fantasy. Each cottage has a separate theme. One resembles a deluxe log cabin and is decorated with numerous pieces of canine-inspired folk art. Another, known as Meadow, has a decidedly Moroccan theme down to a tented ceiling of shaped plaster. Inside each cottage, you'll find a fireplace, a fully stocked complimentary refrigerator/bar, a deluxe featherbed, vast closets, and a luxurious bathroom. Such a comfortable setting forms the perfect venue for a relaxing in-room massage.

If you manage to leave your room, Twin Farms offers many activities. During the fall, the surrounding mountains burst forth with bright colors and beg to be explored. True, you could just jump in your car and drive around, but using one of the bikes is a much better way to observe this splendid phenomenon. You can even arrange to be picked up and brought back to the hotel in time for dinner. During the winter, take advantage of the inn's cross-country ski trails or ice-skating, and in summer, you can golf at the nearby country club. Yes, at Twin Farms, any season is romantic.

Rates: $800–$950 all inclusive

TWIN FARMS
Barnard, VT 05031

Phone	802-234-9999
Toll free	800-894-6327
Fax	802-234-9990

Virginia

FEDERAL CREST INN
Lynchburg

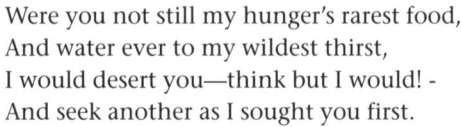

> Were you not still my hunger's rarest food,
> And water ever to my wildest thirst,
> I would desert you—think but I would! -
> And seek another as I sought you first.

> —"Oh, Think Not I Am Faithful To A Vow!" by Edna
> St. Vincent Millay

This elegant 8,000-square-foot Georgian Revival home located in Virginia hunt country was built in 1909 by a prominent Lynchburg attorney, David H. Howard. A few years ago, Phil and Ann Ripley bought the structure. They converted it into a magnificent bed and breakfast which features Flemish bond brickwork on the exterior and mahogany woodwork inside that lend a formal and elegant feeling to the Federal Crest Inn.

As you enter the inn, a pair of classical columns stand sentry to a grand central staircase which leads to the four guest rooms on the second level. Unique mantels adorn the home's seven gas-log fireplaces which are on display in the parlor, dining room, library, and three of the bedrooms. Each of the guest rooms are named for trees native to Virginia and decorated in a motif that reflects the name. All the rooms feature queen-sized beds (two have canopy beds), down comforters, antique furniture, luxurious linens, and terry-cloth bathrobes. A basket of snacks and beverages are placed in the room each night. Private portable telephones, cable television, and a jacuzzi round out the list of amenities.

Guests can play tunes on the jukebox in the "'50s Cafe" located off the dining room on the first floor. You can also relax in front of the sixty-inch large-screen television in a third floor space that also doubles as a meeting room.

Antique shopping, wineries, and golfing are all a

short distance away. Civil War buffs can explore Appomattox and the Confederate Cemetery. Sightseers may want to take a breathtaking drive through the Blue Ridge Mountains.

Rates: Rooms $85–$115

FEDERAL CREST INN
1101 Federal Street
Lynchburg, VA 24504

Phone	804-845-6155
Toll free	800-818-6155
Fax	804-845-1445

THE INN AT LITTLE WASHINGTON
Washington

> My love is such that rivers cannot quench,
> Nor ought but love from thee, give recompense.
> Thy love is such I can no way repay,
> The heavens reward thee manifold, I pray.
> Then while we live, in love let's so persevere
> That when we live no more, we may live ever.
>
> —"To My Dear And Loving Husband" by
> Anne Bradstreet

The Inn at Little Washington is one of the most beautiful country inns in Virginia, and offers a great restaurant as well. The inn is famous for its innovative cuisine and pastoral setting. It's a favorite gathering spot for Washington-types looking to get away from it all and the local squirearchy wanting to get in on the action. Craig Claiborne celebrated his 65th birthday here. Former Senator Eugene McCarthy and syndicated columnist James J. Kilpatrick are regulars (they live nearby).

Each of the inn's ten rooms is furnished in a grand Victorian country-house style. Cookies, fruit, and a bucket of ice make your room instantly comforting. The marble bathrooms have heated towel racks which offer further comfort. Afternoon tea is brought to your room. In the morning, *The Washington Post* is left outside your door. After you read the paper, enjoy a house breakfast served downstairs. There are two suites available and they both have double levels. The first level has a beautiful parlor decorated with exquisite antiques and hand-painted wallpaper. The parlor features a wet bar and stereo for your relaxation and pleasure, as well as a balcony. The first level also has a dressing area with a jacuzzi and a shower. The second level has a king-sized bed and two separate balconies—one facing the garden and the other with a sitting area to enjoy your afternoon tea. Because the inn is such a popular romantic retreat, you might have to make reservations well in advance. But it will be well worth the wait.

Breakfast at the restaurant can include pan-broiled local trout, along with freshly squeezed juices, and hot rolls. Chef Patrick O'Connell is one of the hottest culinary talents on the eastern seaboard. He always uses the freshest ingredients, including home-grown produce in season. And the menu can be incredibly innovative, with items like shad roe served with grapefruit. The wine list includes bottles from France, California, and Virginia vineyards. The best table at the restaurant is number 66, a private space at the end of the enclosed porch, surrounded by two gardens.

The town of Washington can claim to be the only place named after George Washington before he became president. (He surveyed the area in 1749.) This Washington is only sixty-seven miles away from DC. The surrounding countryside is dotted with gorgeous horse farms and parklands. Skyline Drive and the Blue Ridge Mountains are just minutes away.

Rates: Rooms $250–$540; Suites $410–$675

THE INN AT LITTLE WASHINGTON
P.O. Box 300
Middle and Main Streets
Washington, VA 22747

Phone   540-675-3800
Fax   540-675-3100

KESWICK HALL
Keswick

> And when I found your flesh did not resist,
> It was the living spirit that I kissed,
> It was the spirit's change in which I lay:
> Thus mind in mind we waited for the day.
> When flesh shall fall away, and, falling, stand
> Wrinkling with shadow over face and hand,
> Still I shall meet you on the verge of dust
> And know you as a faithful vestige must.
> And, in commemoration of our lust,
> May our heirs seal us in a single urn,
> A single spirit never to return.
>
> —"The Marriage" by Yvor Winters

This Tuscan-style villa is located on 600 acres of rolling hills in the Virginia hunt country just two hours southwest of Washington, DC. If you're looking to be treated like royalty, than this is your destination.

Keswick Hall has been turned into a fine estate in the grand English tradition by owner Sir Bernard Ashley who was married to the late Laura Ashley. Naturally, the villa is decorated with a variety of fabrics and furnishings from the company. You'll also find an ample amount of exquisite antiques from Sir Bernard's personal collection. There are century-old books and paintings as well.

Bedrooms are individually decorated in a variety of color schemes and feature couches, plump chairs, and cushioned window seats. Six of the forty-eight rooms have whirlpool tubs, while the others feature extra-long tubs. You'll also find heated towel racks, terry robes, and thick towels in the bathroom. Some of the rooms also feature a private terrace with views of the golf course.

The public areas include fabulously decorated parlors that lend an exclusive English country-life ambiance to the place. All guests have access to the Keswick Club which offers a variety of activities including an eighteen-hole Arnold Palmer-designed golf course, a fitness center, an indoor/outdoor pool, clay tennis courts, croquet, and bicycles.

Rates: Rooms $325–$545; Master Suite $595

KESWICK HALL
701 Club Drive (Box 68)
Keswick, VA 22947

Phone   804-979-3440
Toll free   800-274-5391
Fax   804-977-4171

▬▬▬

WILLIAMSBURG INN
Williamsburg

> Whether in the bringing of the flowers or of the
>   food
> She offers plenty, and is part of plenty,
> And whether I see her stooping, or leaning with the
>   flowers,
> What she does is ages old, and she is not simply,
> No, but lovely in that way.
>
>   —"Part Of Plenty" by Bernard Spencer

The historic town of Williamsburg is a breathtaking trip back to Colonial America. The attention to detail is so exquisite that if it weren't for the tourists taking pictures, you might think you were in the 1700s, when Williamsburg was the capital of Virginia and a hotbed of the revolution. The town features real stores with the goods for sale back then and shows off artisans practicing crafts (like wigmaking) that have long gone out of fashion.

If you have a passion for history, then Williamsburg is the place for you. And the Williamsburg Inn is where you'll want to stay at this historic burg.

Of course the inn reflects the historical accuracy of Williamsburg itself. The lobby is decorated in Regency style, with fireplaces at each end. From the lobby, you can look out onto the terrace and golf course. The musical instruments played in the dining room can be anything from a harp to piano to string trio. Candles and fresh flowers are always in the dining room, where the entrees can include noisettes of beef tenderloin with fresh oysters or venison in a pepper cream sauce. Two cocktail lounges give you an option for drinks before and after dinner.

But there are also plenty of modern comforts and conveniences, like an indoor and an outdoor pool, tennis courts, and a massage salon. The Golden Horseshoe Golf Course is right outside. And lawn bowling is also available. A few steps from the lobby of the inn, and you're in Colonial Williamsburg.

The lodgings at the inn include a total of 235 guest quarters. Many of those rooms are in the inn itself. But the real experience is to stay in one of the Colonial houses. The houses are situated right in the heart of the restored area. Decorated with period furnishings, they still have all the modern conveniences. Many celebrities and world leaders have stayed at the Colonial houses, including the heads of several countries during the 1983 Summit of Industrialized Nations. But you don't have to run a country in order to enjoy the quaint charm of these historically accurate houses.

> Rates: Rooms $255–$365; Suites $435–$750;
> Colonial houses $185–$840
> (based upon season)

WILLIAMSBURG INN
136 East Francis Street
P.O. Box B
Williamsburg, VA 23185

Phone   757-229-1000
Toll free   800-HISTORY (447-8679)
Fax   757-220-7096

Washington

INN AT LANGLEY
Whidbey Island

> If thou must love me, let it be for nought
> Except for love's sake only. Do not say
> 'I love her for her smile—her look—her way
> Of speaking gently.... '
>
>> —"If Thou Must Love Me, Let It Be For Nought" by
>> Elizabeth Barrett Browning

The Inn at Langley consists of two idyllic cedar-shake Mission-style buildings that overlook Saratoga Passage. The inn's exterior of wood and concrete underscores the harmony between the building and its surroundings. Gardens of flowers and berries grace the grounds.

The interior is decorated in muted tones, and the two dozen guest rooms are decorated with fir, maple, cherry, pine, and wicker furniture. Each amenity-laden guest room includes a fireplace sitting area, waterfront porches, deep whirlpool tubs, and separate shower stalls. All guest rooms have a nearly all-glass wall facing the water that provides romantic vistas of the Cascade Mountains and Camano Island. Those seeking roomier accommodations should request a suite or one of the corner units.

The Cathedral dining room with a stone fireplace serves a continental breakfast to guests only but opens to the public for dinner. Be certain to have one of Innkeeper/Chef Steve Nogal's gourmet five-course dinners featuring regional cuisine.

While your time away beachcombing or exploring the island's antique shops, art galleries, and boutiques.

Rates: Rooms $180–$200; Suites $270

INN AT LANGLEY
400 First Street, Box 835
Langley, WA 98260

Phone	360-221-3033
Fax	360-221-3033

THE SALISH LODGE
Snoqualmie Falls

> With thee conversing I forget all the time,
> All seasons and their change, all please alike.
>
> —from *Paradise Lost* by John Milton

What is it about waterfalls that makes the atmosphere so romantic? Some scientists claim that the water mists put an electrical charge in the air, but that takes the mystery out of the allure of cascading water. Some things are better left unexplained. If you like waterfalls but don't want to brave the crowds at Niagara, try the Salish Lodge at Snoqualmie Falls, the "Niagara of the West."

Located about a half hour east of Seattle, the Salish is situated at the crest of the magnificent Snoqualmie Falls, offering a unique combination of comfort and style in an elegant country inn designed to complement the spectacular natural setting. The falls plunge 268 feet—that's more than 100 feet farther than Niagara.

The Lodge has ninety-one guest rooms with custom-designed furniture, luxurious bedspreads, and down comforters. The walls of each room are wood-paneled in native straight fir, and the floors are made of northwestern slate. All rooms have stone-faced wood-burning fireplaces, two-person whirlpool spa tubs with French doors opening out onto the room, and the spectacular view beyond. Most rooms have balconies or patios overlooking the river. There are four suites with parlors and extra bedrooms.

You can relax in the Curtis Library, named after Asahel Curtis, a turn-of-the-century photographer whose original photos are featured there. Or go shopping at the

Salish country store, featuring designer clothing and accessories and original northwestern art. The Salish fitness center is located on the roof, offering an outdoor spa and sun deck, sauna, and state-of-the-art exercise equipment. Cuisine at the Lodge features regional game, fish and fowl, and an extensive wine list.

There are two lounges. The Falls Terrace opens onto a large outdoor terrace overlooking the falls. The sweeping panorama of the Attic Lounge, located on the roof level, features nightly live entertainment and dancing as well as some of the Northwest's best light jazz and mood music. Sporting activities include golf, fishing, biking, hiking, rock climbing, horseback riding, and cross-country or downhill skiing. Or you can take an unforgettable helicopter picnic and enjoy great Northwest cuisine atop the scenic Mt. Si. The nearby town of Snoqualmie was the inspiration (and provided some of the locations) for David Lynch's avant-garde *Twin Peaks* television series.

The Salish offers a honeymoon special. A romantic riverside room, champagne served in keepsake glasses, and breakfast in bed, all help to set a romantic mood.

Rates: Rooms $180–$210; Suites $500–$575
(based upon season)

SALISH LODGE
6501 Railroad Avenue, SE
Snoqualmie, WA 98065

Phone   425-888-2556
Toll free   800-826-6124
Fax   425-888-2420

West Virginia

THE GREENBRIER
White Sulphur Springs

> How long such suspension may linger? Ah, Sweet,
> The moment eternal—just that and no more -
> When ecstasy's utmost we clutch at the core,
> While cheeks burn, arms open, eyes shut, and lips
> meet!
> —"Now!" by Robert Browning

The Greenbrier is one of the most famous resorts in the country, and deservedly so. A favorite getaway for the Washington power elite, this spectacular retreat is a sprawling establishment set on 6,500 acres in the gorgeous Allegheny Mountains of West Virginia.

In operation for more than 200 years, the Greenbrier has a long-standing tradition of outstanding hospitality. Many of the staff can claim two or even three generations of service at the resort. And some of the chefs are home-grown as well, graduates of the famous Greenbrier Culinary Apprenticeship Program.

The Greenbrier offers a wide range of sporting activities. You can jog, hike, or ride horseback over the miles of woodland mountain trails. There are three eighteen-hole golf courses and twenty tennis courts. Fishing, as well as trap and skeet shooting, are also available. A full-service spa and mineral bath service help revitalize your aching muscles and leave the pressures of life behind you.

But the Greenbrier is not a spa, and the food and beverage service is both generous and exquisite. Tea is served in the afternoon, accompanied by live chamber music. Cocktails in the White Club are a must, followed by dinner in the elegant Main Dining Room where the tables are decorated with fresh flowers and lighted candles. A string ensemble plays romantic music during your meal. Later, return to the White Club for more music and dancing. In the morning, don't worry about being awakened early. Before 9 a.m., the staff actually whispers so as not to disturb their guests.

The Greenbrier offers a wide variety of rooms and suites... in the hotel, as well as in the guest houses that have up to four bedrooms. All the hotel rooms have beautiful views of the gardens and grounds, but only the guest houses have fireplaces. These houses also offer privacy and comfort. Their wide porches with awnings and wicker furniture are the perfect place to enjoy an afternoon cocktail and they overlook some of the most beautiful areas of the resort. The houses have full room-service, so you don't have to ever venture from beyond the front porch, if you don't want to. But if you do, they are located conveniently close to all the resort's many sport and leisure activities.

The Greenbrier offers special honeymoon and anniversary packages. They include: accommodations, breakfast and dinner daily in the Main Dining Room with the options of dinner at Sam Snead's at the Golf Club (seasonal), happy hour hors d'oeuvres in the Old White Club, evening first-run movies, dancing, swimming, a historical presentation or interior tour, complimentary champagne, flowers, and a color photograph to cherish the memories.

Rates: Rooms $406–$525; Suites $660–$4,970
    Guest houses $600–$2,000 (based upon season)

THE GREENBRIER
300 West Main Street
White Sulphur Springs, WV 24986

Phone   304-536-1110
Toll free   800-624-6070
Fax   304-536-7854

▬▬▬▬▬

Wisconsin

THE AMERICAN CLUB
Kohler

> O hurry to the ragged wood, for there
> I will drive all those lovers out and cry -
> O my share of the world, O yellow hair!
> No one has ever loved but you and I.
>
> —"The Ragged Wood" by William Butler Yeats

Consistently ranked as one of the top resorts, not just in the Midwest but throughout the country, The American Club offers luxury and elegance in a friendly atmosphere. Looking at the gorgeous landscaping and gardens, and the stately tudor architecture you'd never think that the Club was originally built for the immigrant workers employed by Kohler in 1918. Carefully refurbished in l981, the Club was reopened as a luxury hotel.

The resort area features nine restaurants, four of which are in the Club. The Immigrant Restaurant is the Club's premier dining room. Serving dinner only, the Immigrant features international cuisine and fine wines, and has been named one of the top restaurants in North America. The adjacent Winery is a comfortable place to enjoy cocktails and fine wines by the glass. Live entertainment is offered on the weekends. The Club's original dining room has been transformed into the elegant Wisconsin Room Restaurant, where breakfast, lunch, and dinner are served amid oak paneling, antique chandeliers, leaded glass panels above French Doors, and original tapestries. The Greenhouse is a charming antique solarium brought over from England and reconstructed here. Now it's a delightful cafe in the fountain courtyard,

151

a great place for afternoon and evening refreshments, including a tantalizing variety of desserts, pastries, coffees, and specialty drinks. Health conscious diners can partake at the Jumping Bean, which overlooks the indoor pool. In the summer a floating dining terrace-the Marine Bean-is set on scenic Wood Lake. The Horse and Plow is a casual pub with turn-of-the-century ambiance.

Blackwolf Run, the resort's two eighteen-hole golf courses, offers challenges for duffers of all skill levels. *Golf Digest* ranked the River Course among the top 100 courses in the country, and the fourth best public course. The Blackwolf Run Clubhouse looks out onto panoramic views of the river valley, providing a comfortable atmosphere for year-round dining or relaxing after a game of golf. River Wildlife, the resort's 500-acre wilderness preserve, offers a rustic retreat plus trails and a meandering river for outdoor activities. Sports Core is a private health and racquet club offering a full-service spa, tennis, swimming, and other recreational activities. Nearby are the shops at Woodlake Kohler, offering a variety of specialties in a scenic lakeside setting.

Rates: Rooms $170-$250; Suites $270-460
(based upon season)

THE AMERICAN CLUB
Highland Drive
Kohler, Wisconsin 53044

Phone   920-457-8000
Toll free 800-344-2838
Fax   920-457-0299

GENEVA INN
Lake Geneva

But our love it was stronger by far than the love
Of those who were older than we—
Of many far wiser than we—
And neither the angels in Heaven above,
Nor the demons down under the sea,

Can ever dissever my soul from the soul
Of the beautiful Annabel Lee—
—"Annabel Lee" by Edgar Allan Poe

This charming inn is located roughly halfway between Milwaukee and Chicago and sits directly on the shores of Lake Geneva. The inn has an elegant European feeling to it and features wonderful craftsmanship in every architectural detail. There is even a three-story raised hearth fireplace in the atrium.

The thirty-three guest rooms feature numerous luxury amenities including oversized antique bathtubs or whirlpool baths, four-poster king-sized beds or queen beds, and balconies that provide breathtaking views of the lake. Additional amenities include fluffy bathrobes, televisions with VCRs and cable, and fully stocked honor-bar refrigerators. For that extra touch, ask for the Lakeside Suite which features a two-person whirlpool tub, king-sized bed, and a private balcony overlooking the lake. Guests staying in the suite can finish a perfect day with chocolates and cognac that are left at turndown.

Romantics will delight in a gourmet candlelit dinner at the inn's Grandview Restaurant. Guests can also watch sunsets from a number of vantage points including the patio, pier, or the piano lounge.

There are plenty of activities to enjoy at the lake regardless of the season. Offerings include a twenty-one-mile trail that encircles Lake Geneva, a championship golf course nearby, parasailing and fishing on the lake, and shopping at local boutiques and galleries. Cold weather activities include cross-country skiing, ice-skating, and snowmobiling.

Rates: Rooms $145–$350

GENEVA INN
N2009 State Road 120
Lake Geneva, WI 53147

Phone   414-248-5680
Toll free   800-441-5881
Fax   414-248-5685

NORTHERN SKY RAIL
Milwaukee

> My beloved is mine and I am his,
>   he pastures his flock among the lilies.
> Until the day breathes
>   and the shadows flee,
> turn, my beloved, be like a gazelle,
>   or a young stag upon rugged mountains.
>
> —Song of Solomon, Ch. 2, by King Solomon

During the golden age of rail, there was no higher symbol of prestige then traveling in your own private rail car, and thanks to Northern Sky, you can recapture this elegance. Northern Sky attaches its renovated rail car to Amtrak trains to transport you throughout the nation.

Capable of holding eight guests in its four staterooms, Northern Sky is best enjoyed with other couples. That's because to rent the car for yourself could be cost-prohibitive. Once you get your group together, you'll enjoy a unique experience in luxury transportation. The highlight of the rail car is the domed upper level. Doubling as the dining room, this room offers uninterrupted views of America's countryside and is the perfect room for a romantic meal, be it breakfast, lunch, or dinner. For service, the car comes with a chef who will prepare your gourmet meals and an attendant to see to your every need.

Northern Sky offers several trips to choose from. Some popular ones include Chicago to New Orleans, Chicago to Los Angeles, and Chicago to Washington, DC. Each trip includes all your meals, drinks, and other costs incidental to rail travel like parking and switching fees.

Rates: $500 per person per day based upon
        eight-person occupancy

NORTHERN SKY RAIL
2816 West Grange Avenue
Milwaukee, WI 53221

Phone   800-414-8050

THE SYBARIS
Mequon

> So huge, so hopeless to conceive
> As these that twice befell.
> Parting is all we know of heaven,
> And all we need of hell.
>
> —"My Life Closed Twice Before Its Close"
> by Emily Dickinson

The Sybaris in Mequon is just one cog in this fantasy-themed Midwest hotel chain. Yet thanks to its ten-acre landscaped setting along the Milwaukee River, it stands above the others.

The Sybaris was born in 1974 when Ken Knudson built a custom-designed bedroom for his wife. After completion, several of their friends commented that they too would like to enjoy such extravagance. Thus, Knudson went on to create these fantasies at the Sybaris. In Mequon, you'll be able to choose from several types of rooms ranging from the Victorian whirlpool suite to the swimming pool suite. For the ultimate experience, try the Sybaris Chalet: a private three-level cottage complete with swimming pool and waterslide.

It should be noted that in addition to room rates, the Sybaris charges an annual $30 membership fee. It does this to discourage uncommitted couples from staying at their hotels.

Rates: Membership $30, Rooms $279–$529

THE SYBARIS
10240 Cedarburg Road
Mequon, WI 53092

Phone   414-242-8000
Fax   414-238-0800

Wyoming

TETON PINES RESORT & COUNTRY CLUB
Jackson

> Yet come to me in dreams, that I may live
>   My very life again though cold in death:
> Come back to me in dreams, that I may give
>   Pulse for pulse, breath for breath:
>   Speak low, lean low,
>   As long ago, my love, how long ago.

—"Echo" by Christina Rossetti

Teton Pines Resort & Country Club is an ideal destination, winter or summer, for a romantic interlude. It borders on some of the most beautiful mountains in the world and is convenient to many of Jackson's activities, most notable the Jackson Hole ski area which is just five miles away.

The resort features sixteen spacious, living units. Very similar to a junior suite, the rooms feature cathedral ceilings, dining and sitting areas, wetbar/refrigerators, and his and her baths. Just outside your room, you'll find eighteen championship holes designed by golf legend Arnold Palmer. During the winter, the links are transformed into a scenic 14K of cross-country skiing trails. For more subdued activities, wander about the wilderness of nearby Grand Teton National Park and enjoy a romantic picnic in a striking alpine setting.

Rates: $160–$425 (based upon season)

TETON PINES RESORT & COUNTRY CLUB
3450 North Clubhouse Drive
P.O. Box 14090
Jackson, WY 83002

Phone   307-733-1005

Toll free   800-238-2223
Fax   307-733-2860

THE WILDFLOWER INN
Jackson

> All right, I may have lied to you and about you, and
>   made a few pronouncements a bit too sweeping,
>   perhaps and possibly forgotten to tag the bases
>   here or there,
> And damned your extravagance, and maligned your
>   tastes, and libeled your relatives, and slandered a
>   few of your friends,
> O.K.,
>   Nevertheless, come back.
>   —"Love 20 Cents The First Quarter Mile" by
>   Kenneth Fearing

Four miles from the Jackson Hole ski area lies the
Wildflower Inn. Housed in a log cabin set amidst three
acres of aspens and ponds, the Wildflower Inn offers the
ideal setting for romance.

With only five bedrooms, this charming bed and
breakfast delivers intimacy in the shadows of the
towering Tetons. During the spring and summer, you can
look out your window and enjoy the splendid hues of
acre after acre of wildflowers. If you're able to rise early
enough, grab your camera and leave the comfort of your
charming room, for nearby you'll be able to observe
many of nature's most beautiful creatures like elk, moose,
bears, and bald eagles. To see these creatures in their
natural habitats reminds you that you are in a northern
version of Eden.

Rates: $120–$170

THE WILDFLOWER INN
P.O. Box 11000
Jackson, WY 83002

Phone   307-733-4710
Fax   307-739-0914

Puerto Rico

HORNED DORSET PRIMAVERA HOTEL
Rincon

> How many loved your moments of glad grace,
> And loved your beauty with love false or true;
> But one man loved the pilgrim soul in you,
> And loved the sorrows of your changing face.
>
> —"When You Are Old" by William Butler Yeats

Built in 1988, the Horned Dorset Primavera Hotel stands astride steep hills overlooking the beautiful Caribbean Sea. Named after a breed of English sheep, the hotel's architecture is classic Spanish neo-Colonial.

The Primavera does not specialize in activities. Besides its secluded beach, its only other amenities are a pool and a delightful restaurant. What the hotel does specialize in is luxurious serenity. The thirty suites feature four-poster mahogany beds, sumptuous baths, and panoramic views. Be sure to bring books, for your room will not have a television, a telephone, or even a radio. Also, don't expect to bring your children. The hotel allows no guest under the age of twelve and doesn't offer much for older children.

Rates: $280–$800

HORNED DORSET PRIMAVERA HOTEL
Rte. 429
Box 1132
Rincon 00742, Puerto Rico

Phone	787-823-4030
Fax	787-823-5580

Anguilla

CAP JULUCA
Maundays Bay

> For each glance of the eye so bright and black,
>   Though I keep with heart's endeavor,—
> Your voice, when you whisk the snowdrops back,
>   Though it stay in my soul for ever!—
>   —"The Lost Mistress" by Robert Browning

This five-star resort of white stucco buildings, soaring Moorish arches, whitewashed domes, parapets, and turrets will have you believing that you're at some Moroccan oasis. The resort is as visually enchanting as it is elegantly romantic and perhaps this explains why it is one of the most photographed resorts in the world.

Cap Juluca is situated on a 180-acre peninsula on its own sheltered bay that looks out to St. Martin. Lush tropical gardens surround the luxurious beachfront property.

There are seventy-one guest accommodations that are a romantic's fantasy. Each of the two-story villas contains three to four guest quarters apiece and all offer a very private setting thanks to some thoughtful landscaping. Guest rooms have a large sitting area, bedroom, dressing area, and bath.

Step up to the suites, and the list of amenities expands significantly. For instance, junior suites have large sitting areas, and a separate marbled bathroom with tub for two complete with terry-cloth pillows. These same bathrooms also feature a glass-walled walk-through shower which opens to a walled solarium suitable for air drying or tanning *au naturel*. In addition, you'll find terry-cloth robes, a king-sized bed on a dais, ceiling fans, air-conditioning, refrigerator, and icemaker. Make your way through the sliding doors and you'll find yourself standing on a private covered seaside patio. There's even

International

159

a complimentary bottle of rum awaiting you on arrival and Godiva chocolates on the pillows at turndown service. Breakfast arrives on your patio each morning at the time you designate.

Larger suites have one to five bedrooms with varying amenities such as a private pool, full kitchen, dining atrium, and oceanview dining terrace.

Guests can also take a dip in the resort's freshwater pool or enjoy the spa and workout room.

Cap Juluca is a romantic's dream!

Rates: Rooms $275–$595; Suites $425–$2,775

CAP JULUCA
P.O. Box 240
Anguilla, British West Indies

Phone	264-497-6666
Toll free	800-323-0139
Fax	264-497-6617

Antigua

CARLISLE BAY CLUB
St. Mary's Parish

> Her lips suck forth my soul: see, where it flies!
> Come, Helen, come, give me my soul again.
> Here will I dwell, for heaven is in these lips,
> And all is dross that is not Helena.

> —"The Face Of Helen" from *Dr. Faustus* by
> Christopher Marlowe

Wonderfully laid-back Carlisle Bay sits on the south shore of Antigua. Once a coconut plantation, this idyllic resort is now home to fifty-five spacious suites. Upon entering your suite, you'll notice the bedroom and its king-sized bed off to your left. The hallway then opens up into a glorious living room with the kitchen tucked in the rear corner of the space. Light spills in from the terrace which is furnished with table and chairs perfect for private and romantic al fresco dining.

Carlisle Bay's beach is famous for its beauty and safety. Its white sand contrasts against the sparkling blue Caribbean. The sand barely descends under the water and the result is a swimming area perfect for wading, swimming, or snorkeling. Immensely popular with the English, Carlisle Bay is also the site of frequent croquet tournaments. At night, you'll often find festive barbecues here complete with steel drum bands.

Rates: $245–$345

CARLISLE BAY CLUB
P. O. Box 1515
St. Mary's Parish
Antigua, West Indies

Phone   268-462-1377
Fax   268-462-1365

Australia

HAYMAN ISLAND RESORT
Hayman Island

> Love hath power over princes
>   And greatest emperors;
> In any provinces,
>   Such is Love's power,
> There is no resisting,
>   But him to obey;
> In spite of all contesting,
>   Love will find out the way.
>
> —"Love Will Find Out The Way" by unknown

Between the north coast of Queensland and the magnificent Great Barrier Reef lies Hayman Island. And on the island is this resort of the same name. Hayman Island Resort's 214 rooms spread out in low, sweeping, terraced wings leaving much of its 900 acres untouched for your enjoyment. Not surprisingly, the rooms at Hayman envelope you in luxury; satellite TV, bathrobes, and terraces are all standard.

With its island location and proximity to the Great Barrier Reef, Hayman Island Resort is able to offer the complete spectrum of water activities. If you're certified, you can scuba dive at the Great Barrier Reef. If you're not, the resort offers excellent snorkeling. And there's whale watching here from July to mid-September when humpbacks migrate from Antarctica to the warmer waters off-shore.

At night, the resort comes alive. There's nightly entertainment in the restaurants and lounges. For an especially romantic meal, try La Fontaine. With a dining room reminiscent of Louis XVI's court, La Fontaine serves exquisite French food using only the freshest ingredients (fresh seafood especially). Live classical and contemporary music serenade guests as you dine on these delectable treats while sipping wine from Hayman's extensive cellar.

Rates: $550

HAYMAN ISLAND RESORT
Hayman Island
Great Barrier Reef
North Queensland, 4801 Australia

Phone   61-79-40-1234
Toll free   800-223-6800
Fax   61-79-40-1234

Bahamas

OCEAN CLUB
Nassau

> Our share of night to bear,
> Our share of morning,
> Our blank is bliss to fill,
> Our blank in scorning.
>
> Here a star, and there a star,
> Some lose their way.
> Here a mist, and there a mist,
> Afterwards—day!
>
> —"The Lovers" by Emily Dickinson

This magnificently restored and exclusive colonial-style resort is a favorite to heads of state and celebrities such as John Travolta, Oprah Winfrey, Kirk Douglas, and Ronald Reagan, who prefer the Ocean Club for its serenity, beauty, and unparalleled service. Pampered service begins the moment you arrive at the Ocean Club. There is someone to open the door of your limo, someone to immediately take your luggage, someone to take your drink order, and someone to direct you to your room. The constant attention makes you feel like royalty.

The hotel offers fifty-nine rooms that vary in size from a suite to a two-bedroom villa. The rooms reflect European elegance with carefully reproduced antique furnishings, chintz fabrics, hand-painted stenciling, and ceiling fans. Spacious balconies afford a view of either the ocean or the vast gardens. Other amenities include large all-marble bathrooms, a twenty-seven-inch television, a mini-bar, bathrobes, scales, ironing board and iron, complimentary bottled water, soaps, and toiletries.

Guests can stroll the Club's Versailles Gardens that feature thirty-five acres of terraced gardens capped by an imported 14th-century cloister purchased from William Randolph Hearst. The more active guests can enjoy tennis at the Paradise Island Tennis Club that features nine lighted courts or play eighteen holes of golf at Paradise Island Golf Club. For those who just want to sun themselves, there is an Olympic-sized pool at the edge of the gardens or a private white-sand beach. Water sports offered include deep-sea fishing, windsurfing, sailing, kayaking, and snorkeling. Scuba diving is available at a sister resort. You also have unlimited access to the facilities at their sister resort, Atlantis, also on Paradise Island, including their casino.

> Rates: Superior $545; Deluxe $645; Superior Suite
> $690; Deluxe Suite $1,060; Villa $1,100

OCEAN CLUB
P.O. Box N-4777
Nassau, Paradise Island, Bahamas

Phone   242-363-3000
Fax   242-363-2424

PINK SANDS
Harbour Island

> Within my reach!
> I could have touched!
> I might have chanced that way!
> Soft sauntered through the village,
> Sauntered as soft away!
>
> —"Almost" by Emily Dickinson

For many romantics, the Bahamas are not their first choice of a destination. They picture the crowded, commercialized streets of Nassau and cringe. Unfortunately, many people fail to realize that the Bahamas' outer islands are among the most attractive and most romantic in the Caribbean. For over forty years, Pink Sands has graced one of these islands while developing a reputation for tranquillity and romance.

Recently renovated, Pink Sands sits amid fifteen acres

of lush, tropical gardens that border a magnificent three-mile stretch of pink-sand beach. Accommodations come in the form of two dozen luxury cottages. Complete with satellite TV and walk-in closets, the cottages also feature ceiling fans, wet bars, tiled baths, and private terraces with teak furniture. These well-appointed rooms make Pink Sands feel more like a private vacation home than a full-time resort.

Activities at Pink Sands have a definite aquatic theme. Of course you can enjoy the sun and surf on the beach or by the freshwater pool. Nearby you'll find scuba outfits and fishing charters. Of special note, Harbour Island offers some of the best bonefishing in the world and is an experience that an angler should not miss. If you tire of the sea, rent a bike or golf-cart (there are no car rentals on Harbour Island) and explore the island's beautiful interior.

For such a small resort, Pink Sands delivers food on a grand scale. Lunch can be had on the beach at the Blue Bar while breakfast and dinner are served at the Club House. Dinner at the Club House is a romantic's delight. You'll enjoy a fabulous four-course meal as you dine by candlelight in an al fresco garden setting.

Rates: $500–$600

PINK SANDS
P.O. Box 87
Harbour Island, Bahamas

Phone	242-333-2030
Toll free	800-688-7678
Fax	242-333-2060

Barbados

CORAL REEF CLUB
St. James Parish

> Crimson nor yellow rose, nor
> The savour of the mounting sea
> Are worth the perfume I adore
> That clings to thee.
>
> The languid-headed lilies tire,
> The changeless waters weary me.
> I ache with passionate desire
> Of thine and thee.
>
> There are but these things in the world—
> Thy mouth of fire,
> Thy breasts, thy hands, thy hair upcurled,
> And my desire!
>
> —"ΕΡΟΣ Δ'ΑΥΤΕ" by Theodore Wratislaw

On the west coast of Barbados, twelve idyllic acres serve as home to the Coral Reef Club. Guests will find this to be one of the Caribbean's most charming and romantic resorts.

Lodgings at the Coral Reef Club come in the form of sixty-nine lovely two-story cottages. These private retreats are set amidst the gardens surrounding the pink main house and feature terraces, living area, kitchenette, and all the other comforts you would expect of such a well-run operation. When the tradewinds are blowing, turn off the air-conditioning, turn on the ceiling fans, and sleep to the sounds of the nearby ocean. Just a few steps from your cottage, you'll find the pink main house which contains the resort's delightful restaurant.

The hotel's beach is spectacular. Just offshore lies a

coral reef that's perfect for snorkeling or diving. For
something different, try one of the hotel's sea kayaks or
windsurfers.

Rates: $300–$645

CORAL REEF CLUB
St. James Beach
St. James Parish, Barbados, West Indies

Phone	246-422-2372
Toll free	800-525-4800
Fax	246-422-1776

Barbuda

K CLUB
Barbuda

> That I did always love,
> I bring thee proof:
> That till I loved
> I did not love enough.
>
> That I shall love always,
> I offer thee
> That love is life,
> And life hath immortality.
>
> —"Renunciation" by Emily Dickinson

Antigua's tiny sister island seems to be more beach than island, yet it is home to the exclusive K Club, a resort owned and operated by the famous fashion designer Krizia.

Set amid a 230-acre park, the K Club consists of a main building and three dozen cottages. Turquoise and white are the dominant color schemes used, a refreshing sight in the Caribbean where pastel peach and yellow confront you at every turn. The cottages are widely spaced so as to afford guests the ultimate in privacy. Each cottage luxuriously features a shower that opens to the beach so as to prevent you from tracking sand into your room.

The beach at the K Club ranks among the best in the world. It's perfect for swimming and snorkeling. While swimming, you will likely see turtles, tropical fish, and small sharks. Indeed, it's not uncommon for guests to catch their own lobsters while snorkeling and then have the resort's chef prepare these delicacies for dinner. Besides sea-based activities, the resort features tennis, and a nine-hole golf course.

Dining at the K Club is elegantly casual. You almost feel guilty eating Mediterranean food so good that if it were being served elsewhere you would have had to don formal attire. You then realize that dinner is just another feature that makes the K Club magical.

Rates: $500–$1,100

K CLUB
P.O. Box 2288
Barbuda, West Indies

Phone   809-460-0300
Fax   809-460-0305

Bermuda

HARMONY CLUB
Paget

> The Sweeping up the heart,
> And putting love away
> We shall not want to use again
> Until eternity.
>
> —untitled by Emily Dickinson

This lovely two-story pink and white cottage-style hotel was built in the 1930s as a private home. The structure was transformed in 1968 to an adults- and couples-only all-inclusive resort that projects the intimacy of a private country hideaway in a setting of lush gardens. The cedar-paneled interior walls lend an elegant feeling to the hotel.

The seventy-one guest rooms are luxuriously decorated with Queen Anne furnishings. Amenities include hairdryers, bathrobes, and coffeemakers. Almost all of the guest rooms have a patio or balcony. A complimentary bottle of champagne awaits your arrival.

You can relax in the club lounge which features a large-screen television and games, swim in the pool, play tennis on one of their two courts, enjoy an invigorating sauna, or take a soothing dip in the hot tub. Guests wishing to golf have complimentary use of the Belmont Hotel Golf and Country Club. Nightlife and fashionable shops are only minutes away.

Your room fare covers all aspects of your stay, from the airport transfers, to the meals and alcohol, to the two-seat scooters.

Rates: Rooms $519–$723 (3 nights); $692–$964 (4 nights); $1,211–$1,687 (7 nights)

HARMONY CLUB
Box PG 299
Paget PG BX, Bermuda

Phone	441-236-3500
Toll free	888-427-6664
Fax	441-236-2624

Brazil

CAESAR PARK CABO DE SANTO AGOSTINHO
Recife

> My heart would wish it broke before,
> Since breaking then, since breaking then,
> Were useless as next morning's sun,
> Where midnight frosts had lain!
>
> —"Till The End" by Emily Dickinson

Situated on a coconut plantation by the crystal clear waters of the warm Atlantic is Caesar Park Cabo de Santo Agostinho, an idyllic resort that combines modern amenities with picture-perfect beaches.

The Caesar Park hotel is actually a tower consisting of 180 spacious guest rooms. Though not decorated in an elaborate fashion, the rooms do feature a separate living room and terrace. Downstairs you'll find wet and dry saunas, and the outdoor pool and terrace bar overlooking the ocean.

Most importantly, the hotel is near some of the best beaches in South America. It sits by its own wide strip of white sand where you can doze under a palm tree or read a book beneath a gigantic umbrella. In this setting, however, you may wish to simply gaze at the many wondrous colors of the Atlantic. Nearby you'll find the Cabo de Santo Agostinho (Handle of Augustine), a natural land formation that is beautiful in its own right.

Rates: Doubles from $200

CAESAR PARK CABO DE SANTO AGOSTINHO
Av. Bernardo Vieira de Melo, 550
54310-001-Piedade-Recife-PE, Brazil

| Phone | 55-81-468-1255 |
| Fax | 55-81-468-2466 |

Canada

BANFF SPRINGS HOTEL & SPA
Banff

> For a touch of her fingers
> In a darkened room,
> For a searching look.
>
> Take courage, lover!
> Could you endure such grief
> At any hand but hers?

— "Symptoms Of Love" by Robert Graves

Modeled after a Scottish baronial castle, the Banff Springs Hotel sits amid tall pines against the backdrop of the Canadian Rockies. This grand hotel is an international symbol of Canadian hospitality, opulence, and fitness.

Operated as a resort since 1969, the hotel has 828 guest rooms that range from spacious bedrooms to elegant suites. All rooms feature cable TV, telephone, mini-refrigerator, wet bar, and scenic valley or mountain views. Guests who want a maximum of amenities should request a Château Deluxe room which comes standard with a king bed.

A multitude of activities awaits you, whether you remain at the hotel, take an hour drive to Calgary, explore Banff, or drive a few minutes to Lake Louise. Cold weather activities include downhill skiing at the Lake Louise ski area, sleigh rides, dog sledding, tobogganing, skating, and cross-country skiing. Tennis, golf (on the hotel's twenty-seven-hole world-class course), and horseback riding are popular in the warmer months. The hotel also features a bowling center, an Olympic-size indoor pool, and an enormous European-style spa. At the spa, you'll find cascading waterfalls, grand fireplaces, solariums, fourteen private treatment rooms, saunas, a steamroom, masseuse, fitness and cardio strength training, and a beauty salon.

Rates: $117–$240

BANFF SPRINGS HOTEL & SPA
P.O. Box 960
Banff, Alberta, Canada T0L 0C0

Phone   403-762-2211
Fax   403-762-5755

CHÂTEAU LAKE LOUISE
Lake Louise

> Love is not just a function of the eyes.
> Beautiful objects will, of course, inspire
> Possessive urges—you need not despise
> Your taste. But when insatiable desire
> Inflames you for a girl who's out of fashion,
> Lacking in glamour—plain, in fact—that fire
> Is genuine; that's the authentic passion.
> Beauty, though, any critic can admire.
>
> —"Love Is Not" by Marcus Argentarius

This chalet-style 511-room landmark hotel is situated at the end of one of Canada's most famous lakes. The views of Mt. Victoria, Lake Louise, and Victoria Glacier are spectacular, whether you're looking from the arched windows in the Lakeview Lounge or from in front of the hotel at water's edge.

The grand three-story hotel lobby makes quite an impression on first-time visitors with its broad vistas and elegant decor. Half of the rooms at this recently refurbished hotel look out on the lake while the other half offer enchanting views of the surrounding peaks in the Rockies.

Guest rooms feature mini-bars, cable TV, and private baths. You may want to splurge and request a duplex suite for added comfort. These suites have two bathrooms, a dining area for four, and a balcony off the upstairs bedroom.

As with other regional Canadian Pacific Hotel properties (the Banff Springs Hotel and the Jasper Park Lodge),
the list of guest activities year-round is virtually limitless.
Cross-country skiing on spectacular Nordic trails, dog
sledding, tobogganing, heli-skiing, and nightly ice-
skating on the oval in front of the hotel are some of the
many wintertime activities. Downhill skiers will delight
in some of the best slopes in North America when they
visit the Lake Louise ski area. Romantics should opt for a
cozy ride up the valley in a sleigh pulled by Belgian Cross
horses.

In warmer weather, guests can rock-climb, hike the
area's many trails (including the one along Lake Louise
that ultimately makes its way up the side of Mt. Victoria),
horseback ride, white-water raft, bike, play tennis, and
fish.

Rates: $81–$113

CHÂTEAU LAKE LOUISE

Lake Louise
Banff National Park
Alberta, Canada T0L 1E0

Phone	403-522-3511
Toll free	800-441-1414
Fax	403-522-3834

JASPER PARK LODGE

Jasper

> Love's not Time's fool, though rosy lips and cheeks
> Within his bending sickle's compass come;
> Love alters not with his brief hours and weeks,
> But bears it out even to the edge of doom.
> If this be error and upon me proved,
> I never writ, nor no man ever loved.
>
> —"Let Me Not" by William Shakespeare

This infamous resort is nestled in 1,000 acres of
Canada's largest mountain park and situated on the

shores of Lac Beauvert. Guests are treated to a beautifully surreal landscape of lofty peaks, cascading waterfalls, and crystal clear lakes.

A variety of guest accommodations are available in 440 rooms in dozens of cedar chalets that surround the log-hewn main lodge. Your choices range from standard rooms with queen beds to deluxe rooms with king or queen beds, lake views, and a sitting area or patio. A number of suites are also available, and each features a jacuzzi bathtub, sitting room, a variety of bed sizes, and a fireplace or wood-burning stove. The suites have either a view of the mountains or the lake. Guests looking for the extra-romantic touch should ask for the Honeymoon Cabin which offers a unique hideaway settled into a corner of the property. The Cabin provides a living room, fireplace, spacious jacuzzi tub, and bedroom.

An exhaustive list of activities awaits you at Jasper Park Lodge including tennis, golfing, hiking, biking, boating or canoeing, fishing, horseback riding, white-water rafting, helicopter sightseeing, high country heli-hiking, and swimming in a year-round heated pool. The winter months offer guests the opportunity for downhill and cross-country skiing, skating on Lac Beauvert, snowmobiling, dog sledding, or riding in a horse-drawn sleigh.

Guests can also enjoy a full complement of exercise equipment at the health club and wind down the experience with a massage at the sports massage center.

Rates: Rooms $104–$488; Suites $192–$610
(rates dependent upon time of year)

JASPER PARK LODGE
P.O. Box 40
Jasper, Alberta, Canada T0E 1E0

Phone   403-852-3301
Fax   403-852-5107

PAN PACIFIC HOTEL
Vancouver

> But true Love is a durable fire
>> In the mind ever burning;
> Never sick, never old, never dead,
>> From itself never turning.
>
> —"Walsinghame" by Walter Raleigh

The award-winning Pan Pacific Hotel with its sleek and sophisticated look sits atop Canada Place on a pier next to the financial and entertainment districts. The downtown waterfont location provides stunning vistas of the harbor and mountains for all of the hotel's 467 guest rooms and thirty-nine suites.

The lobby atrium makes a grand statement with its totem pole and waterfall. Walls of glass at the hotel's award-winning Five Sails restaurant (featured in *Dining by Candlelight*), at the lounge, and at the cafe provide sweeping views of the harbor.

Guest rooms are typical of a luxury hotel chain. Japanese detail and neutral colors add a muted elegance to the rooms. Amenities include in-house movies, cable TV, hair dryer, and bathrobes. Ask for one of the exquisitely-decorated suites if you're looking to make a statement. These spacious quarters feature just about every amenity imaginable and are perfect for a romantic retreat.

Hotel facilities include a health club and spa that offer squash and racquetball courts, massages, an indoor running track, and sprint circuit exercise equipment. There is also an outdoor heated pool and jacuzzi with sun lounges that overlook the harbor.

While essentially a conference center, the location, the efficient and amiable staff, and a suite can make for one very romantic visit.

Rates: $218–$250

PAN PACIFIC HOTEL
300-999 Canada Place
Vancouver, British Columbia, Canada V6C 3B5

Phone   604-689-7777
Toll free   800-810-6888
Fax   604-682-2926

RIPPLECOVE INN
Ayers Cliff

> Therefore the Love which us doth bind
> But Fate so enviously debars,
> Is the conjunction of the mind,
> And opposition of the stars.
>
> —"The Definition Of Love" by Andrew Marvell

Set upon a peninsula overlooking Lake Massawippi in the Eastern Townships of Quebec, the Ripplecove Inn stands as one of Canada's romantic gems. Opened in 1945, Ripplecove built its reputation on the adjacent excellent fishing, but as fishing began to decline, Ripplecove shifted its focus to luxury and became an upscale resort known for fine dining and sumptuous lodging.

All of Ripplecove's rooms exude a romantic ambiance. While all feature designer fabrics, it's best to request a room with a balcony, fireplace, and whirlpool bath. On a cool fall evening, you'll return to your room to find that the thoughtful staff has already begun a fire for your comfort; a luxury that is itself worth the cost of a stay at Ripplecove.

Lake Massawippi still offers excellent fishing though you may not be able to match the catches that are displayed in pictures throughout the hotel. Even if you don't fish, grab a canoe from the inn's beach and enjoy the beauty of this long lake. Equally beautiful, but more dramatic, is the Coaticook Gorge. Just a short drive away, the 165-foot deep gorge spans the Coaticook River and is traversible by the world's longest pedestrian suspension bridge.

Combined with its striking lakeside setting and Victorian ambiance, Ripplecove's dining room serves gourmet cuisine with romantic flair. French cuisine dominates the menu while candles provide the lighting for a divine experience.

Rates: $184–$420

RIPPLECOVE INN
P.O. Box 246
Ayers Cliff, Quebec, Canada J0B 1C0

Phone   819-838-4296
Toll free   800-668-4296
Fax   819-838-5541

▬▬▬▬

VIA RAIL
Vancouver to Halifax

> Who carved Love
>   and placed him by
> this fountain,
>   thinking
> he could control
>   such fire
> with water?
>
> —"A Statue Of Eros" by Zenodotos

Grab a few books, a camera, and jump aboard Via Rail for a transcontinental journey. Traveling from Vancouver to Halifax, Via Rail follows a cross-country route that was completed in 1885 and at the time was called an "act of insane recklessness." Today this trail allows you and your lover to enjoy the solitude of Canada, a country that ranks second in geographic size yet has a population of only 26 million. During your trip, you'll enjoy views of wilderness and countryside that have been largely left untouched.

Via Rail trains offer a wide array of accommodations in their gleaming steel cars. You'll have your choice from basic economy to luxury first-class. For a bit more space and comfort, try a double first-class cabin. It will make your five-day, five-night journey much more enjoyable, and your rate will include your meals and non-alcoholic drinks. You can also wander through the other train cars.

As you travel across Canada, you'll marvel at the beauty of the Rockies, the vastness of the plains, and the lakes of the east. The large-domed observation decks create perfect platforms for taking pictures of the scenery or wildlife-like moose and elk. Meals are delicious and the trains feature a surprisingly deep wine list. After dinner, the observation decks are perfect for star-gazing before you retire to your cabin and let the lazy rocking of the train lull you to sleep.

Rates: $633–$2,352

VIA RAIL
   1161 Hollis Street
   Halifax, Nova Scotia, Canada B3H2P6

   Phone   800-561-3952

Chile

EXPLORA LODGE AT HOTEL SALTO CHICO
Patagonia

> This happy happy love
> Is sieged with crying sorrows,
> Crushed beneath and above
> Between todays and morrows;
> A little paradise
> Held in the world's vice.
>
> —"In Love For Long" by Edwin Muir

At the tip of South America lies Torres del Paine National Park, one of nature's last stands of virgin wilderness. Its white cubical facade contrasts sharply with the green grasses that surround it and the blue waters of Lake Pehoe which it overlooks. It seems as if the architect wanted visitors to remember that this is not their natural habitat. However once you enter the Explora, this feeling recedes into your memory.

The inside of Explora is warm yet airy. Its open modern design is given warmth and character by the extensive use of cypress and other woods. Especially cozy is the bar, where these light woods meet marble and form the perfect place to recount the day's adventures. The hotel's thirty rooms are spacious and appointed with plush carpeting, wicker, imported linens, and goosedown comforters. The bathrooms have floors of Bolivian slate and walls of a variety of cypress that gives off a soft aroma when wet.

When it comes to activities, Explora is not for the sedate. Though you do not have to be a tri-athlete to enjoy Explora, you should enjoy outdoor activities that require some amount of exertion. Explora offers fifteen different excursions. Each of these is rated either easy, medium, or difficult and lasts either a half-day or full day. For example, an "easy" expedition would be a short half-day hike to the peninsula of Lago de Grey. On this hike, you take a suspension bridge to the peninsula where you'll wander through forests and view icebergs as they drift pass the beach. "Difficult" explorations last a full day and require more hiking over more demanding terrain. However, whichever explorations you choose, you will be treated with views of a magnificent landscape that includes mountains, glaciers, icebergs, and the sea.

Rates: Starting at $1,040 for three nights

EXPLORA LODGE

Hotel Salto Chico
Americo Vespucio Sur 80
Piso 5
Las Condes
Santiago, Chile

Santiago Phone	56-2-206-6060
Explora Phone	56-2-699-2922
Fax	56-2-228-4655

HACIENDA LOS LINGUES
Santiago

> Love —thou art deep—
> I cannot cross thee—
> But, were there Two
> Instead of One—
> Rower, and Yacht—some sovereign Summer—
> Who knows—but we'd reach the Sun?
>
> —"Love Thou Art High" by Emily Dickinson

This 450-year-old colonial-style adobe residence is tucked away at the foot of the Andes mountains. Hacienda Los Lingues is Chile's only Relais & Châteaux hotel and was one of Tatler's 101 best hotels in the world in 1996. The historic working farm and horsebreeding facility is part of the Angostura Estate given in 1599 by

King Philip III to the first mayor of Santiago. The property
has been in the same family for over four centuries.

Hacienda Los Lingues offers guests 9,000 acres of
rolling hills and fertile farmlands that serve both as a
playground and a refuge. The main adobe structure with
its broad verandas contains twelve comfortable and
authentic guest quarters. Each unit features hand-carved
period furnishings, oriental rugs, and old-fashioned
baths. Baccarat crystal, exquisite silver and china, oil
paintings, and old family photographs are on display in
the public spaces. A gourmet dinner featuring authentic
Chilean cuisine prepared with a French flair is served in
the formal dining room.

There's plenty of things to do at Hacienda Los
Lingues. Guests can ride horseback or just view the
Aculeguano horses at the breeding farm on the property.
These horses are first cousins of the famed Lippizaner
horses of the Viennese Spanish Riding School. You can
also swim at the outdoor pool or play tennis. Trout
fishing, wind-surfing, water-skiing, and nearby golf are
other enjoyable activities offered.

There are several wineries in the area to visit but you
must remember to bring an English interpreter as many
of the wineries do not have English-speaking guides.

Rates: $435 (double/two nights)

HACIENDA LOS LINGUES
c/o Executive Offices
Av. Providencia Of. 205
Torre C Tajamar
Santiago, 1100 Chile

Phone   56-2-235-5446
Toll free   800-825-2332
Fax   56-2-235-7604

Costa Rica

FINCA ROSA BLANCA
San Jose

> Then be not coy, but use your time,
> And while ye may, go marry:
> For having lost but once your prime,
> You may forever tarry.
>
> —"To The Virgins, To Make Much Of Time" by
> Robert Herrick

When you think of romantic country inns, images of New England or the Smokies come to mind, not Costa Rica. Surprisingly, Costa Rica's Finca Rosa Blanca embodies everything that makes great country inns romantic: intimacy, character, and luxury.

Situated on a high, temperate plateau, Finca Rosa Blanca has six unique rooms which enjoy sweeping views of the valley, coffee plantations, and surrounding mountains. Though each room is different, they do share a couple of unifying themes. Each enjoys cabinets, railings, and floors constructed of fine woods and crafted by the artistic Jampols, a local people of tribal origin. Additionally pre-Columbian artifacts are found throughout the inn. Of the six rooms, the most dramatic is the Rosa Blanca Suite. A spacious duplex boasting a separate living room and wet bar, the Rosa Blanca is high-lighted by the glass-lined canopied tower bedroom. Carved spiral stairs descend from the bedroom to a fantastic bathroom decorated with abundant foliage and murals designed to resemble a jungle. Here you'll find a stone waterfall feeding an extremely large soaking tub. It's the perfect place to bathe with your lover before retiring for a serene night's sleep.

Rates: $175–$225

FINCA ROSA BLANCA (RESERVATIONS)
SJO 1201
P.O. Box 025216
Miami, FL 33102

Phone   506-269-9392
Fax   506-269-9555

HOTEL & BEACH CLUB EL PARADOR
Quepos

> Come quickly—as soon as
> these blossoms open,
> they fall.
> This world exists
> as a sheen of dew on flowers.
>
> —"Come Quickly" by Izumi Shikibu

Hidden away in its own private world of lush jungle and gardens lies Hotel & Beach Club El Parador. El Parador offers romantics a unique combination: Pacific beaches and rainforest. These beautiful pristine beaches back into the rainforest of Manuel Antonio Park. Manuel Antonio's flora and fauna serve as a stage for an abundance of wildlife, most notably monkeys whose chatter fills this lush amphitheater. In addition to the beach and jungle, El Parador can arrange for other activities including sport fishing, white-water rafting, sea kayaking, and even romantic sunset sails.

Back at the hotel, you'll find a collection of fifty-five rooms ranging from standard rooms to the palatial Presidential Suite. Since romance is key, it's best to avoid the standard room and opt for a deluxe room or junior suite. The deluxe rooms are a bit larger than the standard and feature the added luxury of verandas, refrigerators, and tubs. The junior suites enjoy prime views of both the ocean and jungle and offer such luxuries as bathrobes and marble baths with jacuzzi. If you're in the mood to splurge, reserve the Presidential Suite. Actually more of a house, this enormous living compound features three bedrooms, wet bar, dining room, office, kitchen, and leather furnishings.

No matter which room you choose, the most romantic spot at the resort is the infinity pool. At sunset, don your swimsuit, grab a seat at the swim-up bar, order a drink, and enjoy the sunset as the sounds of the jungle increase with the impeding darkness. It's an experience that's somewhat primitive, but extremely romantic.

Rates: $90–$260 (based upon season)

HOTEL & BEACH CLUB EL PARADOR
P.O. Box 284
Quepos, Costa Rica

Phone   506-777-1411
Fax   506-777-1437

TARA
San Antonio de Escazu

> Had we but world enough, and time,
> This coyness, Lady, were no crime.
> We would sit down and think which way
> To walk and pass our long love's day.
>
> —"To His Coy Mistress" by Andrew Marvell

Tara, originally one of Costa Rica's most stately manors, has now become synonymous with luxury, relaxation, and romance. As its name indicates, the hotel is modeled after the extravagant plantation home in *Gone With The Wind*. Its architecture and decor succeed at recreating the graceful feeling of the Old South even at this Central American location.

Nestled high in the Pico Blanco range, Tara enjoys panoramic views of landscaped tropical gardens and the spectacular Central Valley. The green roof of the manor is supported by stylish columns. Inside you'll find a peaceful oasis that will rejuvenate your mind, body, and spirit, for not only is Tara a romantic hotel, it is a world-class spa as well.

Scarlett's Fountain of Youth, the spa at Tara, exists to

make your life more pleasant. Its various treatments are designed to eliminate stress. For an especially romantic experience, order the in-room aromatherapy massage for two. Afterwards you and your lover will be relaxed and ready for a blissful night of sleep wrapped in each other's arms.

Tara offers forty-two guest rooms ranging from standard suites to villas. Each one features the regular amenites, but some do share a balcony. The Superior Suite is particularly romantic. You'll appreciate the additional room and privacy.

Regardless of which room you choose, you will notice Tara's fine service. The attentive staff will pamper you if you let them, or if you're not comfortable with such attentive service, just let them know and they'll try to ease you into it.

Rates: $100–$290

TARA

Apdo. 1459-1250
San Antonio de Escazu, Costa Rica

Phone   506-228-6992
Fax   506-228-9651

England

AMBERLY CASTLE
Near Arundel

> Unlace yourself, for that harmonious chime,
> Tells me from you, that now it is bedtime.
>
> Your gown going off, such beauteous state reveals,
> As when from flowery meads th' hill's shadow steals.
>
> Now off with those shoes, and then safely tread
> In this love's hallow'd temple, this soft bed.
>
> Licence my roving hands, and let them go,
> Before, behind, between, above, below.
>
> To enter in these bonds, is to be free;
> Then where my hand is set, my seal shall be.
> —"To His Mistress Going To Bed" by John Donne

Enclosed by a sixty-foot wall with outlooks and massive fortified gateways is the enchanting Amberly Castle. These features make Amberly unique, but are not the only special assets of this magical abode.

Amberly's fifteen bedrooms are wondrous in their own right. Individually decorated, they feature whirlpool baths and either four-poster or brass beds. Despite being over 900 years old, the castle's public rooms are warm and cozy even with the presence of armor and pikestaffs.

Dinner is taken in the Queens Room restaurant which features a beautiful mural of Catherine of Braganza. Chef Sam Mahoney creates inspired dishes based on carefully researched old English recipes.

Rates: $212–$450

AMBERLY CASTLE

Near Arundel
West Sussex BN18 9ND, England

Phone   44-1798-831992
Fax   44-1798-831998

ATHENAEUM HOTEL & APARTMENTS
London

> Darling, each morning a blooded rose
> Lures the sunlight in, and shows
> Her soft, moist and secret part.
> See now, before you go to bed,
> Her skirts replaced, her deeper red—
> A colour much like yours, dear heart.
>
> —"Corinna In Vendome" by Pierre de Ronsard

This posh five-star family-owned hotel underwent a $12-million renovation a short while ago. The hotel, which overlooks Buckingham Palace and Green Park, has an adjoining enclave of thirty-six apartment units that are virtually a home away from home for a few fortunate guests.

Hotel amenities start off with a uniformed hotel chauffeur who will meet you and your traveling companion at the airport upon arrival. The luxurious hotel guest rooms and suites have monogrammed bedsheets, a private marble bathtub and shower, air-conditioning, direct-dial phones, a CD player, VCR, mini-bar, and a satellite television with Sky Channel and CNN. The much more spacious apartments have one, two, or three bedrooms, fully equipped kitchens, and washers and dryers. International travelers will appreciate the fax/modem capabilities and the USA voltage sockets. Guests who opt for the apartments receive all the benefits and services of the hotel including twenty-four-hour room service.

Guests can relax at the exclusive hotel spa which offers a gymnasium, sauna, steam room, whirlpool, and treatment room.

Rates: One-bedroom apartments $505;
Two-bedroom apartments $750

ATHENAEUM HOTEL & APARTMENTS
116 Piccadilly
London W1V OBJ, England

Phone	44-0-171-499-3464
Toll free	800-335-3300
Fax	44-0-171-493-1860

CLIVEDEN
near Maidenhead

> Tonight I can write the saddest lines.
> I loved her, and sometimes she loved me too.
>
> Through nights like this one I held her in my arms.
> I kissed her again and again under the endless sky.
>
> She loved me, sometimes I loved her too.
> How could one not have loved her great still eyes.
>
> Tonight I can write the saddest lines.
> To think that I do not have her. To feel that I have
>   lost her.
>
> —"Tonight I Can Write" by Pablo Neruda

This palatial mansion-estate set on 375 acres of formal gardens and parkland overlooking the River Thames is Britain's highest rated hotel. Cliveden is the former home of the Prince of Wales, three Dukes, and the Astor family, and it has been at the center of British social and political life for over three centuries—so expect to literally be treated like royalty.

Cliveden's thirty-eight elegantly appointed rooms are decorated with antiques, rich fabrics, and amenity-laden baths. Hallways feature gilded portraits, tapestries, museum-quality art, and rich paneling.

Recreational venues offered to guests include indoor

and outdoor pools, indoor and outdoor tennis courts, a squash court, a hot tub, and a health and beauty spa complete with a fitness gym, and treatment and massage rooms. River cruises, horseback riding, and golf are available by arrangement.

For dinner, try the hotel's Michelin-starred restaurant, Waldo's. This elegant dining room offers attentive service, superb cuisine, and a renowned wine cellar.

Rates: Rooms $365–$655

CLIVEDEN
Taplow
Buckinghamshire SL6 0JF, England

Phone	44-1628-668561
Toll free	800-747-6917
Fax	44-1628-661837

HAMBLETON HALL
Oakham

> But I can find no lilies,
>   Green herbs are all I bring.
> Yet love makes vetches roses,
>   And in their shadowing
> Hide violets fair.
>
> —"To The Lady Radegund, With Violets" by
>   Venantius Fortunatus

Hambleton Hall exudes the charm of the English countryside. Located next to Rutland Water, Britain's largest man-made lake, the gabled facade of this 1881 manor is stately without being ostentatious. The beautiful gardens surrounding the inn add to its appeal and give the brick-and-stone structure a vibrancy that would otherwise be lacking.

Inside this magnificent country inn, you will find fifteen romantic bedrooms and one of England's best restaurants. Each bedroom is individually decorated though they all have an elegant country theme. Their flowering chintzes and fabrics, stripes and soft colors soothe the soul.

Unlike many inns in Britain, Hambleton Hall has pursued fine dining since it began welcoming guests. Its restaurant has won several awards and is now run by Chef Aaron Patterson. The bar with its dark-red lacquer walls and warming fireplace is the perfect spot to enjoy a drink before, or after, dinner. Patterson's seasonal creations use only the finest local ingredients. Thus in the summer, fruit and salads are especially tasty while game dominates the winter menu. To complement your meal, choose from an eclectic mix of over 450 wines.

Rates: $345–$465

HAMBLETON HALL
Oakham
Leicestershire LE15 8TH, England

Phone   44-1572-756991
Fax   44-1572-724721

HOLLINGTON HOUSE HOTEL
Newbury

> One evening the west wind comes bringing showers,
> Scaring, stripping bare flowers, a melancholy pale
>   red.
> Boat prows sever lotus stems, but strands unseen hold
>   fast,
> For lotus roots, lotus seeds, preserve a mutual bond.
> His heart is like the moon, a moon not yet on the
>   wane,
> Clear, bright and full of mid-month days.
>
> —"A Song of Chang Ching-Yuan Picking Lotus
>   Flowers" by Wên T'ing-Yün

Built in 1904, Hollington House Hotel opened as one of England's foremost country-house hotels in 1992. Set in twenty-five acres of woodland gardens, the hotel is adjacent to 250 acres of parkland. Australia's John and Penny Guy run the hotel, and it has a decidedly relaxed and informal atmosphere.

As with many country inns, Hollington House is intimate. Yet its twenty rooms stand above the rest. These luxurious sanctuaries are individually decorated with period antiques and paintings. The spacious bathrooms feature double-headed showers, whirlpool tubs, oversized towels, and robes.

The hotel's public rooms match the charm of the bedrooms. A roaring fire warms the entrance hall and fresh flowers accent the parlors with their deep, comfortable sofas and chairs. The oak-paneled dining room features many traditional dishes and an award-winning wine cellar.

During the day, you can wander about the countryside. The adjacent park is a tranquil oasis perfect for a picnic lunch. If you're looking for something more active, enjoy a game of tennis on the hotel's courts. Afterwards you can take a dip in the outdoor pool, or the indoor pool if the weather refuses to cooperate.

Perhaps Dick Enberg best describes Hollington House. "Not another structure to be seen. Candlelight dinners… need more be said."

Rates: $290–$620

HOLLINGTON HOUSE HOTEL
Church Road
Wolton Hill
Nr. Newbury
Berkshire RG20 9XA, England

Phone   44-1635-255100
Fax   44-1635-255075

LE MANOIR AUX QUAT' SAISONS
Great Milton

You, and only you, I shall glorify in my poems,
As a woman has never been able to do.
And you remember the beloved
For whose eyes you created this paradise,

But I deal in rare commodities—
I sell your love and tenderness.

> —"I Will Leave Your White House" by Anna
>   Akhmatova

Set in secluded private grounds seven miles south of the historic city of Oxford is Le Manoir aux Quat' Saisons. Its rural countryside setting forms the perfect base for exploring the Cotswolds' charming villages or visiting Blenheim Palace.

Understated elegance describes the atmosphere at Le Manoir. All nineteen bedrooms, spread throughout the main house and the converted stables, deliver comfort and luxury. Fresh-cut flowers and attractive, antique furniture fill every room, while some even have their own terraced garden.

Gardens surround the 15th century manor house. Immaculately cared for, the gardens give the grounds an elegant texture. Most importantly, the walled garden outside the kitchen yields fresh herbs and vegetables for the award-winning restaurant.

The manor's proprietor Raymond Blanc and head chef Jonathan Wright oversee the kitchen. Blanc, whose role in the kitchen is that of executive chef, began the hotel's culinary tradition of excellence, and Wright sees to it that this tradition is maintained. The flavor-infused dishes use only the freshest products prepared with precise techniques. As a result, guests are rewarded with delicious meals, served by a gracious staff in a romantic setting.

Rates: $285–$2,245

LE MANOIR AUX QUAT' SAISONS
Church Road
Great Milton
Oxford
Oxfordshire OX44 7PD, England

Phone   44-1844-278881
Fax   44-1844-278847

THE LEONARD
London

> 'Write all my whispers down,'
> She cries to her true love.
> 'I believe, I believe, in the moon!—
> What weather of heaven is this?
>
> 'The storm, the storm of a kiss.'
>
> —"Her Words" by Theodore Roethke

The Leonard is comprised of four late-18th-century Georgian townhouses that were converted into a luxurious oasis located off stylish Portman Square. The lounge and bar are elegantly decorated with antiques and fresh flowers. The extensive reconstruction created five rooms and twenty suites that are exquisitely decorated with rich fabrics and antiques and feature every conceivable amenity.

All rooms are air-conditioned and include full marble baths, a mini-bar, satellite TV, video, CD player, and a fax/modem port. Some of the larger suites have a butler's pantry or a fully-equipped kitchen. Room service is available around the clock.

Several fine restaurants are within a short walk from the Leonard.

Rates: $284–$297

THE LEONARD
15 Seymour Street
London W1H 5AA, England

Phone   44-171-935-2010
Fax   44-171-935-6700

LORDS OF THE MANOR
Upper Slaughter

> And thawing of the Andes melts in kisses
> and mornings on the steppe, beneath the dominion
> of stars that fall in dust, as night goes stumbling
> with bleat growing ever paler, through the village.
>
> And round the straw bed's fevered pain breathe all
> the exhalations of the ancient pit
> and all the vestry's gloomy vegetation.
> And chaos splashes up out of the jungle.
>
> —"Darling, It's Frightening" by Boris Pasternak

This beautifully preserved 17th-century former rectory is set quietly amid eight acres of parkland with a lake and formal gardens on the edge of the picturesque village of Upper Slaughter.

Guest rooms vary in size and all are handsomely decorated with traditional chintz and fine period pieces. Some of the rooms have four-poster beds, and satellite TV is available. The hotel's public rooms are comfortably furnished and guests have a choice of sitting rooms for relaxation.

The elegant and spacious dining room overlooks the walled gardens and terrace and offers excellent cuisine and an extensive selection of wines.

Fishing and croquet are offered at the hotel. Sightseers can visit nearby Blenheim Palace, the Roman City of Bath, the gardens of Hidcote and Kiftsgate, and Stratford-upon-Avon.

Rates: $205–$380

LORDS OF THE MANOR
Upper Slaughter
Cheltenham, Gloucestershire GL54 2JD, England

Phone   44-1451-820243
Fax   44-1451-820696

THE MILLSTREAM HOTEL & RESTAURANT
Bosham

> You are taken in the net of my music, my love,
> and my nets of music are wide as the sky.
> My soul is born on the shore of your eyes of mourning.
> In your eyes of mourning the land of dreams begins.
>
> —"In My Sky At Twilight" by Pablo Neruda

The Millstream Hotel & Restaurant is located in the lovely little village of Bosham on the banks of Chichester Harbour. Comprised of an 18th century malthouse and adjoining cottages linked to the Grange (a small English manor house), the Millstream offers adorable rooms. Accented by chintz fabrics and pastel decor, the rooms have cane and pine furnishings whose light color projects a pleasant warmth. The marble bathrooms are simply luxurious. Though the climate is mild, summer guests should request a room with air-conditioning to guard against the rare hot night.

The candlelit restaurant concentrates on using fresh, local ingredients to create simple yet tasteful dishes. Some of the fresh herbs used come from the garden situated by the stream that runs in front of the hotel. The restaurant, popular with locals as well as hotel guests, allows you to experience the true charm of Bosham and its inhabitants

Rates: $178–$185

THE MILLSTREAM HOTEL & RESTAURANT
Bosham Lane
Bosham PO18 8HL, England

Phone   44-1243-573234
Fax   44-1243-573459

THORNBURY CASTLE
Thornbury

> My downfall: those pink articulate lips
> Divinely flavoured petals to a mouth
> Where soul dissolves… eyes darting
> Beneath black brows, snares for the heart,
> And the milk-white breasts, well shaped,
> The twin rosebuds, fair and beyond other flowers.
>
> —"My Downfall" by Dioskorides

Experience a sliver of England's rich history at Thornbury Castle. In 1511, Edward Stafford, 3rd Duke of Buckingham, began construction on his castle, but ten years later he was beheaded for treason. The castle was never completed but parts of it were livable and hosted the likes of Mary Tudor. Henry VIII stayed here with Anne Boleyn.

Today Thornbury Castle welcomes guests to stay in one of its eighteen rooms and dine at its magnificent restaurants. Stylish fabrics decorate the spacious rooms filled with carved canopy-beds and offering views overlooking the vineyard and England's oldest Tudor garden. Downstairs you can relax by a fireplace in one of the many candlelit salons or enjoy a delicious meal created by Chef Steven Black. Black, now regarded as one of England's best, takes care in preparing his meals and it shows.

Nearby you'll find the lovely seaside town of Bristol. England's first resort town offers numerous shops and a not too shabby nightlife during the high season.

Rates: $370

THORNBURY CASTLE
Castle Street
Thornbury Nr. Bristol
South Gloucestershire BS12 1HH, England
Phone   44-1454-281182
Fax   44-1454-416188

France

CHÂTEAU DU DOMAINE SAINT-MARTIN
Vence

> Your presence here is like a call
> to sit down hastily at midday,
> to read it through from A to Z
> and then write your nearness in it.
>
> —"You're Here" by Boris Pasternak

This Relais & Châteaux property is built atop a hill once occupied by the Knights Templar and legend has it that they buried a treasure here. The real treasure is this Mediterranean-style château garden enclave known as Château du Domaine Saint-Martin that is just twenty minutes from Cannes and Nice.

The château is surrounded by thirty-five acres of well-kept lawns, olive groves, and rose gardens that add to its magnificence.

You will find nothing but old-world refinements here. The thirty-five rooms and junior suites are lavishly decorated with marble floors, antique furnishings, Persian carpets, priceless artwork, and grand private verandas.

Leisure activities include tennis, golf, art museums, sightseeing, or shopping in the nearby town of St. Paul de Vence.

Rates: Rooms and Junior Suites $530–$755

CHÂTEAU DU DOMAINE SAINT-MARTIN
avenue des Templiers
F-06142 Vence Cedex, France

Phone   33-4-93-58-02-02

CHÂTEAU EZA
Eze-Village

> Lying on the bed you sleep.
> Closed eyes unable to conceal your beauty,
> Face clean and pure, needing no adornments.
> You suspend time,
> And for just a moment the whole world is perfect.
> Alas, I must leave for work,
> Trying to remember perfection with an imperfect
>   mind.
>
> —"Tina" by Brent Ruhkamp

This intimate and eminently romantic castle-hotel is the former private residence of H.R.H. Prince William of Sweden. This enchanting spot clings to the rock walls of the 1,000-year-old medieval village of Eze, 1,500 feet above the Mediterranean.

Each of the ten newly decorated guest lodgings are furnished with exquisite antiques, Oriental rugs, timber beams, stone fireplaces, and private balconies that offer breathtaking views of the Côte d'Azur. Every modern comfort has been worked into the rooms including a VCR and CNN.

Guests should visit the ornate gourmet restaurant and scenic dining terrace complete with eagle's nest.

Rates: Rooms $460; Seaview Room $545;
    Seaview Suite $630

CHÂTEAU EZA
rue de la Pise
06360 Eze-Village
Côte d'Azur, France

Phone   33-4-93-41-12-24
Fax   33-4-93-41-16-64

GRAND HOTEL DU CAP-FERRAT
Saint-Jean-Cap-Ferrat

> Here is her portrait, gazing sidelong at me,
> The hair in disarray, the young eyes pleading:

'And you love? As unlike those other men
As I those other women?'

—"The Portrait" by Robert Graves

This glamorous and exclusive hotel is hidden away amid a spectacularly landscaped fourteen-acre private park overlooking the Mediterranean at the tip of Cap Ferrat. The marble lobby and flowering promenades lend an elegant yet relaxed atmosphere to the Riveria's premier hotel.

The traditionally furnished fifty-seven guest rooms feature an abundance of amenities and offer breathtaking vistas of the sea, tropical gardens, or woodlands.

A suspended cable car will take you down the cliff to an Olympic-sized saltwater pool that seems to drop right off into the Mediterranean. There is also an alfresco poolside bar and restaurant.

Tennis and water sports are some of the typical leisure activities offered at the hotel.

Rates: Rooms $490–$595; Terrace Rooms and Suites, prices available upon request

GRAND HOTEL DU CAP-FERRAT

71 boulevard General de Gaulle
06230 Saint-Jean-Cap-Ferrat, France

Phone   33-4-93-76-50-50
Fax   33-4-93-76-04-52

HÔTEL DE PARIS
Monte Carlo

'Tis this—invites—appalls—endows—
Flits—glimmers—proves—dissolves—
Returns—suggests—convicts—enchants—
Then—flings in Paradise—

—"The Love A Life Can Show" by Emily Dickinson

The Hôtel de Paris is one of Europe's last grand hotels. This hotel, located in the heart of Monte Carlo, exudes gold-plated charm and has hosted the rich and famous for over a century.

The posh 200 guest rooms are decorated with period furnishings and marble baths. Make certain that you ask for a balcony suite with breathtaking views of the Riviera.

The hotel features a cliffside heated pool and a state-of-the-art health club. Other hotel charms include Rococo public salons and the Louis XV restaurant with its superb cuisine and extensive wine cellar. There is also an award-winning rooftop grill for a more relaxed atmosphere.

> Rates: Rooms $405-475; Junior Suite $610–$715;
> Full Suite, prices upon request

HÔTEL DE PARIS
Place du Casino
98007 Monte Carlo, Monaco

Phone	377-92-16-30-00
Toll free	800-221-4708
Fax	377-92-16-38-49

HÔTEL RITZ
Paris

> I love to hear her speak, yet well I know
> That music hath a far more pleasing sound;
> I grant I never saw a goddess go;
> My mistress, when she walks, treads on the ground.
>> And yet, by heaven, I think my love as rare
>> As any she belied with false compare.
>
>> —"My Mistress' Eyes Are Nothing Like The Sun" by
>> William Shakespeare

This venerable and opulent hotel located in chic Place Vendome introduced the adjective "ritzy" into the English vocabulary. The Ritz has been the choice of the most demanding international travelers since it opened its doors in 1898. Every aspect of this grand hotel—accommodations, amenities, service, and dining—is of the highest caliber.

The posh interior is adorned with gilt and crystal chandeliers, silk, and tapestries. There are 142 rooms and forty-five suites that are named after former residents of the Ritz such as Marcel Proust and Coco Chanel. All the guest rooms and public areas are decorated in Louis XV and Louis XVI period furniture. The guest rooms have a mini-bar, wet bar, an enormous whirlpool tub, balcony or patio, fireplace, hair dryer, and safe.

Guests can enjoy the hotel's health club and relax with a massage or sauna. The Louvre, Tuileries, and fashionable shops are all nearby.

Guests should make a point of dining at the two-Michelin-star L'Espadon. This gastronomic delight features the cuisine of Chef Auguste Escoffier who is known as the "king of chefs and the chef of kings." There's also the Hemingway Bar, whose namesake used to frequent this cozy and elegant spot.

Rates: Rooms $495–$525 (single), $595–$665 (double)

HÔTEL RITZ
15 pl. Vendome
75001 Paris, France

Phone	33-1-43-16-30-30
Toll free	800-223-6800
Fax	33-1-43-16-36-68

██████

LA RESERVE DE BEAULIEU
Beaulieu-sur-Mer

> Who shall hear of us
> in the time to come?
> Let him say there was
> a burst of fragrance
> from black branches.
>
> —"Love Song" by William Carlos Williams

This Italian Renaissance-inspired villa is the gem of the French Riviera. Created in 1880, this rose-pink villa offers luxuriously intimate accommodations for a handful of fortunate guests.

Elegance, refinement, pleasant living, and comfort are all factors that influenced the decoration of the thirty-six bedrooms and nine suites of this beautiful Florentine residence. The rooms are appointed in rich fabrics and period furniture, and offer remodeled marble baths.

Other hotel amenities include a heated saltwater pool and a sundeck that looks onto the beach. There's also a sauna and a massage room.

Diners should visit the gourmet restaurant and terrace that overlook the Mediterranean. The cuisine here is top-notch and the experience memorable.

Rates: Rooms $390–$560; Junior Suites $595–$715

LA RESERVE DE BEAULIEU
5 boulevard General Leclerc
06310 Beaulieu-sur-Mer, France

Phone   33-4-93-01-00-01
Fax   33-4-93-01-28-99

SAINT JAMES PARIS
Paris

Love is a child and does not hide the truth:
You may be proud, and rich in beauty too,
But not enough to scorn a heart that's true;
I can't re-enter April and my youth.
Grey though my head is now, love me today,
And I shall love you when your own is grey.

—"Sonnet for Helen" by Pierre de Ronsard

This lovely 100-year-old château-hotel is the only château in Paris and is particularly unique for the walled garden that surrounds it. The interior has a gentrified club-like appearance to it but the large and attentive staff make you feel at home.

Saint James Paris has forty-eight guest rooms and suites which are spacious, quiet, and air-conditioned. The rooms are decorated in either art deco or a more traditional style with flowers and plants. Bathrooms feature a lovely gray mosaic tile.

The public areas are magnificent. You'll love the beautiful library bar and restaurant that is available for guests only. You can enjoy a romantic meal in the walled gardens during the warmer months.

Sightseeing is certainly an option for guests with the Arc de Triomphe just a few minutes away. Relax in the sauna or jacuzzi in the luxurious health club after a long, activity-filled day.

Rates: Rooms $260–$326; Suites $425–$620

SAINT JAMES PARIS
43 Avenue Bugeaud
75116 Paris, France

Phone   33-1-44-05-81-81
Fax   33-1-44-05-81-82

French Polynesia

BORA BORA LAGOON RESORT
Bora Bora

> Awakening spring: how many leaves!
> Rustling dawn: how many branches!
> Does she know the pangs of love?
> Never a time she wouldn't dance.
>
> —"Willow" by Li Shang-Lin

Bora Bora is French Polynesia's (aka Tahiti) most beautiful island. Located in a fabulous lagoon lies Bora Bora Lagoon Resort. Here you'll be able to view magnificent coral reefs and the island's mist-enshrouded peaks. To complement this natural beauty, the Bora Bora Lagoon Resort has created heavenly rooms from which you can enjoy a variety of activities.

Lodging at Bora Bora Lagoon Resort comes in the form of eighty thatched roof villas, fifty of which are built over the lagoon. It's these villas that are the most romantic. Like the other bungalows, they feature high-peaked ceilings with exposed beams, soft soothing color schemes, sitting areas, and private sundecks. Yet unlike the others, their sundecks have stairs descending right into the lagoon and their sitting areas feature illuminated glass coffee tables. At night, you can turn on the table and observe the marine life below. In fact, you can move the table and feed tropical fish right from your own sofa, an experience that is as surreal as it is romantic.

Also perched over the water is the resort's equally romantic restaurant. It's the perfect place to enjoy a brilliant sunset.

Rates: $547–$863

BORA BORA LAGOON RESORT
Motu Toopua
B.P. 175
98730 Vaitape
Bora Bora, French Polynesia

Phone 689-604001
Fax 689-604003

HOTEL BORA BORA
Bora Bora

> What happens afterwards, none need enquire:
> They are poised there in conjunction, beyond time,
> at an oak-tree top level with Paradise.
>
> —"Conjunction" by Robert Graves

Paradise. That one word best describes the Hotel Bora Bora. Situated on Point Raititi, Hotel Bora Bora hugs the shores of a crystal clear lagoon. Perched over this lagoon are a handful of the fifty-five thatched roof bungalows that serve as the accommodations at Hotel Bora Bora. Though the over-water bungalows are the most sought after, all the bungalows at Hotel Bora Bora are romantic. Some are located on the beach, while others are nestled among the resort's lush tropical gardens. Each bungalow is quite spacious featuring a bedroom, living room, bathroom, and sundeck; eight have their own private pool. The furnishings are simple yet elegant and the canopied beds are especially romantic.

If you manage to leave your bungalow, you'll be amazed by the natural beauty that surrounds the resort. The white-sand beach is perfect for tanning. Filled with neon-colored fish, the lagoon is great for swimming, snorkeling, or diving. You can sail to nearby islands on the resort's fifty-foot catamaran, enjoy a lovely sunset cruise, or partake in exciting saltwater flyfishing.

The Matira Terrace Restaurant overlooks the lagoon and serves breakfast and casually elegant dinners. During the day, you can have a boxed lunch prepared for you or sit down at the Pofai Beach Bar for food and drink. At night, you can stroll along the beach hand in hand with your lover as the stars' reflections dance in the water and you hope that your vacation never ends.

Rates: $415–$736

HOTEL BORA BORA
Point Raititi
B.P. 1
Bora Bora, French Polynesia

Phone   689-604460
Toll free   800-421-1490
Fax   689-604466

Germany

BRENNER'S PARK HOTEL & SPA
Baden-Baden

> Then Phyllis slightly raised her head
> (her lips were full & wet & red)
> to kiss the sweet eyes full of her:
> 'Corydon mine, with me prefer
> always serve unique Amor:
> my softer flesh the fire licks
> more greedily and deeper sticks.'
>
> —"Phyllis and Corydon" by Catullus

This stately 19th-century health-spa and hotel has won international acclaim as Europe's premier resort spa. The tranquil setting in its own park in the Black Forest facing the River Oos and the variety of leisure activities have attracted a loyal following for the hotel.

Brenner's Park Hotel & Spa has seventy elegantly decorated guest rooms and thirty-two suites. The spacious salons are filled with antiques that enhance the elegant old-world ambiance.

Guests can enjoy a variety of activities including swimming in the indoor pool, sunning in the solarium, relaxing with a soothing massage and sauna, working out in the fitness studio, playing tennis, riding horses, fishing the River Oos, golfing, or gambling at the elegant casino. Ladies can also visit the famed beauty clinic on the premises.

Rates: Rooms $190-$435; Junior Suite $470-$620;
Full Suite from $720

BRENNER'S PARK HOTEL & SPA
Schillerstrasse 6
D-76530 Baden-Baden, Germany

Phone   49-07221-9000
Fax   49-07221-38772

KEMPINSKI HOTEL ADLON BERLIN
Berlin

> In former days we'd both agree
> That you were me, and I was you.
> What has now happened to us two,
> That you are you, and I am me?
>
> —"In Former Days" by Bhartrhari

The new Hotel Adlon sits upon the site of the infamous Hotel Adlon that burned down in 1945. The new hotel carries on a tradition of world-class luxury. Old or new, the elegant Adlon has been the hotel of choice for heads of state, artists, politicians, and personalities. Noted figures from Theodore Roosevelt to Albert Einstein to Lawrence of Arabia have all stayed at the Hotel Adlon.

Like all the Kempinski hotel properties, the Hotel Adlon features a combination of luxury and technology in each of the hotel's 337 rooms and forty-seven suites. Each room has ISDN Internet access as well as PC and fax connections. Guests can also order in-room movies while relaxing in their lavishly decorated surroundings.

The elegant hotel dining room features French and German cuisines. Diners are afforded a spectacular view overlooking the Brandenburg Gate. Private dining rooms are available for that extra-romantic touch. Guests can also enjoy the Wintergarden, piano lounge, or American bar.

Hotel guest facilities include a fitness center with massages, sauna, solarium, pool, whirlpool, and steam bath. Jogging is available in the park next door and golf courses, tennis courts, and horseback riding are just an hour away at a resort in Bad Saarow.

Rates: Rooms $232–$436; Suites $555–$2,380

KEMPINSKI HOTEL ADLON BERLIN
Unter den Linden 77
D-10117 Berlin, Germany

Phone   49-30-2261-0
Fax   49-30-2261-2222

Greece

GRAND BRETAGNE
Athens

> She let herself be loved: then drowsy-eyed,
> Smiled down from her high couch in languid ease.
> My love was deep and gentle as the seas
> And rose to her as to a cliff a tide.

> —"The Jewels" by Charles Baudelaire

Athens, the birthplace of democracy, stands as one of the most historically important cities in the world. It's filled with an abundance of landmarks, foremost among them the Acropolis. Unfortunately there are only a handful of luxurious hotel rooms with views of the Acropolis, but now you know where to find them, Grand Bretagne.

Originally built as a private residence, Grand Bretagne has been a popular gathering place in Athens for over a century. Located near the Royal Palace and opposite of Parliament, Grand Bretagne remains a gathering place for Greece's most powerful people.

The hotel's prestige is reflected in the marble lobby, decorated with antiques, Oriental rugs, plush sofas, ornate chandeliers, and tapestries. Upstairs you'll find the 364 rooms and suites that serve as the hotel's guest quarters. The twelve-foot ceilings give even the hallways a touch of drama. Elegantly decorated, the rooms are luxurious in every detail from the linens to the marble bath. For views of the Acropolis, request a Syntagma room. Downstairs you'll find the hotel's restaurant, GB Corner. Known more for its powerful clientele than the food, the restaurant is an excellent place to people-watch while enjoying Greek cuisine.

Rates: Doubles from $380

GRAND BRETAGNE
Vasileos Georgiou A'1
Syntagma Square
Athens 10563, Greece

Phone   30-1-331-4444
Fax   30-1-322-8034

PERIVOLAS
Oia-Santorini

> Love, till dawn sunder night from day with fire
> Dividing my delight and my desire,
>   The crescent life and love plenilune,
> Love me though dusk begin and dark retire;
>   Ah God, ah God, that day should be so soon.
>
> —"In the Orchard" by A.C. Swinburne

Created by a volcano, the island of Santorini rises from the Aegean Sea in a series of steep cliffs. For centuries, life on this island was hard, with earthquakes toppling buildings with relative frequency. Finally, after a 1956 earthquake, the Greek government stepped in and decided to modernize the island. This brought with it a great surge in tourism. Now the island is home to booming discos and large hotels, yet the most romantic spot in the Aegean lies carved into a cliffside. This spot is the innovative and charming hideaway of Perivolas.

With only fourteen rooms, Perivolas is dwarfed by the island's large hotels. Each room is housed in a tiny little cottage called a skafta. The skaftas are carved out of the cliff face and are decorated with elegant simplicity. Each vaulted-ceiling skafta features a bedroom, a sitting area, a well-equipped kitchenette, and a domed bathroom. Most importantly, each has its terrace with magnificent views of the Caldera which serves as the perfect place to hold hands and enjoy a romantic sunset. After a blissful night's sleep, descend down the steps to the pool and the breakfast skafta, and enjoy a hearty meal as the rising sun begins to dance on the sea's surface.

Rates: Very Expensive

PERIVOLAS
Oia-Santorini 84702, Greece

| Phone | 30-286-71-308 |
| Fax | 30-286-71-309 |

Honduras

POSADA DEL SOL
Guanaja

> She opened her eyes, and green
> They shone, clear like flowers undone
> For the first time, now for the first time seen.

> —"Green" by D.H. Lawrence

Posada del Sol sits on a hillside, tucked between a mountain ridge and the Caribbean Sea. Set on seventy acres, the Spanish mansion and cabins are connected by stone walkways to beaches, a boathouse, and a spacious sun-drenched deck surrounding the freshwater pool.

The rooms at Posada del Sol are simple. They have no telephone. They have no television. They simply wisely provide a comfortable place to stay amidst paradise. Indeed, man-made luxuries would not be able to match the beauty of the surrounding jungle or the nearby sea.

As beautiful as the island of Guanaja is, Posada del Sol's main attraction lies beneath the surface of the Caribbean. Just offshore lies the world's second largest barrier reef. Expert and novice scuba divers will enjoy the fifty world-class dive sites that lie nearby from the Caribbean's largest shipwreck, the Jado Trader, to the breathtaking coral formations of the reef. Marine life abounds in this paradise and you'll have opportunities to view moray eels, giant grouper, silversides, and countless other species. Also just offshore are salt-flats perfect for flyfishing.

Though not as spectacular as the reef, the island does offer several attractions. You can hike the mountain to a waterfall, explore an archeological dig, lift weights, or enjoy a game of tennis. Whichever activity you choose, you'll likely work up a strong appetite. Thankfully the rate includes three hearty meals a day with a strong emphasis on fresh seafood.

Of special note, Posada del Sol offers couples a unique attraction. They will take you to a nearby uninhabited island for an afternoon complete with champagne lunch and private hammocks.

Rates: $150-$190

POSADA DEL SOL (RESERVATIONS)
1201 US Highway 1
Suite 210
North Palm Beach, FL 33408

Phone	561-624-3483
Toll free	800-642-3483
Fax	561-624-3225

Hong Kong

KOWLOON SHANGRI-LA
Hong Kong

> I wonder by my troth, what thou and I
> > Did, till we loved? Were not weaned till then?
> But sucked on country pleasures, childishly?

> —"The Good Morrow" by John Donne

This magnificent waterfront hotel is frequently credited with being one of the top ten hotels in the world. The Kowloon Shangri-La has won a number of accolades including *Conde Nast Traveler's* "Gold List," *Travel & Leisure's* "Top twenty-five hotels in Asia," and Laura McKenzie's "Best of '97 Award."

Each of the 725 modern and elegant guest rooms and suites are decorated in pastels and offer breathtaking views of Victoria Harbour or Hong Kong Island. Rooms come with a variety of bedding options but many have king beds. The rooms also feature the latest technology including in-house movies, satellite TV, and three international direct dial telephones and voice mail. Guests will also find a fully stocked mini-bar and refrigerator, and a luxury marble bath. Complimentary tea and coffee-making facilities and twenty-four-hour room service are also available.

Guests can make use of the hotel's state-of-the-art health club which features massage, an indoor pool, sauna, solarium, and gym. Kowloon's commercial and shopping districts are a short walk from the hotel.

Rates: Rooms $316–$490; Suites $568–$2,195

KOWLOON SHANGRI-LA
65 Mody Road
Tsimshatsui East
Kowloon, Hong Kong

Phone   852-2721-2111
Fax   852-2723-8686

THE PENINSULA
Hong Kong

> And, as he walk'd, t'himself alone he smiled,
> To think how Venus' Arts he had beguil'd;
> And when he slept, his Rest was deep:
>> But Venus laugh'd, to see and hear him sleep:
>>> She taught the am'rous Jove
>>> A magical Receipt in Love,
> Which arm'd him stronger, and which help'd him
>   more,
> Than all his Thunder did, and his Almighty ship
>   before.

> —from *Odes,* Book Three, 15, "Love and Gold" by
>   Horace

Two densely packed miles from Kai-Tak Airport stands the Peninsula, one of the grandest hotels in the world. A stay here is a case study in class, luxury, and service. Rarely will you find these ingredients perfectly blended in such abundance. As a result, you will be rewarded with romantic memories sure to last a lifetime.

Built in 1928, the Peninsula stands guard over the South Kowloon shoreline. Its wings spread out to form a towering thirty-story landmark. The wings were added only several years ago and regained the Peninsula's famous views and nearly doubled the hotel's capacity. Inside you'll find 300 rooms and suites that combine luxurious period furnishings with high-tech features like dataports and other items that are not important for a romantic experience.

The hotel's gracefully elegant lobby sets the tone for the entire hotel with its columns and gilt cornices. Here you'll find the concierge and be able to enjoy tea while watching other guests or marveling at the efficiency of the valets attending to the guests' needs. Just outside the lobby, you'll discover the hotel's Rolls Royces which you can use for a price (a high price). At the top of the tower is Felix, one of Asia's most romantic restaurants boasting a commanding view of Victoria Harbour and the business district's skyscrapers. Felix serves delicious and elegant cuisine in this idyllic setting and is an experience that you must indulge in even if you are not staying at the hotel.

In addition to the Felix, the Peninsula features four other fine restaurants: Imasa, serving Japanese cuisine; Spring Moon, for authentic Cantonese; Verandah, specializing in continental cuisine; and the famous Gaddi's, one of the region's best French restaurants. When not eating, you can relax at the new, terraced pool or the spa which is located in the tower.

Rates: $425-$710

THE PENINSULA

Salisbury Road
Tsimshatsui
Kowloon, Hong Kong

Phone	852-2366-6251
Toll free	800-223-6800
Fax	852-2722-4170

THE REGENT
Hong Kong

> How many kisses satisfy,
> How many are enough and more,
> You ask me, Lesbia. I reply,
> As many as the Libyan sands
> Sprinkling the Cyrenaic shore
>
> —"How Many Kisses" by Catullus

This luxurious hotel is regularly listed among the top hotels in the world, and it's easy to see why. This very modern, elegant, and sophisticated palace sits at the edge of Victoria Harbour. The lobby features impeccably maintained polished granite floors and forty-foot-high glass walls that offer a panoramic vista of the Hong Kong skyline. The walls are adorned with exquisite Oriental art.

The 660 guest rooms and suites are lavishly decorated and feature large bathrooms with oversized sunken tubs and separate showers.

Guests can enjoy the hotel's health spa, a scenic outdoor pool, the fitness club, and a shopping arcade. Romantics must remember to take a dip in the secluded outdoor hot tub which affords a twinkling vista of the city skyline. One end of the hot tub looks like it literally falls into the harbor.

Plume is where you go for a romantic meal that makes a statement. This split-level restaurant located in the lobby level of the Regent Hotel is award-winning in every respect. Here you can enjoy spectacular views of Hong Kong Island's glittering lights and its postcard skyline.

Guests can finish off the perfect stay in the perfect locale with a ride to the airport in a Daimler from the hotel's fleet of twenty-one chauffeur-driven limousines.

Rates: Rooms $535; Junior Suite $710; Full Harbor View Suite, prices available upon request

THE REGENT
18 Salisbury Road
Tsimshatsui, Kowloon, Hong Kong

Phone   852-2721-1211
Fax   852-2739-4546

Indonesia

AMANDARI
Ubud

> To cheat the eyes
>> of stern
> leering prudes
> adds honey to
>> love's cup.
>> —"Our Kisses" by Paulos

Known as the "Island of the Gods," Bali is a place of immense beauty. From gorgeous beaches to lush highlands, Bali's beauty overwhelms the senses. Ubud is a cultural center of this paradise. Not far from Ubud lies the village of Kedewatan, home of Amandari.

Amandari, Sanskrit for "the place of peaceful spirits," is one of the world's best hotels. Created by Adrian Zecha, Amandari was designed to embody the characteristics of a typical Balinese village. Overlooking the Ayung Gorge, the hotel is actually a collection of villas built of teak and volcanic rock. Each thatch-roofed villa is surrounded by its own courtyard, providing you with romantic privacy. Cool marble floors, sliding glass walls, local furnishings, and a large outdoor sunken bath add to the ambiance.

The public rooms at Amandari enhance the hotel's luxurious atmosphere. Dark-green tiles line a pool shaped like a terraced rice padi, giving it the illusion of spilling into the gorge below. Overlooking the pool is the Verandah restaurant. Considered the best restaurant on the island, this open-air gem serves inspired dishes that mix the best of Indonesian and Western cuisine. Verandah also showcases Amandari's excellent service, a luxury that you might not otherwise notice but will definitely appreciate.

No wonder Amandari is a favorite of celebrities like Kate Mulgrew.

Rates: $450-$850

AMANDARI

P.O. Box 33
Ubud 80571
Bali, Indonesia

Phone	62-361-975333
Toll free	800-421-1490
Fax	62-361-975335

FOUR SEASONS JIMBARAN BAY
Bali

> Love, ah Love, when all your slipknot's drawn,
> We can but say, 'Farewell, good sense.'
>
> —"The Lion In Love" by Marianne Moore

Located on the idyllic island of Bali, Four Seasons Jimbaran Bay features every amenity a romantic could hope for. The resort rises up a hillside from a beach on picturesque Jimbaran Bay and covers thirty-five acres with its luxurious villas.

The heart of the Four Seasons Jimbaran is its collection of 147 villas. Each thatched roof villa covers 2,100 square feet and features every luxury imaginable. You enter your villa through a pair of carved Balinese doors. Stepping stones are surrounded by shining green pebbles and lead to your own private plunge pool overlooking the bay. Next to the pool, a dragon fountain drowns out any sounds—not that there are many. Also outside is a lovely bamboo-pipe shower, where you can take a nighttime bath beneath the stars, and you need not to worry about privacy since the other three sides of your compound are surrounded by a high wall. Inside the villa, you'll find a bathroom with a large marble soaking tub and separate shower. Living and dining areas overlook the pool and encourage generous use of the hotel's excellent room service. The bedroom features a peaked bamboo ceiling and soft, luxurious linens.

If you find reason to leave your bungalow, you can enjoy a number of activities at the resort. Due to its size, Four Seasons Jimbaran offers golf-cart taxis to whisk you from one end of the resort to the other. The beach features the typical array of water sports while the dramatic pool is fed by a twenty-foot waterfall. Golfers can tee up at a nearby course. If you tire of eating in your villa, the resort boasts three excellent restaurants that are open to the breezes and overlook the bay.

Rates: $475-$2,200

FOUR SEASONS JIMBARAN BAY
Denpasar 80361
Bali, Indonesia

Phone	62-361-701010
Toll free	800-332-3442
Fax	62-361-701020

IBAH
Ubud

> Sweet one I love you
> for your lovely shape,
> for the art you make
> in paint and bed and rhyme,
> but most because we see
> into each other's hearts,
> there to read secrets
> and to trust,
> and cancel time.
>
> —"Reasons" by Tom McGrath

Bali has long been known as a tropical paradise rich in culture. The center of the island's cultural and artistic community is Ubud, a Balinese word that means medicine and refers to the healing powers of the area.

Ibah lies on the outskirts of Ubud on the Campuhan River. Owned by the Prince of Ubud, Ibah opened in 1995 so visitors from around the world could enjoy

Ubud's rich culture. Situated on a lush hillside, Ibah's property is dotted with lotus ponds and forms the perfect base for exploring the island. You'll stay in one of ten traditional Balinese villas featuring teak beams and thatched roofs. When not in your villa, you can enjoy a tiled pool or take a relaxing therapy at the spa.

Just a short walk away, downtown Ubud offers a bustling scene of restaurants, cafes, and shops. For the ultimate romantic excursion, grab one of the resort's mountain bikes and go explore the countryside. Here you'll be able to see rice paddies and coconut groves as well as the monkeys who inhabit the surrounding forests.

Rates: $195-$250

IBAH
Puri Tjampuhan
Ubud
Bali, Indonesia

Phone   62-361-974466
Fax   62-361-974467

Ireland

BLUE HAVEN HOTEL
Kinsale

> O heart! O heart! If she'd but turn her head,
> You'd know the folly of being comforted.
>
> —"The Folly Of Being Comforted" by W.B. Yeats

Near the city of Cork on the Irish Sea lies the village of Kinsale. This grouping of pastel-colored buildings was once primarily a fishing village. While fishing remains important, Kinsale is now better known as the gourmet capital of Ireland. Indeed, its palms trees have even earned the village and the surrounding area the reputation of being an Irish version of the Riviera. The best and most romantic place to stay in Kinsale is the Blue Haven Hotel.

A stay at the Blue Haven Hotel immerses one in the culture of modern Ireland. Brian and Anne Cronin greet each guest and immediately make you feel at home. Though many of the rooms are small, they are all immensely charming and feature such comforts as teapots and homemade Irish whiskey marmalade. Downstairs locals and guests gather in the pub to down a pint of Guinness and engage in colorful and animated discussions. Later on at dinner, you'll enjoy the hotel's fresh seafood and shellfish all excellently prepared. And in the morning, you'll be able to fill up on eggs, homemade yogurt, poached fish, sausage, and Irish bacon.

Rates: $56-$240

BLUE HAVEN HOTEL
3/4 Pearse Street
Kinsale
County Cork, Ireland

Phone   353-21-772209
Fax   353-21-774268

THE CLARENCE
Dublin

> From sullen earth, sings hymns at heaven's gate;
>> For thy sweet love rememb'red such wealth brings,
>> That then I scorn to change my state with kings.
>
> —"When In Disgrace" by William Shakespeare

First opened in 1852, the Clarence was one of Dublin's finest hotels, and remained so for many years. Unfortunately though, the years took their toll on the Clarence, and it began to lose its clientele. However, this cloud had a silver lining. Just as the Clarence was losing its following, its neighborhood, Temple Bar, was enjoying an artistic revolution. Thus many artists and musicians began to frequent the Clarence and became quite attached. Two of these regulars happened to be Bono and The Edge of the rock band U2 who purchased the hotel in 1992 and restored it to its former glory.

Each of the fifty rooms and suites has been individually decorated. The combinations of earth tones and simple furniture give the rooms a simplistic elegance vaguely reminiscent of America's Shaker movement. Yet the simplicity of the oak furnishings and colors of the fabrics does nothing to detract from the luxury of other appointments such as Egyptian cotton linens, and glass-lined wrought-iron bedside lamps.

Downstairs you'll find the Tea Room and its spectacular mosaic and marble Octagon bar. Tall windows flood the room with light and allow you to view the hustle and bustle of Temple Bar while enjoying a quiet romantic meal. After dinner, explore Temple Bar. Who knows? You might just see the next U2 before they become famous.

Rates: $270-$315

THE CLARENCE
6-8 Wellington Quay
Dublin 2, Ireland

Phone   353-1-670-9000
Fax   353-1-670-7800

THE KILDARE HOTEL & COUNTRY CLUB
Straffan

> And like this stream our passions flow,
>   Our love goes by;
> The violence hope dare not show
> Follows time's beat which now falls slow.
>   Night may come and clock may sound,
>   Within your shadow I am bound.
>
> —"The Mirabeau Bridge" by Guillaume Apollinaire

The Kildare Hotel & Country Club offers the best of Ireland. Set on 330 acres, the hotel allows you to enjoy the finest of Ireland's countryside. Yet the hotel is near enough to Dublin that if you tire of the countryside you can drive to Temple Bar for a night out on the town.

This hotel only opened in 1991, and was known earlier as Straffan House. Yet despite its modern conversion from mansion to luxury hotel, much of the original charm has been preserved. Overlooking the River Liffey, the hotel still boasts wide hallways, bow windows, high ceilings, and grand sweeping staircases. The forty-five bedrooms and suites have each been individually decorated. Antiques and paintings combine with luxurious modern appointments to form a timeless style of elegant comfort. New to the old property is the Arnold Palmer-designed eighteen-hole championship golf course, already considered one of Ireland's best. The hotel has also added squash courts, and an indoor pool and tennis courts.

Rates: Two nights from $428

THE KILDARE HOTEL & COUNTRY CLUB
Straffan
County Kildare, Ireland

Phone	353-1-627-3333
Toll free	800-221-1074
Fax	353-1-627-3312

THE PARK HOTEL KENMARE
Kenmare

> A single flow'r he sent me, since we met.
>   All tenderly his messenger he chose;
> Deep-hearted, pure, with scented dew still wet -
>   One perfect rose.
>
> —"One Perfect Rose" by Dorothy Parker

Ireland is a nation known for its natural beauty. Rich, lush greens grace craggy hills and low mountains that dot the countryside. One of the most beautiful regions of Ireland is the Beara Peninsula. Located on a finger of land jutting out to the Atlantic, the Beara is one of Ireland's least known and unspoiled regions. Due to its proximity to the Gulf Stream, the Beara's climate borders on subtropical, yet because of its narrow roads, tour buses avoid the area. As a result, a room at the Park Hotel Kenmare serves as a perfect base for exploring the beautiful countryside.

Built in 1897 as railway hotel, the Park Hotel Kenmare compliments its beautiful surroundings. Ivy climbs the stone walls trying to reach the dormered windows high above. Its steep roofs are dotted with slab-chimneys, and oddly enough, the palm trees that dot the grounds do not seem out of place.

Once you pass the tennis court and croquet lawn and step into the hotel, you realize that you are in a place of unique luxury. A fire glows below the grand staircase and the hallways are fashionably cluttered with antique bureaus, armoires, and paintings. As is expected with all Relais & Châteaux hotels, the rooms are luxurious. Each room is individually decorated and extremely comfortable, but rooms overlooking the Kenmare Estuary are the most romantic.

Downstairs, the hotel's restaurant serves world-class cuisine. For a special Christmas, the hotel offers a three-day Victorian holiday package, but be sure to make your reservations well in advance for rooms go quickly.

Rates: $195-$680

THE PARK HOTEL KENMARE
Kenmare
County Kerry, Ireland

Phone   353-64-41200
Fax   353-64-41402

Italy

HOTEL CIPRIANI & PALAZZO VENDRAMIN
Venice

> I hid my love in field and town
> Till e'en the breeze would knock me down;
> The bees seemed singing ballads o'er,
> The fly's bass turned a lion's roar;
> And even silence found a tongue,
> To haunt me all the summer long;
> The riddle nature could not prove
> Was nothing else but secret love.
>
> —"I Hid My Love" by John Clare

Nestled along the coast of the Adriatic, Venice has long been considered one of the most romantic cities in the world. Once a city-state made wealthy by trade, this city of islands remains rich in culture, boasting many fine collections of art and other cultural treasures. It is among this backdrop that the Cipriani treats lovers to romantic repasts.

In this magical city, the Cipriani enjoys an enchanting setting: its own island at the mouth of the Grand Canal with views of the lagoon and the Basilica of San Giorgio. With 105 rooms in the main hotel and seven suites in the Palazzo Vendramin, Cipriani is a sensualist's oasis. Posh rooms pamper you in luxury, and each one is magically romantic. For a special treat, reserve one of the suites in Vendramin. Outside the hotel, you'll find Venice's most striking pool set amid lush gardens.

Another treat of staying here is the hotel's restaurant. You'll marvel at its architecture and decor that set it apart from others. Most dramatic is the steepled ceiling, and its arches which appear to hang without any support. Underneath these arches are tables appointed with white tablecloths, set with fine china and crystal, and adorned with fresh flowers. When not marveling at the ceiling, enjoy the view from one of the many windows draped with Fortuny curtains. It's in this setting that you'll enjoy a menu full of tempting dishes. For example, you might wish to try blinis Russian style with Scottish salmon for an appetizer followed by roasted monkfish perfumed with rosemary and served with sautéed eggplant. Meals at the Cipriani are remembered as romantic experiences, rich in visual and palatable treats.

Rates: $665-$775

HOTEL CIPRIANI & PALAZZO VENDRAMIN
Giudecca 10, 30133
Venice, Italy

Phone	39-41-520-7744
Toll free	800-223-6800
Fax	39-41-520-3930

HOTEL HASSLER
Rome

> And what they mean to wayfarers,
>   I scarcely heed or mind;
> He has won that storm-tight roof of hers
>   Which Earth grants all her kind.
>
>   —"She Hears The Storm" by Thomas Hardy

After a day of viewing monuments in the area and shopping in Rome's elegant boutiques, Hotel Hassler offers the perfect romantic setting for relaxing together.

Located at the top of the Spanish Steps, Hotel Hassler is a romantic's dream. The rooms and suites are richly decorated, and many are highlighted by frescoes. After unpacking, go downstairs and enjoy a cocktail with your lover in the garden courtyard amidst vine-covered walls, flowers, and statues. After your drink, proceed to the rooftop restaurant. Immediately you'll understand why the Hassler Roof continually receives praises as one of Rome's most romantic spots. The view from this perch is breathtaking and sets the stage for a magical evening. You'll enjoy the fine Italian cuisine.

Rates: $250-$430

HOTEL HASSLER
Trinita Dei Monti, 6
00187 Rome, Italy

Phone	39-6-678-2651
Fax	39-6-678-9991

HOTEL SAN PIETRO
Positano

> It seemed that ancient joys were flying over,
> sunset of dreams once more embraced the wood.
> But happy people do not watch the clocks;
> it seems they only lie in pairs and sleep.
>
> —"In The Wood" by Boris Pasternak

Positano was once a powerful commercial town. Its pastel-and-white houses perched above the sparkling azure sea now create a serene scene fitting of postcards. Perched also on these cliffs is the award-winning Hotel San Pietro and its dining room.

Actually the Hotel San Pietro is carved out of a cliff. To reach it, you park your car in a nondescript lot near a tiny stone chapel on top of a lonely cliff. Here a member of the staff will greet you and show you to the elevator that will take you down through the cliff to the Hotel San Pietro. Exiting the elevator, you understand why this hotel is named after Saint Peter, guardian of the gates of heaven, for you feel as if somehow a little bit of heaven has been captured here on earth. Every public room, from the lobby to the dining room, is exquisitely decorated and highlighted by an abundance of flora and fauna which give the rooms a very lush quality.

The bedrooms at San Pietro equal the public rooms in their opulence. Hand-painted doors set the tone for these magnificent rooms which are stacked in tiers. The "special" rooms at San Pietro are a romantic's dream.

These are highlighted by tiled floors, and beds with canopies of real vines. The bathrooms are especially luxurious with at least one room boasting a sunken Roman tub the size of a small pool with depths of up to nine feet.

It is in this earthly Eden that you will enjoy magical romance. During the day, you can descend via elevator through the cliff and enjoy San Pietro's private beach. After a day by the sea, savor the fresh pastas, fresh vegetables, and especially the fresh fish that are the staples of the hotel's lovely dining room. The hotel actually has fishermen who work exclusively for it. After dinner, linger and dance under the bougainvillea or drink a nightcap on the terrace as the moon and stars' reflections shimmer on the sea.

Rates: $300-$600

HOTEL SAN PIETRO
Via Laurito 2
84017 Positano, Italy

Phone   39-89-875-455
Fax   39-89-811-449

HOTEL SANTA CATERINA
Amalfi

> Choose now among this fairest number,
> Upon whose breast would for ever slumber:
> Choose not amiss since you may where you will,
>   Or blame yourself for choosing ill.
> Then do not leave, though oft the music closes,
> Till lilies in their cheeks be turn'd to roses.
>
> —untitled by William Browne

Hotel Santa Caterina clings to the edge of a cliff overlooking the azure-colored Gulf of Salerno. As with many cliffside hotels in Italy, the lobby of Hotel Santa Caterina fronts the road and reveals little of what lies beyond. Indeed, though the Hotel's lobby is tasteful, it could easily be mistaken for the reception area of a large restaurant, not a world-class hotel famous for its romantic ambiance.

Built in the early 1900s, the hotel has slowly evolved over the years. Lush flowering vines now twine around the hotel's arches and lemon trees perfume the air with their sweet citrus scent. Individually decorated rooms represent an eclectic mix of 20th-century decor. Antiques are placed beside contemporary furnishings and tiled floors lead to whirlpool baths. The overall effect is one of playful luxury that continually reminds you that you are here to have fun and to enjoy the company of someone special.

For activities, descend in elevators down to the seashore where you can enjoy a pool and private beach attended by a staff decked out in boat-neck shirts with stripes. Or you can lounge by the pool beneath lemon trees up at the main level of the hotel. Above this pool is a magical open-air restaurant that serves as the perfect place to enjoy a meal and an enchanting sunset.

Rates: $78-$555

HOTEL SANTA CATERINA
S.S. Amalfitana 9
84011 Amalfi, Italy

Phone   39-89-871012
Fax   39-89-871351

HOTEL SPLENDIDO
Portofino

> Before a joy propos'd, behind a dream,
>> All the world well knows yet none knows well;
>> To shun the heaven that leads men to this hell.
>
> —"Th' Expense of Spirit" by William Shakespeare

Portofino's shops are filled with postcards featuring pictures of its dazzling harbor dotted with yachts from around the world. Tourists gazing at these postcards often ask where they were shot, only to receive the same answer, "La Terraza," the fabulous terrace restaurant at the luxurious Hotel Splendido.

Indeed, the panoramic views from other parts of this Relais & Châteaux are equally stunning. Perched on a hill overlooking Portofino's harbor, Splendido is surrounded by olive groves and pine trees that give way to the world-famous view that you can enjoy from your the private balcony attracted to your luxury room. Romantic frescoes and rare furniture dot the common areas of the hotel that are nearly as beautiful as the views.

Rates: $420-$800

HOTEL SPLENDIDO
16 Viale Baratta
16034 Portofino (GE), Italy

Phone   39-185-269551
Fax   39-185-269614

LA POSTA VECHIA
Ladispoli

> This ecstasy doth unperplex
> (We said) and tell us what we love,
> We see by this, it was not sex,
> We see, we saw not what did move:

> —"The Ecstasy" by John Donne

Priceless paintings, tapestries, antiques, and carpets adorn this world-class hotel on the outskirts of Rome. However, since La Posta Vechia once served as the private residence of John Paul Getty, such appointments seem natural, not ostentatious.

With only seventeen rooms, accommodations at La Posta Vechia are not easy to come by. You will have to make your reservations well in advance, but La Posta Vechia is well worth it. Your individually decorated, luxurious room will be filled with many museum-quality pieces of art and furniture. In fact, the basement of La Posta Vechia is a museum housing a collection of Roman antiquities found on the site and unparalleled floor mosaics.

On the main level of the building, you'll enjoy La

Posta Vechia's intimate dining room. With one side facing the sea and the other the garden, this dining room is decorated with 17th-century marble tables and boasts high ceilings obviously crafted by fine artisans. Once settled in at your table, you will be treated to traditional Italian cuisine full of the flavors that made this nation's cooking famous. Also on the main floor is the magnificent indoor pool with its ceiling-high arched windows with breathtaking views of the sea below.

Rates: Expensive

LA POSTA VECHIA
00055 Palo Laziale
Ladispoli, Italy

Phone   39-6-994-9501
Fax   39-6-994-9507

LE SIRENUSE
Positano

> And all her face was honey to my mouth,
>   And all her body pasture to mine eyes;
>   The long lithe arms and hotter hands than
>   fire,
> The quivering flanks, hair smelling of the south,
>   The bright light feet, the splendid supple thighs
>   And glittering eyelids of my soul's desire.
>
> —"Love And Sleep" by A.C. Swinburne

Besides the Hotel San Pietro, Positano also hosts the charming deluxe hotel Le Sirenuse. As with every building in Positano, Le Sirenuse is perched on a cliff, and it overlooks the sea and the islands of the Sirens.

Le Sirenuse opened in 1951 and gradually expanded to its present size. Before it became a hotel, it had served the noble Neapolitan family, Marchese Sersale, as a summer house. Today, the family still owns the hotel and has taken great care to preserve its grand past, thus rewarding its guests with the romantic elegance of a bygone era.

Painted a rosy red, the original house at Le Sirenuse serves as the hotel's nucleus. Here you'll find the Presidential Suite, the drawing rooms, and the bar. Surrounding it are a number of new buildings equally charming. Their rooms range from the gloriously spacious to intimately small. Most have balconies overlooking the sea in addition to jacuzzi tubs, while all are dotted with antiquities to remind you that you are the guest of Italian nobles.

Rates: From $380

LE SIRENUSE
Via Colomo 30
84017 Positano, Italy

Phone   39-89-875-066
Fax   39-89-811-798

TORRE DI BELLOSGUARDO
Florence

> We look and understand
> We cannot speak
> Except in trifles and
> Words the most weak.

> —"No One So Much As You" by Edward Thomas

The name of this hotel describes its beauty. Translated, it means "Tower of a Beautiful View." Indeed, the site for the hotel was chosen by Guido Cavalcanti—a nobleman and friend of Dante's—specifically because he felt it was the most beautiful site in all of Florence. It's on this site that a 13th-century tower was built, and 200 years later, the villa that is now the hotel.

Today you approach Torre di Bellosguardo via an avenue lined with cypress. Soon the stone entrance, topped by a Charity with two toddlers, comes into view, and you begin to realize that Cavalcanti was right. This is the most beautiful spot in Florence. If you have any lingering doubts, they will most certainly be erased by the views from your window; beneath you lies the tiled roofs, steeples, and domes of Florence. Surrounding the hotel is an immacuately landscaped garden and a terraced pool overlooking Florence. Though the hotel has no nighttime restaurant, it does serve breakfast year-round and lunch during the summer months.

Rates: From $208

TORRE DI BELLOSGUARDO
2 Via Roti Michelozzi
50124 Florence, Italy

Phone   39-55-229-8145
Fax   39-55-229-008

Jamaica

ROUND HILL HOTEL & VILLAS
Montego Bay

> Soul and body have no bounds:
> To lovers as they lie upon
> Her tolerant enchanted slope
> In their ordinary swoon,
> Grave the vision Venus sends
> Of supernatural sympathy,
> Universal love and hope;
> While an abstract insight wakes
> Among the glaciers and the rocks
> The hermit's sensual ecstasy.
>
> —"Lullaby" by W.H. Auden

Opened in the 1950s, the Round Hill Hotel & Villas was the Carribean's first super resort. Once a pineapple plantation, Round Hill's 100 acres have welcomed some of the world's most famous and powerful people; JFK and Jackie honeymooned here. Today Round Hill remains one of the Carribean's top resorts and one of the world's most romantic places.

As its name suggests, Round Hill offers both typical hotel rooms and villas for lodging. In the old Pineapple House, you'll find thirty-six pleasant rooms, but to experience the real grandeur of Round Hill, try to secure a villa. Not only will you enjoy the extra privacy, but you'll like the luxury of having breakfast served to you on your own terrace.

Not surprisingly, activities at Round Hill center on the sea. Located on a peninsula, Round Hill's private white-sand beach offers a pristine setting for sunning and swimming in the crystal clear waters. Additionally, many of Round Hill's all-inclusive packages offer rafting trips, massages, and even scuba dives.

Dining at Round Hill leaves pleasant memories. Each night has a different theme ranging from a beach bonfire to a gala dinner dance on Saturday night (for which a jacket and tie must be worn). The chefs at Round Hill combine fresh local ingredients, especially seafood, to create continental dishes with a Jamaican flare. After dinner, dance to lively Calypso music and enjoy the romance of a warm Jamaican evening.

Rates: $220-$520 (all inclusive)

ROUND HILL HOTEL & VILLAS
P.O. Box 64
Montego Bay, Jamaica, West Indies

Phone	876-952-5150
Toll free	800-972-2159
Fax	876-952-2505

Kenya

OLERAI HOUSE
Lake Naivasha

> and yet no such song have
> I heard in the darkness of night before,
> (where does this tenderness come from?):
> here, on the ribs of a singer.
>
> —"Where Does This Tenderness Come From?" by
> Marina Tsvetaeva

Unfortunately, sub-Saharan Africa, with the exception of South Africa, does not seem to be on many romantics' radar screen. As a result, they are missing the wondrous beauty of the African plains. Dotted with lakes and forests, this vast expanse is home to exotic wildlife like elephants and hippos. Located near Lake Naivasha, Olerai House serves as the perfect base to explore this land.

Olerai House is a family affair. Run by Oria and Iain Douglas-Hamilton, the retreat was built by her parents in the 1930s. After her parents' death, it lingered for some years and fell into disrepair. Structurally there was little damage—the house was designed by the chief architect of the Panama Canal—but cosmetically the place was a wreck. Then Oria and Iain came onto the scene and lovingly restored the grand house. Today the black-and-white marble floors shine as never before. Vases of wild sage and rushes fill the rooms and artworks by Oria's mother are proudly displayed. The living room looks out on a long avenue of cypress leading to the lake. The bedrooms feature intricately carved furniture and canopied beds. Even without its setting, the house would be very romantic.

Considered to be the world's leading authorities on the African elephant, the Douglas-Hamiltons are fountains of knowledge. They'll assist you in viewing the local wildlife. You can travel via horseback to the surrounding hills, or walk down to the lake. Here you can watch the hippos, take a boat to the Crescent Island game preserve, or simply admire the many species of birds that call Lake Naivasha home. For a special treat, join the couple on one of their Cessna safaris, an experience that allows you to truly grasp the vastness and glory of the bush.

Rates: Rooms from $380

OLERAI HOUSE (MAILING ADDRESS)
Box 54667
Nairobi, Kenya

Phone   254-2-33-4868

Macau

HOTEL BELA VISTA
Macau

> Shall I see her again to-day, then?
> There's one hour to the train. That's all.
> But that one hour's held by the apathy of sea, of
>   rumbling storm, of hell.
>
> —"Cape Mootch" by Boris Pasternak

Getting a room at the Hotel Bela Vista is not easy. Recently restored in 1992, this century-old mansion features only eight suites behind its elegant facade. Located at the top of a grand staircase, these eight rooms rank among the most prized and most romantic in Southeast Asia. Each luxurious suite blends Oriental touches with Portuguese charm, and each features dramatic views of the city and Praia Grande Bay.

The restaurant at the Bela Vista hotel is a true gem of the Far East. Hidden away from the city bustle, this Portuguese-style mansion overlooking the Praia Grande has all the ingredients for a very romantic evening: colonial setting, a breathtaking column-and-arch veranda, linen tablecloths, ceiling fans, chandeliers, and potted plants. The windows of the restaurant are doorways to the veranda and let in a nice subtle breeze.

If you're in this part of the world soon, you must experience the Bela Vista before it closes its doors. Sadly, the Bela Vista will become the Portuguese consulate after Macau reverts to China in December 1999.

Rates: $325–$440

HOTEL BELA VISTA
8 Rua do Comendador
Kou Ho Neng, Macau

Phone   853-965-333
Fax   853-965-588

Mexico

HOTEL BEL-AIR
Puerto Vallarta

> I loved you first: but afterwards your love
> > Outsoaring mine, sang with such a loftier song
> As drowned the friendly cooings of my dove.
> > Which owes the other most? My love was long,
> And yours one moment seemed to wax more
> > strong;

— "I Loved You First" by Christina Rossetti

Hotel Bel-Air's sixty-seven rooms are the best in Puerto Vallarta, a town with 15,000 hotel rooms. Why? First off, forty-two of the rooms are suites while the other twenty-five are villas. As a result, even the smallest rooms at Hotel Bel-Air are spacious. Additionally, each villa and suite has its own private terrace and is decorated with sculptures by Sergio Butamonte, while many have private pools and jacuzzis.

Service and location complete the Hotel Bel-Air experience. The hotel's staff prides itself on attention to detail and it shows. Day-to-day activities are run with seamless precision and always with a smile. The service compliments the hotel's location in Marina Vallarta, a yachting community with an excellent golf course at which hotel guests receive reduced greens fees. The hotel itself offers a freeform swimming pool, tennis, and complete exercise facilities.

At Hotel Bel-Air's restaurant, you'll have your choice of indoor or outdoor dining. Tempting dishes are served ranging from Continental to regional Mexican. After dinner, retire to the Terrace Bar, have a drink, and enjoy nightly entertainment.

Rates: $110–$435

HOTEL BEL-AIR
311 Pelicanos
Marina Vallarta
Puerto Vallarta
Jalisco 48354, Mexico

Phone   52-322-10800
Fax   52-322-10801

LAS ALAMANDAS
Near Manzanillo

> 'If this be not perfection,' Love would sigh,
> 'Perfection is a great, black thumping lie....'
> Endearments, kisses, grunts, and whispered oaths;
> But were her thoughts on breakfast, or on clothes?
>
> —"Friday Night" by Robert Graves

Secluded, exclusive, and breathtaking, Las Alamandas's four villas house a maximum of twenty-two people. These twenty-two rank among the luckiest vacationers in the world, for only they will be able to enjoy the 1,500 breathtaking acres that make up this resort.

The staff at Las Alamandas strive to make you feel at home. They'll pick you up at the airport for the long drive to the villas. Once you arrive at Las Alamandas, the staff transports your bags to your casita. Each casita is individually decorated with Mexican oil paintings and hand-painted bath tiles. On your king-sized bed, you'll find *bienvenidos* spelled out in flower petals your first day. At night, you'll drift into a blissful sleep while the ocean pounds against the shore.

The sheer size of Las Alamandas makes any day here an adventure. Three beaches serve as the perfect spot for tanning, swimming, or enjoying lunch. Guided horseback tours will take you to the resort's lagoons which many tropical birds call home. You can take the launch to nearby Bird Island, nesting spot of the exotic bobo bird and home to a cove filled with tropical fish.

Dining at Las Alamandas is a flexible affair. Breakfast

will be brought to your casita each morning. For lunch, the staff can prepare a box lunch if you are exploring or going to the beach. For dinner, choose from the resort's excellent dining room, the beach, or your casita. Whichever you select, the staff will ensure that your meals are as romantic as the rest of Las Alamandas.

Rates: $365–$499

LAS ALAMANDAS (RESERVATIONS)
P.O. Box 1753
Costa Mesa, CA 92628

Phone   800-223-6510

LAS BRISAS
Acapulco

> Oh, when I was in love with you,
>   Then I was clean and brave,
> And miles around the wander grew
>   How well I did behave.
>
> —"Oh, When I Was In Love" by A.E. Housman

Tiered into a hillside overlooking Acapulco Bay, Las Brisas specializes in romance. Its 300 casita-style rooms command excellent views of the harbors and are appointed in a luxurious fashion. The refrigerator and mini-bar allow you to mix a drink to enjoy on your spacious veranda or by your own private, or semi-private, pool (there are over 250 pools in all). To enhance the luxury of your private pool, the staff at Las Brisas places fresh hibiscus blossoms on it each morning. It should be noted that the rooms further up the hill offer more peace and quiet for they are a greater distance from the road.

Las Brisas's excellent service makes enjoying the resort easy and pleasurable. During the peak winter months when service at other resorts suffers, Las Brisas increases its staff so that there are three staffers to every guest. Even more amazing is the resort's "no tipping" policy, something that comes in very handy at the posh Lo Concha Beach Club where guests are granted membership during their stays. The Beach Club is the perfect place to spend the day before heading to Belavista, the resort's romantic restaurant.

Rates: $380–$635

LAS BRISAS
Apdo. Postal 281
39868 Acapulco, Gro., Mexico

Phone   52-74-84-15-80
Toll free   800-228-3000
Fax   52-74-84-22-69

Morocco

LA MAMOUNIA
Marrakech

> Then talk not of inconstancy,
>   False hearts, and broken vows;
> If I, by miracle, can be
> This lifelong minute true to thee,
>   'Tis all that heaven allows.

> —"Love And Life" by Lord Rochester

Downtown historic Marrakech would seem an unlikely place to find a tranquil oasis, but that is exactly what La Mamounia is. This hotel was built between 1922 and 1924 on the grounds of an 18th-century palace owned by Mohammed III, a sultan who used Marrakech as his capital. Not surprisingly, Mohammed surrounded his palace with beautiful gardens (thirty-two acres' worth), which are still maintained today.

It is this combination of space amidst the cramped confines of an old city that makes La Mamounia special. It most definitely influenced Winston Churchill who came every winter until 1952. The rooms in which Churchill stayed remain pretty much the same. True, much of the furniture has been reupholstered and touched up, but their charm remains intact. You can still find many of Churchill's personal effects here ranging from walking sticks to signed Churchill oil paintings. The hotel even has a Churchill Suite that you can rent for around $1,200 a night. Nearby you'll hit upon more history in the Jman El Fna Square, a bustling tangle of markets and historic landmarks.

Even without the Churchill connection, La Mamounia would still offer an enchanting experience. Upon arrival, you'll be greeted by staff adorned in baggy white pants and pointed yellow slippers. They'll take your bags through the spacious public areas featuring marble floors, Rabat carpets, massive chandeliers, and intricate stucco arches. The hotel's public areas also include four restaurants serving everything from Moroccan to French cuisine.

Rates: $375–$720

LA MAMOUNIA
Avenue Bab Jdid
Marrakech, Morocco

Phone	212-4-448981
Toll free	800-223-6800
Fax	212-4-444940

PALAIS JAMAI
Fez

> Don't hurry with their tender dew,
> Sweetness complete and incomplete;
> For I have lived to wait for you:
> My heart was your approaching feet.
>
> —"The Footsteps" by Paul Valéry

Northern Africa is home to some of the world's most ancient cities, such as Cairo and Fez. It's in the ancient walled city of Fez that you'll find one of the Arab world's most haunting and exotic souks, a type of marketplace. Nearby, you'll also find the Palais Jamai.

Palais Jamai benefits from its distinctive city-setting. Built in the 18th century, the hotel has a definite Moorish influence. This is most evident inside where public areas are highlighted by gilded arches lit by sparkling chandeliers. For such an old hotel, the rooms are remarkably comfortable and feature many modern amenities not found in other old hotels in the area. Best of all, many of the rooms overlook the exotic city or the hotel's terraced pool surrounded by charming gardens.

Rates: $245–$500

PALAIS JAMAI

Bab El Guissa
Fez, Morocco

Phone	212-6-634331
Toll free	800-888-4747
Fax	212-6-635096

███████

Nevis

FOUR SEASONS RESORT NEVIS
Charlestown

> 'Tis not thy love I fear to lose,
>   That will in spite of absence hold;
> But 'tis the benefit and use
>   Is lost, as in imprison'd gold:
> Which though the sum be ne'er so great,
> Enriches nothing but conceit.
>
> > —"To Mrs. M.A. Upon Absence" by Katherine
> > Philips

The Four Seasons Resort Nevis delivers the romantic promise of the Caribbean. Located on 350 breathtaking acres, the resort will exceed your expectations for luxury, a remarkable feat considering the high expectations that come with the Four Seasons name.

Accommodations lie in a dozen two-story cottage-like annexes. Each of these buildings contains a dozen or so rooms that have to rank among the most spacious in the Caribbean. A combination of wicker and mahogany furniture give the rooms a feeling of Caribbean elegance. Depending upon the weather, you can either use the air-conditioning, or open the doors to your veranda, turn on the ceiling fan, and enjoy the soothing sounds of the nearby surf as you and your lover enjoy a night of serene sleep.

With a half-mile of white-sand beach just steps from your door, you would think that water sports would be the main attraction at this resort. However this is not the case. The beach and freeform pools are forced to share top-billing with the resort's eighteen-hole championship golf course. Designed by Robert Trent Jones II, the golf course winds its way up the slope of Nevis Peak and offers views as splendid as the course is challenging.

After a long day in the sun, you'll be ready for a good meal. For this, you could always go to the Dining Room and find superb cuisine, impeccable service, and an elegant decor. But for a truly romantic setting, order room service and enjoy dinner on your veranda as the rolling surf serenades you.

Rates: $450–$1,025 (seasonal & package sensitive)

FOUR SEASONS RESORT NEVIS

P.O. Box 565
Pinney's Beach
Charlestown, Nevis, West Indies

Phone	869-469-1111
Toll free	800-332-3442
Fax	869-469-1040

NISBET PLANTATION

St. James Parish

> Sorrow was there made fair,
> And Passion, wise; Tears, a delightful thing;
> Silence, beyond all speech, a wisdom rare;
>   She made all her sighs sing,
> And all things with so sweet a sadness move;
> As made my heart both grieve and love.
>
> —"I Saw My Lady" by Anonymous

Enjoy the romance of a Caribbean plantation at this tropical retreat. Once a sugar plantation, the grounds are now covered with towering pines and dotted with the guest lodgings and an overgrown sugar refinery. Most of the guest lodgings are located in duplex villas amid the palm groves. Peaked beam ceilings and white-washed walls give the rooms a spacious feeling while ceiling fans and louvered windows provide cross-ventilation.

As you walk through the palm groves, the ground turns to sand and soon you are standing on Nisbet's glorious beach. A half-mile long, Nisbet's secluded white-sand beach ranks among the best in the Caribbean. In the opposite direction from the beach, the old plantation house dominates the landscape. Stonework, timber flooring, antiques, and mahogany furnishings fill the grand old estate. The dining terrace serves as the stage for romantic dinners at night, while during the day you can enjoy lunch on the beach.

Rates: $295–$525

NISBET PLANTATION
Newcastle Street
St. James Parish, Nevis, West Indies

Phone	869-469-9325
Fax	869-469-9864

New Zealand

HOTEL DU VIN
Pokeno

> I've become the most forgetful of all the forgetful,
> Quietly the years sail by.
> Those unkissed lips, unsmiling eyes
> Will never return to me.
>
> —"Instead Of Wisdom" by Anna Akhmaatova

Just forty-five minutes from Auckland, Hotel de Vin is the perfect place from which to base a romantic vacation in New Zealand. Colorful gardens interlaced with brick pathways surround forty-six lavish rooms in chalets featuring such amenities as bathrobes and VCRs. While all rooms receive daily plates of fresh fruit, the Executive Suites with extended living areas and soaking tubs are well worth the extra cost.

Hotel du Vin sits alongside the De Redcliffe Winery, and the Huna National Forest is within walking distance. Thus you're able to hike through the forest in the morning, observing many species of waterfowl as you go, and then return for an afternoon wine tour and tasting. If you're an angler, the hotel offers guided flyfishing tours at nearby lakes and streams. At night, you can eat at the hotel or drive into Auckland and enjoy its nightlife.

Rates: $190–$225

HOTEL DU VIN
Lyons Road
RD 31 Pokeno
South Auckland, New Zealand

Phone   64-9-478-0274
Fax   64-9-479-7968

HUKA LODGE
Taupo

> - Oh, the first flowers—what a scent they have!
> And what a charm breathes in the murmuring
> Of the first yes that comes from the lips you love!
>
> —"Nevermore" by Paul Verlaine

Today's visitors to Huka Lodge would never guess its beginnings as a humble fishing lodge if not for its setting in a natural wonderland. Indeed, Huka was born more than sixty years ago when Alan Pye cut a path through the heart of North Island's bush so that he could enjoy tranquillity while fishing on the Waikato River. Since then, Huka has developed into a world-class resort deserving of its membership in Relais & Châteaux.

Staying at Huka Lodge combines the best of New Zealand hospitality with the ambiance of the region. Accommodations consist of twenty junior suites housed in a series of duplex cottages. Accented by cathedral ceilings, these spacious rooms are furnished with king-sized beds and wicker furniture, and feature sitting areas, mini-bars, furnished verandas, and skylit baths.

Though fishing is still a major attraction at Huka, the resort features a full array of activities. At the resort, you can enjoy tennis, croquet, and river flyfishing. Just a short distance away, you'll find the striking Huka Falls and the beautiful Lake Taupo where you can fish or take an exhilarating jet-boat ride.

For such a small resort, Huka's restaurant is a surprise. Its chef prepares delicious five-course meals. Arrive before the 8 pm seating, and take a tour of the impressive wine cellar. Here you'll find many rare vintages that will compliment your wonderfully delicious and romantic meal.

Rates: $510–$745

HUKA LODGE
Box 95
Taupo, New Zealand

Phone   64-7-378-5791
Fax   64-7-378-0427

Republic of Palau

PALAU PACIFIC RESORT
Palau

> Somewhere or other there must surely be
> > The face not seen, the voice not heard,
> The heart that not yet—never yet—ah me!
> > Made answer to my word.
>
> —"Somewhere Or Other" by Christina Rossetti

Once a territory of the United States, the Republic of Palau hugs the border of Asia and is comprised of 350 islands of which only nine are populated. Those who used to watch Jacques Cousteau have probably seen the islands as they were one of the scientist's favorite dive sites. Indeed, Palau has long been known as one of the world's top dive destinations.

In addition to diving, guests can now enjoy first-class accommodations at the Palau Pacific Resort. A favorite with the likes of John F. Kennedy Jr. and Daryl Hannah, the resort covers sixty-four acres and houses 160 rooms and suites. Be sure to request one of the ocean-front rooms; they enjoy spectacular views of the sea and there's nearby coral reefs beneath the ocean surface.

Surprisingly the resort offers much more than diving. On the grounds, you'll find tennis, hiking trails, a fitness center, and a driving range. Of course, diving is the main attraction and non-divers can even attend *Splash,* the resort's dive school. Or you can even forgo the scuba gear and enjoy the beauty of the reefs by snorkeling. In these reefs, there are 1,500 species of fish, 700 varieties of coral, and giant clams. For a more relaxing activity, you can lounge around the pool, or savor delicious meals of seafood and Pacific Rim cuisine at the resort's restaurant.

Rates: $235–$600

PALAU PACIFIC RESORT
Koror
Republic of Palau 96940

Phone	680-488-2600
Toll free	800-327-8585
Fax	680-488-1601

St. Kitts

RAWLINS PLANTATION
St. Kitts

> The blood runs thinner, yet the heart
> remains as ever deep and tender.
> O last belated love, thou art
> a blend of joy and of hopeless surrender.
>
> —"Last Love" by Fyodor Tyutchev

Built from the ruins of a 17th-century sugar cane plantation, this resort enjoys an idyllic perch 350 feet up the slopes of Mount Liamuiga at the undeveloped northern end of St. Kitts. From this setting, you'll be able to gaze off into the distance at the neighboring islands.

The outbuildings of the old plantation have been converted into guest quarters. They are set amid twenty acres of beautifully landscaped grounds and surrounded by the sugar cane that was once the life-blood of the plantation. In this setting of tropical flora and fauna, you'll stay in a delightfully unpretentious room with wood floors, stone walls, and a four-poster bed. Keeping with the original feeling of the plantation, the rooms lack air-conditioning, telephones, and television, but the trade winds and ceiling fans are usually enough to make the rooms comfortable. Even if you're not a honeymooner, try for the honeymoon suite located in an old windmill.

Breakfast and dinner are included in the rates, but unlike some hotels, this is a welcome luxury not a trap. Owner/Chef Claire Rawson and her staff take incredible care to select only the freshest ingredients from the plantation's gardens, local markets, and local fishermen. As a result, you'll be rewarded with flavor-infused dishes with strong West Indian influences.

Due to its remote location, it's a good idea to rent a

car to explore the island. The best beaches are at least sixteen miles away. However, also due to its location, the plantation is the perfect place to be lazy, relax in a hammock, and enjoy a good book.

Rates: $275–$420

RAWLINS PLANTATION
Box 340
St. Kitts, West Indies

Phone   869-465-6221
Fax   869-465-4954

Scotland

TURNBERRY HOTEL
Turnberry

—Can you recall our ecstasy of long ago?
—Why stir the memory? Why do you want to know?

—Does your heart beat at just my name, as ever?
Do you still see my spirit in your dreams?—No. Never.

—O lovely days of speechless happiness
When our mouths met!—Speechless? Perhaps it was.

—How blue the sky was and what hopes we had!
—Hope ran away to the black sky, defeated.

   —"An Exchange Of Feelings" by Paul Verlaine

Nestled along the sea, the Turnberry Hotel cuts a striking image. The long white building stands in stark contrast to the deep, perfectly green grass surrounding it. Building on the contrast, Turnberry's muted red roof is dotted with white chimneys. Indeed, Turnberry's impressive facade raises your expectations before you ever step inside. Thankfully, Turnberry delivers.

Designed in the grand Edwardian style, the Turnberry sits amid two of the world's finest eighteen-hole championship courses. Though the Turnberry houses 132 guest rooms, be sure to request one with a view of the sea. Refurbished just a few years ago, the traditionally appointed rooms include such luxurious trappings as fabrics by Colefax and Fowler and soaking tubs. Suites have whirlpool baths.

Besides the two golf courses, Turnberry features a full-service spa and three excellent restaurants. At the spa, you can receive any combination of the twenty-five treatments available or enjoy the indoor pool or squash courts. Afterwards, you can relax at the spa's low-fat restaurant, the Bay. Turnberry's main dining room serves more traditional dishes amidst Edwardian decor and Ionic columns. Or if you're looking for a simple, hearty meal, try a roast at the Clubhouse. Whichever you choose, your meals at Turnberry will only enhance your romantic stay.

Rates: $395–$595

TURNBERRY HOTEL
Turnberry
Ayrshire, Scotland KA26 9LT

Phone   44-1655-331000
Fax   44-1655-331706

Singapore

RAFFLES
Singapore

> And there on the much-used, lowly bed
> I had the body of love, I had the lips,
> the voluptuous and rosy lips of ecstasy -
> rosy lips of such ecstasy, that even now
> as I write, after so many years!
> In my solitary house, I am drunk again.
>
> —"One Night" by C.P. Cavafy

Raffles is a hotel steeped in history. It was originally a tiffin house, a restaurant serving light lunches. In 1886, it began operating as a hotel and has since served as one of Asia's premier destinations. The hotel has been especially popular with authors and has hosted the likes of Joseph Conrad, Somerset Maugham, Noel Coward, and Rudyard Kipling.

Several years ago, Raffles underwent an extensive renovation and emerged as glorious as ever. The rooms in this rambling estate feature high molded ceilings, Oriental carpets, ceiling fans, and period furnishings.

Excellent service makes staying at Raffles even more enjoyable. Courteous, prompt, attentive, and unobtrusive are the hallmarks which each staff member lives by. From the famous Longbar—home of the Singapore sling—to the restaurants, to the shops, the gracious staff pampers you and ensures that your stay at Raffles is as memorable as the hotel's history.

Rates: From $650

RAFFLES
1 Beach Road
Singapore, 189673

Phone	65-337-1886
Fax	65-339-7650

South Africa

THE CELLARS HOHENORT
Constantia

> Trust me, I mind not, though Life lours,
>> The bringing me here; nay bring me here again!
> I am just the same as when
> Our days were a joy, and our paths through flowers.

> —"After A Journey" by Thomas Hardy

The Constantia Valley has long been known for its superb wines. The vintages produced here have dazzled many famous palates, among them Napoleon's and Jane Austen's. You would think that such magnificent wine country would be isolated, but this beautiful little valley is only fifteen minutes from Cape Town.

The country house at Cellars Hohenort once served as the Cape governor's wine cellar in the 1700s. Today this lovely Relais & Châteaux hotel sits amid nine acres of glorious formal gardens. Here you'll find fifty guest rooms perfect for romance but the garden suites are prized for their spacious layouts and private gardens. The public rooms feature original works of art and many period antiques. Equally attractive is the hotel's gourmet French restaurant and less formal bistro.

Rates: $410–$590

THE CELLARS HOHENORT
15 Hohenhort Avenue
Constantia, South Africa 7848

Phone 27-21-794-2137
Fax 27-21-794-2149

ELLERMAN HOUSE
Cape Town

> I cannot say what loves have come and gone;
> I only know that summer sang in me
> A little while, that in me sings no more.
>
> —From "What Lips My Lips Have Kissed"
>   by Edna St. Vincent Millay

Built by shipping magnate Sir John Ellerman in the early 1900s, Ellerman House is now one of South Africa's top hotels and one of the world's most romantic.

Nestled on the slopes of Lion's Head at stunning Bantry Bay, Ellerman House commands breathtaking views of the bay and the sea as well as the mountains. Ellerman's refined architecture sets a romantic mood. Graceful masonry work is highlighted by arches, and palm trees dot the beautifully landscaped grounds. The hotel's public rooms are done in an intimate Edwardian style that continues into its cozy guest rooms and suites. Behind the hotel, a simple pool is made breathtaking by the plush green lawn surrounding it and its views of Bantry Bay beyond.

Ellerman's Edwardian-style dining room maintains the inn's theme of intimacy. Decorated with care and detail, the dining room reflects an elegance rarely found in today's newer restaurants. A world-class staff makes dining here reminiscent of an era when top-flight service was the rule not the exception. Lastly, the flavorful food is skillfully prepared and is easily matched with many of the fine local vintages found on the wine list.

Rates: $625–$650

ELLERMAN HOUSE
180 Kloof Road
Cape Town, South Africa 8001

Phone   27-21-439-91-82
Fax   27-21-434-72-57

THE GRANDE ROCHE
Paarl

> Rose leaves, when the rose is dead,
> Are heaped for the beloved's bed;
> And so thy thoughts, when thou art gone,
> Love itself shall slumber on.
>
> —"Music" by Percy Bysshe Shelley

A stay at the Grand Roche is a magical experience. Located in the heart of South Africa's wine country, the highlights of this Relais & Châteaux hotel are its sumptuous rooms and its gourmet restaurant.

The lodgings at the Grand Roche have a definite country-house feeling. Numbering 35, they can be found in tastefully renovated stables, coach houses, and several newer structures with vine-covered terraces. Each room combines a high level of privacy and luxury to create a romantic haven where you and your lover can sleep late into the morning. Just outside your room, you'll find a brick pathway leading to the main house where the hotel's restaurant is located.

Recently reopened after a $350,000 renovation, the hotel's restaurant, Bosman's, remains one of South Africa's most romantic restaurants. Bosman's views—of the Paarl Rock, Drakenstein Mountains, and the vineyards stretching off into the distance—inspire romance. Inside, the ambiance of the region continues to dominate. You can choose from many local as well as international vintages on the wine list; there are 300 or so choices. Chef Frank Zlomke's creations are continentally inspired. Zlomke uses local ingredients to produce light and healthy dishes including a series he calls Flavors of the Cape. This series will allow you and your lover to enjoy low-cholesterol and vegetarian dishes in this idyllic setting.

Rates: $350–$450

THE GRANDE ROCHE
Plantasie Street, Paarl
P.O. Box 6038
Paarl, South Africa 7620

Phone   27-21-8-632727
Fax   27-21-8-632220

THE PALACE OF THE LOST CITY
Sun City

> Let me not to the marriage of true minds
> Admit impediments. Love is not love
> Which alters when it alteration finds,
> Or bends with the remover to remove.
>
> —"True Love Not At The Mercy Of Time And
> Circumstance" by William Shakespeare

Pure romantic fantasy best describes the Palace of the Lost City. Located in rugged desert about 100 miles from Johannesburg, the Palace's Angkor Wat-inspired architecture does a good job of giving the resort a dated feeling. Surrounding the complex is a man-made jungle complete with 1.6 million trees and over 10,000 orchids.

The interior of the hotel matches the exterior in both flair and in style. Its 340 luxurious rooms and suites feature hand-carved furniture and colorful fabrics designed especially for the hotel. Particularly nice are the spacious amenity-laden baths, a welcome luxury after a long day in the sun. Downstairs you'll find grand sweeping staircases, striking sculptures, frescoes, inlaid marble floors, furniture crafted of pear, mahogany, and ebony, and beautiful mosaics. There's also the hotel's two top-flight restaurants to discover.

Outside you'll rejoice in the playful design of the pool. Here you can catch one of the pool's seven-foot-high waves and ride it all the way up to the white-sand beach. Or you can try the water slide or simply relax on a tube as you drift down the Sacred River. If the pool and its attractions begin to bore you, try one of the resort's two eighteen-hole championship golf courses at the Gary Player Country Club. A world-class golfing destination, this club hosts the Million Dollar Golf Challenge. Just watch out for the hazard on hole 13… live crocodiles.

Rates: $367–$4,030

THE PALACE OF THE LOST CITY
P.O. Box 30
Sun City
Bophuthatswana, South Africa SC0316

Phone   27-1465-73000
Fax   27-1465-73111

SANDTON SUN & TOWERS INTER-CONTINENTAL
Johannesburg

> Let me confess that we two must be twain,
> Although our undivided loves are one;
> So shall those blots that do with me remain,
> Without thy help, by me be borne alone.
>
> —"Let Me Confess" by William Shakespeare

South Africa's vibrant commercial capital, Johannes-burg, is modern and cosmopolitan. Increasingly, it is becoming the destination of business trips. Unfortunately, many businesspeople fail to realize how exciting this city can be and leave their spouse at home. I urge you not to make the same mistake.

Originally a gold-mining town, Johannesburg still ranks as one of the best places to shop for gold and gems. Its shops, both in the city and suburbs, offer a dazzling array of jewelry and present the opportunity to make a purchase for that someone special in your life. If jewelry isn't your thing, ask the concierge about the Crocodile Ramble, a monthly event in the surrounding countryside where you can buy antiques. For the more adventurous, the concierge can arrange an airplane charter to Madikwe Game Reserve on the Botswana border.

While you're enjoying all that Johannesburg has to offer, you'll be glad you stayed at the Sandton Sun. One of South Africa's best hotels, the Sun is as modern as they come. From its steel and glass construction to its curved front desk of light-colored wood, the hotel makes no apologies for being contemporary. Yet despite its contem-porary decor, the hotel has one old-fashioned amenity that will never go out of style… service! From the always-helpful concierge, to the attentive valets, service at the Sandton Sun is rarely equaled elsewhere.

Rates: Doubles from $250

SANDTON SUN & TOWERS INTER-CONTINENTAL
P.O. Box 784902
Sandton 2146
Johannesburg, South Africa

Phone   27-11-780-5000
Fax   27-11-780-5002

SINGATA PRIVATE GAME RESERVE
Johannesburg

> Alas! madam, for stealing of a kiss,
> Have I so much your mind then offended?
> Have I then done so grievously amiss,
> That by no means it may be amended?
> Then revenge you, and the next way is this:
> Another kiss shall have my life ended.
> For to my mouth the first my heart did suck,
> The next shall clean out of my breast it pluck.
>
> —Untitled by Sir Thomas Wyatt

With 35,000 acres and a maximum capacity of twenty-eight guests, Singata Private Game Reserve might be the most private resort in the world. Located at the southwestern edge of Kruger National Park, this vast expanse of land serves as your private playground. Just a short drive in a Land Rover will bring you near many of the continent's great animals like leopards, lions, giraffes, rhinos, hippos, and crocodiles.

A base for your excursions is the grand main house of Singata. Constructed of stone, wood, and thatch, the house is decorated with game trophies, antiques, and native folk art. You'll dine on refined cuisine accompanied by the finest South African vintages. After dinner, you'll retire to one of fourteen suites. There you'll be ensconced in luxurious appointments like ebony beds, clawfoot tubs, indoor and outdoor showers, and stone fireplaces. No wonder this is considered by many to be the world's best resort. Singata is a member of the prestigious Relais & Châteaux group.

Rates: From $950

SINGATA PRIVATE GAME RESERVE
Private Bag X27
Benmore
Johannesburg, South Africa 2010

Phone   27-11-784-7077
Fax   27-11-784-7667

Spain

HACIENDA BENAZUZA
Seville

> Being myself captived here in care
> My heart, (whom none with servile bands can tie
> But the fair tresses of your golden hair)
> Breaking his prison, forth to you doth fly.
>
> —"Being Myself Captived Here" by Edmund Spenser

On a hilltop just outside of Seville sits the ancient Hacienda Benazuza. Built in the 10th century by the counts of Benazuza (members of a noble Moorish family), the hotel has hosted nobility throughout its history. In fact, until recently, only nobility were invited to stay in its luxurious rooms.

Hacienda Benazuza's architecture reflects its Moorish past. Moorish arches are found throughout as are wide corridors preferred by the Moors. These long tiled corridors are carpeted in Berber rugs which absorb the sounds of foot traffic. True to its Spanish heritage, the hotel has its own chapel and the grounds are actually an olive grove. You'll enjoy these tasty olives at Alqueria, the hotel's restaurant, where marinated olives and freshly baked bread begin the meals.

Each of the hotel's forty-four rooms is unique. You'll find such historical treasures as 500-year-old closet doors and paintings by Spanish aristocrats. Thankfully though the bathrooms are tiled and equipped with all the modern luxuries you would expect.

Rates: $250–$425

HACIENDA BENAZUZA
Virgen de las Nieves
41800 Sanlucar la Mayor
Seville, Spain

Phone   34-5-570-3344
Fax   34-5-570-3410

TERMES LA GARRIGA
La Garriga

> My love for him is growing and shall grow
> Throughout my life as long as there's a part
> Where it can grow to greatness in that heart;
> Then at the last my love may show
> So very clearly he shall have no doubt.
>
> —"My Love For Him Is Growing" by Mary,
>   Queen of Scots

For Americans, Spanish spas are remarkably different from their American counterparts. Operators of Spanish spas see pure and total relaxation as a health treatment, while many of their American counterparts integrate health food and exercise into their regimens. Well, you'll find that Termes La Garriga holds true to the Spanish spa tradition.

Originally built in 1891, Termes La Garriga is located just outside of Barcelona. The rooms are tastefully decorated and very private, but the highlight of a stay here is the regimen of relaxation. The day begins with breakfast which guests can enjoy between 8:30 and 10 a.m. After breakfast, it's time for treatments like massage and hydrotherapy. Around 2 p.m. or so, a large lunch is served with plenty of wine, and this is followed by a siesta in your room or out by the pool. After siesta, guests return to the spa for another round of "medical service." Finally, it's time for another delicious meal. After dining, you can retire to your room, or travel into Barcelona and dance until the wee hours of the morning.

Rates: $150–$400

TERMES LA GARRIGA
Calle Banys 23
08530 La Garriga
Barcelona, Spain

Phone   34-93-3-871-7086

Switzerland

BADRUTT'S PALACE
St. Moritz

> So, when love speechless is, she doth express
> A depth in love and that depth bottomless.
> Now, since my love is tongueless, know me such
> Who speak but little 'cause I love so much.
>
> —"To His Mistress Objecting To Him Neither Toying
>   Nor Talking" by Robert Herrick

Majestically situated amid breathtakingly beautiful and unspoiled scenery, Badrutt's Palace is the perfect place to enjoy a romantic stay. The map says it's in St. Moritz, but your heart will likely tell you that you're in Nirvana.

In order to fully enjoy the splendor of the Swiss Alps, it's important that you select the right room. While all rooms at Badrutt's are beautifully decorated and feature such luxuries as bathrobes and fresh roses, you should request a "maximum double" facing the mountains. This will allow you to rise in the morning, venture out onto the balcony, and enjoy the brilliant reflection of the sun as it bounces off the snow-capped peaks. It's a good idea to wear sunglasses when doing this.

During the winter, the mountains beckon to be skied. The ski areas surrounding St. Moritz are among the best in the world, and the hotel even has its own ski school to help you improve your skills. After a couple of days skiing, your legs will probably need some time off. That is the perfect opportunity to discover the vast array of activities at the hotel. You can enjoy the warm waters of "Acapulco," the indoor pool fed by waterfalls and boasting alpine views through its large wraparound window. If this doesn't bring your legs back, try the sauna or a massage. Regardless, Badrutt's will definitely leave memories of Swiss elegance and romance.

Rates: $321–$489

BADRUTT'S PALACE
CH-7500
St. Moritz, Switzerland

Phone	41-81-837-10-00
Fax	41-81-837-29-99

GRAND HOTEL VICTORIA-JUNGFRAU
Interlaken

> O, were I loved as I desire to be!
> What is there in the great sphere of the earth,
> Or range of evil between death and birth,
> That I should fear,—if I were loved by thee?
>
> —"O, Were I Loved As I Desire To Be!" by Alfred,
> Lord Tennyson

When it comes to alpine settings, it's hard to imagine a prettier place than Interlaken, a village sitting on an isthmus between two lakes. Here you'll find the Grand Hotel Victoria-Jungfrau, a stately structure set against the Jungfrau Mountain range.

Famous for its high level of service, the Victoria-Jungfrau has welcomed guests for over 130 years. While the public rooms underwent a recent renovation in 1992, only a portion of the guest rooms underwent the same treatment. As a result, some of the 216 rooms have a decidedly modern feeling while others retain their old-fashioned charm. For romance's sake, choose an unrenovated room with a view of the mountains.

The public areas of the Grand Hotel Victoria-Jungfrau rival the world's best. The lobby produces an ambiance of refined elegance in its art nouveau setting, while the salons add grandeur with their belle epoque styling. La Terrasse with its marble columns and inlaid marble floor serves French cuisine in a formal atmosphere while a pianist provides soothing music. For a more relaxed dining experience, try the cozy Jungfrau-Stube specializing in traditional Swiss fare.

Besides its beautiful mountain setting, great food, and great service, the main attraction of the Victoria-Jungfrau is its spa. The highlight of the spa, from an architectural standpoint, is the indoor pool with its arched ceiling supported by marble columns and its natural light provided by a large arched window. When you're not swimming laps, you can relax in the Turkish baths, fresh and saltwater whirlpools, and saunas. Of course, you could also opt for a soothing massage. For the more fanatical fitness buffs, the spa can even perform complete stress evaluation tests to find your body's physical limits.

Rates: $285–$585

GRAND HOTEL VICTORIA-JUNGFRAU
3800 Interlaken, Switzerland

Phone	41-33-828-2828
Fax	41-33-828-2880

Thailand

AMANPURI
Phuket

> Love is its own great loveliness always,
> And takes new lustre from the touch of time;
> Its bough owns no December and no May,
> But bears its blossom into Winter's clime.
>
> —"Love" by Thomas Hood

Terraced above a beautiful beach in Phuket is the luxury resort named Amanpuri, a Sanskrit word meaning "Place of Peace." Indeed Amanpuri is a peaceful private retreat favored by celebrities like Fergie and Mick Jagger. Musician Carol Conners visited here with her best friend and says, "Not a minute of the day went by that I did not wish to be with someone I loved. Romantic beyond romantic."

Inspired by Buddhist temples, the forty private pavilion suites and twenty-eight villas serve as your own private hideaway. The open and airy floorplan allows you to fully enjoy your view of the beach. Keeping with its Buddhist influences, the decor is simple and uncluttered but still extremely comfortable.

Activities at Amanpuri are centered around the water. Down the steps from your room is a fabulous 100-foot-long black-tiled pool perfect for a morning dip. Further down the hill is the beach where you can sun, swim, surf, and sail. Amancruises, the resort's charter service, offers private excursions to nearby islands and bays. Back up the hill, you'll find a complete health and beauty salon. At night, take advantage of the excellent room service and enjoy a romantic meal in the privacy of your own room.

Rates: $510–$775

AMANPURI

P.O. Box 196
Phuket 83000, Thailand

Phone	66-76-324-333
Toll free	800-421-1490
Fax	66-76-324-100

BANYAN TREE
Phuket

> But true Love is durable fire
> In the mind ever burning;
> never sick, never old, never dead,
> From itself never turning.
>
> —"Walsinghame" by Walter Raleigh

Located in the idyllic region of Phuket, Banyan Tree is a world apart. The grounds of this spa resort hug the private beach of Bang Tao Bay. The treatments at the spa pamper the body and the soul. Indeed stress disappears from your life as you and your lover achieve total relaxation together. In addition to the world-class spa, the resort features a complete fitness center and tennis courts where you can exert your newly relaxed muscles.

The rooms at Banyan Tree rank among the most luxurious in the world. Lodgings consist of ninety-eight villas spread throughout the lush grounds and each feature raised king-sized beds, private gardens, and sunken open-air tubs. Forty-six villas even have their own private swimming pools.

Another luxury of Banyan Tree is its relationship with four neighboring hotels. As a result, guests can choose from a wide array of restaurant and additional recreational activities. With these additional amenities, Banyan Tree offers you the possibility to do everything, or if you choose, you can always relax and do nothing.

Rates: $125–$316

BANYAN TREE
33 Moo 4
Stisoonthorn Road
Cherngtalay
Amphur Talang
Phuket 83110, Thailand

Phone   66-76-32-4374
Fax   66-76-32-4375

MANOHRA SONG
Bangkok

> You think I give myself to you?
> Not so, my friend, you do not see
> My single purpose and intent -
> To make you give myself to me.
>
> —"Giving" by Nora B. Cunningham

If you're going to be in Thailand for a more than a week, you might want to consider a cruise on the *Manohra Song*. Originally a rice barge, the forty-year-old Manohra Song travels the famed Menam Chao Phraya, "The River of Kings." Kathleen Heinecke has renovated the *Manohra Song* from the teak deck on up. Each of the four deluxe, high-ceiling staterooms feature raised beds so that you and your lover can gaze out the oversized windows. The two-day cruises go from Bangkok to the ancient capital of Ayutthaya and back. The price is all-inclusive and covers all meals, drinks, and guides.

Rates: $372

MANOHRA SONG
257 1/3 Charoen Nakorn Road
Thonburi
Bangkok 10600, Thailand

Phone   66-2-4760021

POPPIES SAMUI
Koh Samui

> What is it that Love chaunts? thy perfect praise.
> What is it that Love prays? worthy to prove.
> What is it Love desires? thy length of days.
> What is it that Love asks? return of love.
>
> —"Music, And Frankincense Of Flowers" by Julian
> Fane

Located on Thailand's southern island, Koh Samui, Poppies Samui offers lovers romance in a tropical paradise. The resort's two-dozen cottages are hidden in lush gardens laced with streams. Additionally, each cottage has its own private garden and is appointed with solid teak furniture, Thai silks, and sunken marble tubs.

Poppies sits on beautiful Chaweng Beach. Considered one the most pristine in the world, its powder-fine, white sand embraces your bare feet. The particular stretch of Chaweng that Poppies occupies is extra special since it has no coral reef. This allows you and your lover to wade out into the surf without fear of cutting your feet. Nearby is Angthong Marine National Park consisting of forty-seven islands, and it's well worth a day's excursion.

Rates: $132–$220

POPPIES SAMUI
P.O. Box 1
Chaweng Beach
Koh Samui 84320, Thailand

Phone   66-077-422-419
Fax   66-077-422-420

SHERATON GRANDE LAGUNA BEACH
Phuket

> Therefore the Love which us doth bind
> But Fate so enviously debars,
> Is the conjunction of the mind,
> And opposition of the stars.
>
> —"The Definition of Love" by Andrew Marvell

The Sheraton Grande Laguna Beach is a sprawling resort featuring every luxury a romantic could hope for. Centered on an island in the lagoon, the resort spreads out onto the white-sand beach of Bang Tao Bay. The Sheraton Grande boasts a wide array of activities to keep you busy during the day. Physical activities include tennis, windsurfing, golf on an eighteen-hole championship course, swimming laps in Asia's longest pool, and scuba diving. Additionally, the resort offers such diversions as deep-sea fishing and sailing.

After a long day in the sun and surf, you will have quite an appetite. Thankfully, Sheraton Grande Laguna Beach houses nine restaurants to satisfy your every craving. Especially romantic is Chao Lay. Located on the beach, Chao Lay serves delicious southern Thai food with a heavy emphasis on fresh seafood. While you dine, live classical music serenades you.

After dinner, you'll probably be ready to retire to your room. All of the resort's 292 rooms and thirty-six suites offer views of water. Some overlook the ocean, some the lagoon, and others the pool. The rooms are comfortable, and when combined with the overall ambiance of the hotel, romantic enough. But for those of you who want a little more, this resort offers a special lodging option, the Grande Villas.

The Grande Villas are an exclusive world within the resort. Set in a lushly landscaped garden, the villas face either the ocean or the lagoon and share a freeform pool. Staying at the Villas comes with certain luxuries not found elsewhere at the Sheraton Grande: in-room check-in, packing and unpacking, video and CD players, and turndown service. Most importantly, the Villas come with twenty-four-hour on-call service to ensure that your every need is satisfied no matter what the hour.

Rates: $287–$836

SHERATON GRANDE LAGUNA BEACH
Bang Tao Bay
Phuket, 83110, Thailand

Phone	66-76-324-101
Fax	66-76-324-108

Turkey

CIRAGAN PALACE
Istanbul

Keep your eyes open when you kiss: do: when
You kiss. All silly time else, close them to;
Unsleeping, I implore you (dear) pursue
In darkness me, as I do you again
Instantly we part... only me both then
And when your fingers fall, let there be two
Only, 'in that dream-kingdom': I would have you
Me alone recognize your citizen.

Before who wanted eyes, making love, so?
I do now. However we are driven and hide,
What state we keep all other states condemn,
We see ourselves, we watch the solemn glow
Of empty courts we kiss in. Open wide!
You do, you do, and I look into them.
        —Untitled by John Berryman

Istanbul has long been considered one of the world's great cities. Perched on both sides of the Bosphorus—the crossroads between Asia and Europe—Istanbul enjoys a long and glorious history (including being the capital of the Ottoman Empire).

Completed in 1876, the Ciragan Palace is itself steeped in history. It is here that Sultan Abdul Aziz killed himself and here that Sultan Muran V was imprisoned after he was deposed. Yet despite this troubled past, which also includes a fire, the Ciragan has been remarkably preserved and restored so that you may enjoy its ostentatious luxury just as the Sultans did. Just be sure to book one of the twelve suites in the Sultan's palace so that you may enjoy uninterrupted views of the Bosphorus from your elegant room.

280

In addition to its rich history and luxurious rooms, Ciragan is also home to the world-famous Tugra restaurant. Tugra's high ceilings and ornate crystal chandeliers set the mood for an evening of romance. However, if it is warm outside, forgo the dining room and enjoy your meal on the terrace. Overlooking the Bosphorus, the terrace is flanked by the palace's marble columns and may be Turkey's best dining spot. However, regardless of your seating location, the food will be excellent. With many recipes taken from the Sultans' cookbooks, Tugra serves classical Ottoman cuisine with flair and style fitting for such an elegant setting.

Rates: $395–$650

CIRAGAN PALACE
Ciragan Cad. 84
Istanbul, Turkey

Phone   90-216-258-3377
Toll free   800-223-6800
Fax   90-216-259-6687

Zanzibar

ZANZIBAR SERENA INN
Stone Town

> Then think I love more than I can express,
> And would love more could I but love thee less.

> —"No, No, Fair Heretic" by Sir John Suckling

Off the coast of Tanzania in the Indian Ocean lies the island of Zanzibar. Surrounded by the bluest sea imaginable, Zanzibar is ringed by white, powder-fine beaches. The area's warm, salty ocean waters are known for their ability to enhance relaxation and erase tension.

In such idyllic settings, the best hotels are the ones that make the most of their surroundings. Zanzibar Serena Inn is such a place. Located in the coastal community of Stone Town, Zanzibar Serena Inn is housed in two converted stucco buildings—one being the former British consulate. Many of its fifty-one rooms feature private balconies, while all offer uninterrupted views of the sparkling Indian Ocean. Throughout the hotel, you'll find antique Dutch porcelain and English ceramic tiles. Especially romantic is the private beach and the hotel's seafront restaurant.

Rates: $180

ZANZIBAR SERENA INN
Stone Town, Zanzibar

Phone   255-54-31015

Cruises and Alternate Travel

CRYSTAL CRUISES
Around the World

> You ask me what since we must part
> You shall bring back to me.
> Bring back a pure and faithful heart
> As true as mine to thee.
>
> You talk of gems from foreign lands,
> Of treasure, spoil, and prize.
> Ah love! I shall not search your hands
> But look into your eyes.
>
> —"Gifts" by Juliana Horatia Ewing

Crystal Cruises began with a lofty mission: to bring the golden-age qualities of the grand ocean liners into today's market. This meant that Crystal's ships would have to capture the elegance and personalized service of the past. Thankfully, the company delivered.

Its first ship, *Crystal Harmony,* was launched in 1990 and exceeded the company's expectations. Nearly the size of most superliners, *Crystal Harmony* carries only one-third the number of passengers. As a result, you'll be rewarded with a spacious cabin decorated with luxurious appointments straight from Rodeo Drive. Many of the rooms have their own veranda. With the size of a superliner, the *Crystal Harmony* and her sister ship, *Crystal Symphony,* offer all the amenities you'd expect, except that there are fewer people to share them with!

Depending upon the season, you can cruise nearly every region of the globe. For a little something off the beaten track, try the world cruise in the winter or Alaska in the summer.

Rates: $303–$835

CRYSTAL CRUISES
2121 Avenue of the Stars
Los Angeles, CA 90067

Phone   310-785-9300
Fax   310-785-3891

SEABOURN CRUISE LINE
Around the World

> Who carved Love
> and placed him by
> this fountain,
> thinking
> he could control
> such fire
> with water?
>
> —"A Statue of Eros" by Zenodotos

When was the last time you took a cruise and the only choice you had for a room was a suite? "Never," you say. Then you have never cruised on Seabourn.

On Seabourn, 90% of the rooms are standard suites spreading out to cover a spacious 277 square feet—palatial by cruise-line standards. In your suite, you'll find such luxurious appointments as plush terry towels and robes, marble bath, TV, VCR, a walk-in closet, and a bar stocked to your taste. Even your coffee table converts into a dining table so that you can enjoy course-by-course in-suite service. If you don't care for the standard suite, choose a larger one (many feature private sundecks).

Seabourn offers the standard array of cruise activities: health club, jogging, pools, deck games, driving platforms. It also features activities that other cruise lines don't. On all Seabourn cruises, you'll enjoy cuisine rivaling the best land-based restaurants. More importantly, you can enjoy this cuisine virtually anywhere, thanks to Seabourn's excellent service offerings. Additionally, select cruises will feature fellows from the Hoover Institute—a world renowned think tank at Stanford—to give lectures and host tables at dinner.

As for selection, Seabourn features three ships—*Spirit, Legend,* and *Pride.* Each are equally luxurious and cruise virtually every corner of the globe.

Rates: $535–$1,629

SEABOURN CRUISE LINE
55 Francisco Street
San Francisco, CA 94133

Phone	415-391-7444
Toll free	800-929-4747
Fax	415-391-8518

SILVERSEA CRUISES
Around the World

Time, who is knocking at the gate,
Cannot make you all his boast:
Our garden shall be desolate
But you—a ghost
Timeless; as beauty's timeless norm
You are in passion and in form.

—"Recollection Of First Love" by William Soutar

With service first offered in 1994, Silversea is a relative newcomer to the cruise market, yet its cruises have a timeless quality about them. Their attentive, precise, personal service gives passengers an opportunity to enjoy the grandeur of cruising the world's oceans. Afterall, with water covering three-fifths of the earth's surface, doesn't it make sense that you should be able to enjoy all of mankind's luxuries at sea?

The secret to Silversea's success starts in your cabin. The smallest room is a suite. Most importantly, you can upgrade to one of the many cabins with a veranda. Yet as comfortable as your room is, you'll want to explore the ship's public areas as well. They have an atmosphere of understated elegance that nicely compliments the laid-back attitude of the majority of passengers.

Silversea features two identical ships: *Silver Cloud* and *Silver Wind.* Each can carry up to 296 passengers and cruises most regions of the world (save the Pacific Coast of Mexico and Alaska). Especially nice about cruising Silversea is their all-inclusive prices which cover airfare as well as accommodation at a deluxe pre/post cruise hotel if necessary.

Rates: $494–$894

SILVERSEA CRUISES
110 East Broward Boulevard
Ft. Lauderdale, FL 33301

Phone   954-522-4477

QUEEN ELIZABETH 2
Around the World

> If I stare at you,
> driving slate seas,
> it is because I want to draw from you
> all your loveliness into my own face.
>
>   —"The Straits" by Valerie Gillies

The Queen Elizabeth 2, flagship of the Cunard cruise line, stands as the lone survivor of grand style of ocean travel. When other cruise lines launch new luxury ships, it is the QE2 they are trying to imitate. Yet, in many ways, they never will succeed. The new ultra-luxury yachts lack the QE2's more economic levels of service, and thus only those with a deep wallet can experience them. This leads to a rather homogenous mix of clientele that gives them a feeling of a floating country club. Not on the QE2. The QE2 is a floating city with all of its wonderful color and diversity.

Another unique aspect of the QE2 is its itinerary; it's the only ship to provide regularly scheduled transatlantic service. Thus you'll be able to cruise the waters of the Atlantic in style and enjoy its full majesty. From January to April, the QE2 rounds the world.

As previously mentioned, the QE2 offers several choices when it comes to how much money you wish to spend. Since the levels of service differ between transatlantic and transworld itineraries, reserving a cabin can become a bit confusing. As general rule, first class is always safest; you'll enjoy the spaciousness of your cabin. But if you feel like saving some money, simply ask the following question: "Will that category of service allow me to dine in the Queen's Grill?" If the answer is, "No," then choose something more expensive, for cruising on the QE2 and not dining at the Queen's Grill is like going to the top of the Eiffel Tower but not looking out over Paris. Also, while you're on board, be sure to make use of the Steiner Health Spa, the world's first sea-based full-service spa.

Rates: $198–$669

CUNARD CRUISE LINES
555 Fifth Avenue
New York City, NY 10017

Phone	212-880-7500
Toll free	800-528-6273
Fax	212-949-0915

ORIENT EXPRESS TRAINS
Europe and Asia

> That you and I from Love may never part
> While still these jeweled monuments remain.
> These monuments, wrought out of hours, contain
> The wound inflicted on me by Love's dart.
>
> —"Bridal Day" by Compton Mackenzie

There are trains, and then there is the Orient Express. In fact, there are two Orient Expresses. The first—the Venice Simplon Orient Express—tours Europe. The second—the Eastern & Oriental Express—tours Southeast Asia.

The Venice Simplon Orient Express carries passengers across Europe in the grand style of a bygone era. Its seventeen shining blue-and-gold cars stretch a quarter-mile and recapture the opulent luxury of the 1920s. Passengers are attended to by cabin stewards who deliver attentive yet discreet service. Each compartment becomes a comfortable bedroom complete with damask cotton bed-linens. Cities on this line include: London, Paris, Venice, Rome, and Dusseldorf.

The Eastern & Orient Express is the crown jewel of train travel in Southeast Asia. From the moment you come aboard, a gracious staff will cater to your every need. The green-and-cream cars feature three types of compartments, each with an in-room shower. In the dining cars, you'll enjoy an inventive combination of European and Asian cuisines that results in flavorful dishes that your palate will not soon forget. Cities on this line include: Singapore, Kuala Lumpur, and Bangkok.

Rates: Venice Simplon, $1,850; Eastern & Orient, $1,300–$3,6000

ORIENT EXPRESS TRAINS
1520 Kensington Road
Oakbrook, IL 60523

Phone   800-524-2420

Appendix

RECOMMENDED ROMANTIC ALBUMS

Album	Artist
Tidal	Fiona Apple
Rimsky-Korsakov Scheherzade Symphonic Suite	Bernstein NY Philharmonic
Body & Soul	Rick Braun
Butterfly	Mariah Carey
Daydream	Mariah Carey
Carpenters	Carpenters
The Singles, 1969-1973	Carpenters
Yesterday Once More	Carpenters
Karen Carpenter	Karen Carpenter
The Three Tenors in Concert 1994	Carreras, Domingo, Pavarotti
The Best of Ray Charles: Rhino Years	Ray Charles
Ray Charles: His Greatest Hits Vol. 1	Ray Charles
Unforgettable	Natalie Cole
Favorite Ballads	Nat King Cole
Love is the Thing (And More)	Nat King Cole
Songs for Two In Love (And More)	Nat King Cole
Ten Best of Nat King Cole	Nat King Cole
We Are in Love	Harry Connick, Jr.
Bolero	Denver Symphony
Falling Into You	Celine Dion
Let's Talk About Love	Celine Dion
Paint the Sky with Stars	Enya
Whitney Houston	Whitney Houston
1100 Bel Air Place	Julio Iglesias
Heart Shaped World	Chris Isaac
The Best of Johnny Mathis	Johnny Mathis
Johnny Mathis: 16 Most Requested Songs	Johnny Mathis

Album	*Artist*
If I Don't Stay the Night	Mindy McCready
Gently	Liza Minelli
Love Songs for a Rainy Day	Peter Nero
Love Songs	101 Strings
Pensami Per Te	Anna Oxa
Amore	Luciano Pavarotti
Pavarotti's Greatest Hits	Luciano Pavarotti
Joy	Teddy Pendergrass
Life Is A Song Worth Singing	Teddy Pendergrass
TP	Teddy Pendergrass
Truly Blessed	Teddy Pendergrass
Cinema Serenade	Itzhak Perlman
30th Anniversaire	Edith Piaf
Selection of Edith Piaf	Edith Piaf
Back to Front	Lionel Richie
Dancing on the Ceiling	Lionel Richie
Louder than Words	Lionel Richie
Truly—The Love Songs	Lionel Richie
Take Me Higher	Diana Ross
Gypsy Legend	Los Reyes
The Very Best of the Righteous Brothers	Righteous Brothers
Violin Romances	Gil Shaham
Come Dance With Me	Frank Sinatra
Frank Sinatra's Greatest Hits	Frank Sinatra
Sinatra Reprise: The Very Good Years	Frank Sinatra
Softly As I Leave You	Frank Sinatra
The Very Best of Frank Sinatra	Frank Sinatra
Humoresque	Isaac Stern
Barbra Streisand's Greatest Hits	Barbra Streisand
One Voice	Barbra Streisand
China Girl—The Classical Album 2	Vanessa-Mae
The Classical Album	Vanessa-Mae
The Violin Player	Vanessa-Mae
Sarah Slightly Classical	Sarah Vaughan
All Time Greatest Hits	Barry White
Best of Love Unlimited Orchestra	Barry White
Just Another Way to Say I Love You	Barry White
Sheet Music	Barry White
Songs for Someone You Love	Barry White

Album	*Artist*
The Icon is Love	Barry White
Next	Vanessa Williams
Bolero and Other Sensuous Classics	various artists
Candlelight Magic—50 Romantic Piano Favorites	various artists
Erotic Dreams	various artists
Gypsy Passion	various artists
A Little Night Music	various artists
Love is in the Air	various artists
Mellow Gold	various artists
Music for a Bachelor's Den	various artists
Music from the Motion Picture Titanic	various artists
Tribute to Edith Piaf	various artists
Romantic Piano Volume I	various artists
Romantic Piano Volume II	various artists
The Romantics	various artists
Secret Love	various artists
Spotlight on Violin	various artists
World's Greatest Love Songs	various artists

If you have a favorite hideaway that you would like us to consider for our next edition of *Bed & Champagne,* please send us your suggestions. Also, if you have something to add to the resorts that are included in this edition, or you believe we have missed the target on any resort, please let us know.

I'd also like to hear your answer to the age-old question—what is romance?

Boru Publishing
11212 Ladera Drive
Austin, TX 78759